# The Guide to the Path *of* Righteousness

Path of the Banī ᶜAlawī

Volume 1

Compiled by

Rizwana Sayed

*(B.A. Hons Arabic, M.A. Islamic Studies From the University of London, SOAS)*

Under the guidance of

Sheikh Muḥammad Ṣādiq ᶜAlawī

SAKINA

ISBN 978-0-9566146-2-9

Published by Sakina, UK

www.sakinapublishing.com

Compiled by: Rizwana Sayed

1st Edition

*Printed in Great Britain*

# DEDICATION

This book is dedicated to Sayyidinā al-Faqīh al-Muqaddam Muḥammad b. ᶜAlī ﷺ (574AH-653AH)

بسم الله الرحمن الرحيم

# TRANSLITERATION

| | | | | | |
|---|---|---|---|---|---|
| ء | ʾ | س | s | م | m |
| أ | a | ش | sh | ن | n |
| ب | b | ص | ṣ | ه | h |
| ت | t | ض | ḍ | و | w |
| ث | th | ط | ṭ | ي | y |
| ج | j | ظ | ẓ | | |
| ح | ḥ | ع | ʿ | | |
| خ | kh | غ | gh | | |
| د | d | ف | f | | |
| ذ | dh | ق | q | | |
| ر | r | ك | k | | |
| ز | z | ل | l | | |

Long vowels are represented as: ā, ī, ū

May Allah bless him and grant him peace ﷺ

May Allah be pleased with him رضي الله عنه

May Allah be pleased with her رضي الله عنها

May Allah be pleased with them رضي الله عنهم

# Contents

## Section 3: Keeping Good Company



## Section 4: Summarised biographies of some of the eminent figures amongst the Sāda Bā ʿAlawī

# Volume 2



## Section 1: The Virtues of Dhikr

## Section 2: Beneficial Supplications



## Section 3: Daily Supplications

## Section 4: Qasā'id

# Introduction

Praise be to Allah, and may peace and blessings be upon His chosen Messenger, his family and Companions.

In recent times the form of the Bā ᶜAlawī Ṭarīqa has changed. Traditionally, it was a ṭarīqa that was maintained amongst the *Sāda* (sing. Sayyid) of Ḥaḍramawt. The preservation of the religious structure of this ṭarīqa was through practical embodiment, oral tradition, and spiritual transmission from senior masters to disciples. The Sāda travelled across the shores to other lands to spread the teachings; these teachings were transmitted through the creation of large Sufic communities which ensured the transmission of learning to subsequent generations. The last century has witnessed an extensive rise in numbers towards the Bā ᶜAlawī Ṭarīqa.

With followers to be found in almost every country, away from the original protective environment of the valleys of Ḥadramawt, elements of the etiquettes of the ṭarīqa have moved away from their original feature. Knowledge of the great masters remains in the Arabic language as it was originally aimed for the Ḥaḍramī people, with enough detail to suffice their understanding. Bearing this in mind, I felt the need to compile a short manual portraying the main aspects of the Bā ᶜAlawī Ṭarīqa, which would be useful for all the dedicated seekers who wish to benefit from the knowledge and guidance of the illustrious Sāda Bā ᶜAlawī.

The aim of this work is to enlighten and help those who are on the path to improve, elevate and ascend to greater heights that can be reached through the *mashā'ikh* of this ṭarīqa. In order for this to occur, it is vital that the seeker acquaints himself with them, how the blessings have been passed down from generation to generation, initiated from the time of the Messenger of Allah ﷺ and then transmitted from father to son and to loyal murīds up until the present day.

We have been blessed with a Path that has been proven sound in the light of the Quran and the Sunna. Upon it are Masters who have made their lives the Quran and their practice the Sunna, who lived and breathed only for the sake of Allah. It is through their fountain that the seeker receives the blessings, which ignites the flame of imān in his heart.

By Allah's bounty, many seekers have been guided and acknowledged by Sheikh Muḥammad Ṣādiq ᶜAlawī, who has been ordained by the Great Quṭb, al-Ghawth, al-Fard: Sayyidinā al-Imām al-Ḥabīb Aḥmad Mashhūr b. Ṭāha al-Ḥaddād رضي الله عنه to continue his teachings and works and to follow the path of the pious predecessors, and it is through his hands that many drink from the fountain of the Sāda Bā ᶜAlawī.

When Allah has associated us with such great Masters, it is our responsibility to value, appreciate and be nurtured with excellence. This can only be achieved when the seeker is aware of how to acquire the blessings and beware of the pitfalls upon the path. Hence, the need arose to outline the main principles upon the path, and illustrate the conduct of the seeker to receive the blessings and elevate to higher ranks.

The first part of this work is a brief history outlining the formation of the Banī ᶜAlawī Ṭarīqa, mentioning the key figures who contributed in serving the religion of the Messenger of Allah ﷺ. This is followed by an explanation of the principles and the ideology of the ṭarīqa, indicating the outlook that is required by the seeker in order to be successful upon the path. This section has been translated from the book: *Al-Manhaj al-Sawī* by Ḥabīb Zayn b. Aḥmad b. Sumaiṭ.

The second part is about adab. Adab in this context is referring to good manners and etiquette; which is vital not only for seekers of the Banī ᶜAlawī Ṭarīqa, but for seekers of any ṭarīqa. Key points have been mentioned in detail because adab is the yardstick that will determine your place upon the path, as Abū Ḥafs ؓ said:

> *Taṣawwuf, all of it is adab, at all times it is adab, in all states it is adab, and at every level it is adab.*

This section was cited from the book '*Manhaj al-Ṣufī wa'l-Ḥayāt ul-ᶜAṣrīya*' by Fawzī Muḥammad Abū Zayd, who mainly refers to the writings of Imam ᶜAbd ul-Wahhāb Shaᶜrānī, may Allah be pleased with him.

The third part emphasises the importance of keeping good company, this can affect and influence the Seeker as Ḥabīb Aḥmad b. ᶜUmar b. Sumait ؓ said:

> *Good and evil are seeded within a human; it does not appear until one mingles with others. So if he mingles with the good, then good actions will appear from him, and if he mingles with evil, then evil actions appear from him.*

The fourth part includes summarised biographies of some of the great mashā'ikh to familiarise the seeker of their practices, rank and mastery in the religion. Most of the mashā'ikh remain unknown, in spite of ascending to the greatest levels in sainthood, since the prevailing feature of this Ṭarīqa is the desire to seek obscurity.

The final part – vol. 2 explains the litanies of the path and its importance. The invocations have been structured with additional supplications by Sheikh Muḥammad Ṣādiq to be recited throughout the day. Finally I have included some poetry of the Mashā'ikh that is often recited to receive the *baraka.* In some of the poems, the local Ḥaḍramī dialect has been used; here the couplets have been translated in order to convey the general meaning rather than a literal translation.

I pray to Allah that this will help and increase the determination of all the seekers upon the path, and I seek forgiveness for any shortcomings on my part, and I hope that this work will be accepted and pleasing to the Messenger of Allah ﷺ and all the Sāda Bā ᶜAlawī, may Allah be pleased with them all and keep us in their company in this world and the hereafter.

# Section 1

# Historical background and ethics of the Sāda Bā ʿAlawī

*"I am leaving behind with you two weighty things: the Book of Allah and my family"*

The Prophet ﷺ

## ~ Chapter 1 ~

# History of the Sāda Bā $^{c}$Alawī

Imam $^{c}$Alī al-$^{c}$Uraydī, the son of Imam Ja$^{c}$far al-Ṣādiq, son of Muḥammad al-Bāqir, son of $^{c}$Alī Zain ul-$^{c}$Ābidīn, son of Imam Ḥusain, son of Sayyidinā $^{c}$Alī ibn Abī Ṭālib, may Allah be pleased with them all, was born and raised in Madina. After the passing away of his father, he moved to the town Al-$^{c}$Urayd, where he became the sheikh for the Banī Hāshim and the leader (*naqīb*) of the descendents of the Prophet ﷺ. He was a devout worshipper, surpassed in knowledge, very generous and transmitted many hadiths. He lived for approximately 100 years, until the era of his brother Mūsā al-Kādhim's great grandson $^{c}$Alī al-Hādī. He passed away in Al-$^{c}$Urayd, where he is buried.

His son, Imam Muḥammad, also born in Madina, moved to Basra in Iraq after his father passed away. He was a man of great learning, he preferred isolation and was known for his abstinence (*zuhd*). In Basra he became the leader of the Ahl al-Bayt. His son Imam $^{c}$Īsā followed in his footsteps and assumed his father's position of responsibility and took the Ahl al-Bayt under his wing. He was also a man of great knowledge and a Gnostic.

Thereafter his son, Aḥmad b. ᶜIsā had taken on the responsibility of his father. He was a man of great spiritual insight; he was renowned for his generosity, kindness and knowledge. During his time there was internal strife, bloodsḥed and confusion in Iraq, where a number of the Ahl-al-Bayt were persecuted by the ruling Abassids. At that time, Imām Aḥmad b. ᶜIsā left Basra for the sake of the religion and to protect the descendents of the Prophet ﷺ in the year 317AH (929CE), this is how he acquired the title "*Muhājir ila-Allāh*", i.e. the one who emigrated for the sake of Allah. He migrated with seventy people, which were his family members and close companions. He first went to Madina and Makka, and then from Makka to Yemen at around 319AH.

Henceforth, Imām Aḥmad settled in the valley of Ḥaḍramawt, which became the homeland for his blessed progeny. The Āl Bā ᶜAlawī[1] are named after the grandson of Imām Aḥmad, who was called **ᶜAlawī b. ᶜUbaydillāh b. Aḥmad.**

After Imām Aḥmad b. ᶜĪsā passed away, his children moved to Tarīm in 521AH (1127CE), the first one to settle there was **Imām ᶜAlī b. ᶜAlawī**, more famously known as **Khāliᶜ Qasam** and his brother **Sālim.** Thereafter, Tarīm became renowned for the noble and pious offspring that emerged; and many institutions of learning and mosques were established.

## *The Establishment of the Bā ᶜAlawī Ṭarīqa*

The ṭarīqa became more formally established during the time of **Imām Muḥammad b. ᶜAlī**, renowned as **Sayyidinā al-**

[1] The term 'Banī ᶜAlawī' means the Clan of ᶜAlawī, it is synonymous with the name 'Bā ᶜAlawī', this is a Hadramī acronym of Banī ᶜAlawī, both terms are the same in meaning.

**Faqīh al-Muqaddam** 🕊, the great grandson of **ʿAlawī**. All of the family lines amongst the Bā ʿAlawī go back to the father of Sayyidinā al-Faqīh al-Muqaddam, named ʿ**Alī** and his brother ʿ**Alawī**, more famously known as ʿ**Amm al-Faqīh al-Muqaddam'** (uncle of al-Faqīh al-Muqaddam).

The ʿAlawī Ṭarīqa has two lines of transmission: one which is passed on through the family line, as they are direct descendents of the Messenger of Allah 🕊, the other was transmitted through the *khirqa*[2] that was sent to Sayyidinā al-Faqīh al-Muqaddam from Morocco by Shuʿayb Abū Madyan al-Gawth 🕊. Sheikh Abū Madyan sent one of his foremost students, named ʿAbd al-Raḥmān b. Muḥammad al-Ḥaḍramī al-Maghribī towards Ḥaḍramawt. Before reaching Ḥaḍramawt he stopped at Makka, where he met a Maghribi Sufi named ʿAbdallāh al-Ṣāliḥ al-Maghribī. ʿAbd al-Raḥmān never reached Ḥaḍramawt, as he passed away in Makka, before his death he instructed ʿAbdallāh al-Ṣāliḥ to go to Tarīm, where he was told that he would find Muḥammad b. ʿAlī, namely Sayyidinā al-Faqīh al-Muqaddam, and he was instructed to pass on the *khirqa* of Sheikh Abū Madyan to him.

Hence, the ʿAlawī Ṭarīqa is based on a dual transmission, the initial *Muḥammadī* transmission which goes from father to son, and the *Madyaniyya* transmission infused into the ṭarīqa by the Great Quṭb,[3] Sheikh Abū Madyan al-Gawth 🕊.

After Sayyidinā al-Faqīh al-Muqaddam 🕊 the ṭarīqa continued; the children followed in the footsteps of their blessed father, and the spiritual blessings and secrets were being passed down from father to son. However, the Bā ʿAlawī

---

[2] The Khirqa is the initiatory cloak of the Sufi chain of spirituality, with which there is a spiritual transmission of knowledge and *baraka* from the Master to the disciple.

[3] The *Quṭb* is described as being the Axial Saint, the highest authority in sainthood at that given time.

were inclined towards obscurity and secrecy, it remained this way until the era of **al-ᶜAydrūs** (d.864AH) and his brother **Sheikh ᶜAlī** (d. 892AH), when the ṭarīqa started to gain prominence and the need for literature arose. Compositions such as: '*Min al-Mu'allifāt fī Ādāb al-Ṭarīqati wa Maᶜālim al-Sulūk fī hā*', '*Kibrīt Aḥmar*', '*Juz il-Laṭīf*', '*Maᶜārij*', and '*Barqah*' emerged.[4]

Gleaming from the dignitaries of this ṭarīqa were men who stood out amongst their peers with proficiency and advancement in knowledge and action, to the extent that some of them reached the rank of mujtahid; while others demonstrated amazing aspects of sainthood similar to their predecessors, such as the Quṭb: ᶜ**Abd al-Raḥmān al-Saqqāf** (d.819AH), he was known as "**Muqaddam al-Thānī**", and his son Imam al-Ghawth ᶜ**Umar al-Miḥḍār** (d.833AH), the Quṭb **al-ᶜAydrūs** ᶜ**Abdallāh b. Abī Bakr** (d.865AH) and his son **Abū Bakr al-ᶜAdanī** (d.914AH) who is buried in Aden, **Sheikh Abū Bakr b. Sālim**, renowned by the name "*Fakhr al-Wujūd*" (d.992AH), and al-Imām ᶜ**Umar b.** ᶜ**Abd al-Raḥmān al-ᶜAṭṭās** (d.1072AH) and so forth, until the ṭarīqa reached its peak when the great *mujaddid* (renewer of the religion) appeared: the Great Imam and Quṭb ᶜ**Abdallāh b.** ᶜ**Alawī al-Ḥaddād** (d.1132AH), may Allah be pleased with them all.

The Bā ᶜAlawī Ṭarīqa adopted a new form at the hands of Imam al-Ḥaddād ﵁ and he called it "*Ṭarīqa Ahl al-Yamīn*" (The Path of the People of the Right). He saw that the people of that era required encouragement towards obedience and their faith had to be revived advancing it to the levels of excellence

[4] *Kibrīt Aḥmar wa'l-Iksīr al-Akbar* was written by Al-ᶜAydrūs al-Akbar ᶜAbdallāh b. Abī Bakr, *Juz' al-Laṭīf fī'l-Taḥkīm al-Sharīf* was written by his son Sheikh Abū Bakr al-Adanī, *Maᶜārij al-Hidāya* and *Barqat ul-Mashīqa bi dhikri libās al-khirqat ul-anīqa* were both written by Sheikh ᶜAlī b. Abī Bakr al-Sakrān, the brother of al-ᶜAydrūs al-Akbar.

(*iḥsān*). This method produced the most excellent results in calling people to Allah, improving the states for the general people. The Bā ᶜAlawī Ṭarīqa became renowned in many places and it continues to be the most exemplary way in calling people to Allah up until the present day.

Imam al-Ḥaddād ﷺ has had a tremendous influence upon the ummah; his litanies, supplications, words of wisdom, counsels and poetry are upon the tongues of the Muslims in many countries around the world.

His literature was simplified, with an ease and flow in his writings. It has been said that his books are the essence of previous Sufi literature, such as the "*Iḥyā ᶜUlūm al-Dīn*" by Imam al-Ghazālī. He was an excellent example and a perfect model, and he was like a teacher for the scholars and the pious people. For that reason, his Sheikh, Habib **ᶜUmar b. ᶜAbd al-Raḥmān al-ᶜAṭṭās**, ﷺ said: "Al-Sayyid ᶜAbdallāh al-Ḥaddād is an ummah in himself". A point to note – the age of Imam al-Ḥaddād when his Sheikh passed away was 28, so he must have been younger when his Sheikh mentioned the above.

After Sayyidinā Imam al-Ḥaddād, the great figures that continued in his footsteps, propagating the faith and calling people to Allah were his students that excelled, such as the great scholar Ḥabīb **Aḥmad b. Zayn al-Ḥabshī** (d.1144AH), Imam **ᶜAbd al-Raḥmān b. ᶜAbdallāh Ba'l-Faqīh** (d.1162AH), who was renowned by the name "The scholar of the world," (*ᶜAllāmat il-dunyā*) and the exceptional Imam **Muḥammad b. Zayn b. Sumaiṭ** (d.1172AH), in addition to the children of Imam al-Ḥaddād, who were a representation of their father's upbringing, may Allah be pleased with them all.

Following the generation of Imam al-Ḥaddād's students, another generation of great men emerged continuing the role of eradicating falsehood and calling people to Allah. This was the generation of the Great Saint, Ḥabīb ᶜ**Umar b. Saqqāf al-Saqqāf**, who was known as "*Sheikh al-Aqṭāb*", (the Sheikh of the Aqṭāb) and his students: Ḥabīb **Aḥmad b.** ᶜ**Umar b. Sumaiṭ** (d.1257AH), Ḥabīb ᶜ**Abdallāh b. Ḥusain b. Ṭāhir** (d.1272AH) and his brother Ḥabīb **Ṭāhir b. Ḥusain b. Ṭāhir** (d.1241AH), Ḥabīb **Ḥasan b. Ṣāliḥ al-Baḥr al-Jifrī** (d.1273AH), Ḥabīb ᶜ**Abdallāh b.** ᶜ**Umar b. Yaḥyā** (d.1265AH). And the outstanding students of this generation were: the great muḥaddith and scholar Ḥabīb ᶜ**Aydrūs b.** ᶜ**Umar al-Ḥabshī** (d.1314AH), the author of the great book: "ᶜ*Iqd ul-Yawāqīt al-Jawhariyya*", which contains all the lines of transmissions (*isnāds*) within the Sāda Bā ᶜAlawī.

The most distinguished figures amongst the Bā ᶜAlawī in the following generation were three: the great mufti of Ḥaḍramawt, Imam ᶜ**Abd al-Raḥmān b. Muḥammad al-Mashhūr** (d.1320AH) and the great ᶜAllāma al-Ḥabīb **Aḥmad b. Ḥasan al-**ᶜ**Aṭṭās** (d.1334AH), his renown and reputation in the sphere of knowledge extended beyond Ḥaḍramawt reaching as far as Egypt, Syria and the Hijaz. And the one who espoused and encouraged the love for the Messenger of Allah ﷺ: Ḥabīb ᶜ**Alī b. Muḥammad al-Ḥabshī** (d.1333AH), who was also a Master in literature and a great Sufi, may Allah be pleased with them all.

Leading up to the most recent generation, the outstanding figures, who have followed in the footsteps of their predecessors, continuing their efforts, some who have passed away and some who are still alive are the following: Sheikh ul-Islam Ḥabīb ᶜ**Abdallāh b.** ᶜ**Umar al-Shāṭirī** (d.1361AH), who was a reviver of the religious sciences of his time, the Gnostic Ḥabīb ᶜ**Alawī b.** ᶜ**Abdallah b. Shihāb al-Dīn** (d.1386AH), Ḥabīb **Sālim b. Ḥāfiẓ** (d.1378AH), and the master of great renown Ḥabīb ᶜ**Umar b. Aḥmad b. Sumaiṭ** (d.1397AH) whose mastery excelled his and the previous generation, and produced the greatest *akābir* of our time such as Ḥabīb ᶜ**Abd al-Qadir b. Aḥmad al-Saqqāf,** Ḥabīb **Aḥmad Mashhūr b. Ṭāha Al-Ḥaddād**, Ḥabīb **Abī Bakr** ᶜ**Aṭṭās al-Ḥabshī**, Ḥabīb **Muḥammad b.** ᶜ**Abdallāh al-Ḥaddār**, Ḥabīb **Muḥammad b. Sālim b. Ḥāfiẓ** and Ḥabīb **Ibrahīm b.** ᶜ**Umar b.** ᶜ**Aqīl b. Yaḥya,** May Allah be pleased with them all.

This is just a brief summary of some of the most renowned figures amongst the Sāda Bā ᶜAlawī, there are many more who had also reached great spiritual and scholarly heights. This is the distinct feature of the Sāda Bā ᶜAlawī, the transmissions from the time of the Messenger of Allah ﷺ are passed down in a continual chain from father to son and loyal murids,[5] hence there are so many *ṣāliḥīn*, *ṣiddīqīn*, *aqṭāb* and *abdāl* that mentioning them all would amount to volumes. I have merely mentioned some of the names that a murīd of the Bā ᶜAlawī Ṭarīqa should be familiar with. Moreover, when mentioning the names of the ṣāliḥīn there is an emission of baraka, as it has been said, "*Dhikr ul-ṣāliḥīn tanazzal ur-raḥma*", 'Mercy descends upon the remembrance of the righteous.'

## *Ideology of the Banī ᶜAlawī*

The Sāda Bā ᶜAlawī have followed the fiqh of Imam al-Shāfiᶜī ﷺ since the time of *Muhājir illa Allah* Imam Aḥmad b. ᶜĪsā. With the course of time, amongst the Sāda were many fuqaha specialising in Shāfiᶜī fiqh, and there still remains to be specialists in this field. As for belief, the Sāda are Sunni and have always followed the doctrine (*ᶜaqīda*) of Imam al-Ashᶜarī

[5] Although the transmissions were from father to son, other murīds who were not from Ahl al-Bayt also received and were people of great rank such as: Sheikh Saᶜīd b. ᶜIsa al-ᶜAmūdī ﷺ.

ﷺ. In summary, the following explains the way of the Banī ᶜAlawī:

> To spend time occupied in good deeds, by completely emulating the Messenger of Allah ﷺ, and perfecting the actions with sincerity removing doubts and vices. And purifying the heart from every blameworthy trait, adorning it with every praiseworthy trait, having mercy and compassion towards the believers, exerting one's efforts in teaching and guiding them towards that where there is success. Being wary of the unlawful and doubtful things, and not having too much involvement in permissible acts of desire (*shahawāt*), to seize the opportunity of being in seclusion, only mixing with people to learn and to teach, for the Friday prayer, and for prayer in congregation, or to visit close friends, making social visits useful by learning beneficial knowledge. Maintaining relations with the brothers, being kind to everyone and maintaining good relations with them, commanding the good and forbidding the evil, helping the grieved with care, compassion and humility, fulfilling promises, being ascetic, and having trust in Allah.

These are some of the spiritual teachings of the Banī ᶜAlawī, they are explained in detail in the *Iḥyā'* of Imam al-Ghazālī, and are also mentioned in the books of Imam Al-Ḥaddād, may Allah be pleased with them both.

The Banī ᶜAlawī Ṭarīqa embraces the other spiritual paths, as long as they remain within the boundaries of the Sharia, and has respect for them and does not rebuff them. In fact, they benefit from their spiritual knowledge to the extent that the masters of the Path have said that the Banī ᶜAlawī are outwardly Ghazālı and inwardly Shādhilī. Imam ᶜAbd al-Raḥmān Ba'l-Faqīh ﵁ has said: "The outward is what Imam al-Ghazālī has explained with regards to knowledge and action which will lead to the right way, and the inward is what the Shādhilī's have explained with regards to achieving reality and pure tawḥīd.[6] The most part of this is striving to purify the heart, and preparing it to receive the breaths (*nafaḥāt*) of nearness, and gaining intimacy with Allah.

[6] "Pure tawḥīd" is taṣawwuf in its essence, it involves the sublime spiritual levels having interaction with Allah ﷻ. This involves removal of all human (*bashari*) traits in order to witness the Divine manifestations, this occurs towards the later stages of the spiritual path.

# ~ Chapter 2 ~

## THE PRINCIPLES OF THE BANĪ ᶜALAWĪ

The path is based on three traits: adherence to the Quran, compliance to the Sunna, and following the pious forefathers (*salaf*). This is the 'path of righteousness' (*ṣirāṭ al-mustaqīm*), indicated in Allah's statement, Exalted is He: "*This is My path and it is straight, follow it...*"[7]

Abu'l-ᶜĀliya[8] related, with regards to the verse: "*Guide us to the straight path, the path of those whom You have favoured...*"[9] that this refers to the offspring of the Messenger of Allah ﷺ.

Imam ᶜAbdallāh al-Ḥaddād said:

> The Banī ᶜAlawī Ṭarīqa is the most upright and balanced ṭarīqa. Their conduct is the best and most exemplary, they are upon the most admirable way, broad and vast, with clear legislation; it is the most sound and successful path. The successors are not allowed to adopt any other way that differs from the forefathers, neither incline to any other ṭarīqa or conduct, because this ṭarīqa is that

[7] Sura Anᶜām 6:153

[8] Abū'l-ᶜĀliya was one of the great scholars amongst the Tābiᶜīn, he was one who had memorised the Quran, a scholar and a commentator on the Quran (*mufassir*), he passed away in 93AH.

[9] Sura al-Fātiḥa 1: 6-7

> which has been proven correct in the light of the Quran and the blessed Sunna, the accepted traditions, and the conduct of the perfect forefathers. The successors (*khalaf*) have received these teachings from the ancestors (*salaf*), and fathers have received it from grandfathers going all the way up to the Messenger of Allah ﷺ.

Imam Aḥmad b. Ḥassan al-ᶜAṭṭās - may Allah make us benefit from him - was asked to describe the ᶜAlawī Ṭarīqa, he said:

> Outwardly it is Ghazālī and inwardly Shādhilī, in other words, its outward is to remove all blameworthy traits and adorn it with praiseworthy traits. Its inward is to witness the blessings of Allah, Exalted is He. He further said, 'It is as Imam ᶜAbd al-Raḥmān Bā'l-Faqīh has said, "Compliance to the texts in a specific way,"' (the texts refer to the Quran and Sunna.) And Imam Aḥmad also said, "The way of the ancestors is to act where action is required, to abandon where abandonment is required, and to intend where intention is required..."

He رضي الله عنه also said:

> The household of the Prophet ﷺ (*Ahl al-Bayt*), their way is action, they do not take any knowledge except that which will lead them towards performing good acts and protecting them, as for the remaining knowledge they learn it for blessings, and they only acquire that knowledge which enforces God consciousness (*taqwā*), this is indicated in Allah's saying: "*Fear Allah, and Allah will teach you*"[10]

---

[10] Sura al-Baqara 2: 282

> We should be careful, especially those who are from Ahl al-Bayt, not to disregard the practice of the pious forefathers, and to adopt another ṭarīqa, other than the Banī ᶜAlawī. How can we abandon this ṭarīqa, whose soundness has been proven in the light of the Quran and Sunna, and by the leaders who have been approved by the majority? Therefore, all good is in following them, in their speech, deeds and beliefs.'

Imam ᶜAbdallāh al-Ḥaddād said:

> Our Sāda Bā ᶜAlawī, their affairs are regulated upon the Sunna and good traditions. One who turns away from it, there is hardly any virtue in such a person.

Imam Aḥmad b. Ḥassan al-ᶜAṭṭās said:

> One who adopts a path other than that of the Sādāt al-ᶜAlawiyyīn - this is in reference to the Ahl al-Bayt - abandoning the conduct of their forefathers, they will not benefit, or advance no matter how much their knowledge and deeds increase.

Know, that it is imperative for everyone and especially for those who are from Ahl al-Bayt to be concerned about acquiring knowledge of the sharia, adorning oneself with the traits of the Messenger of Allah ﷺ and removing blameworthy traits, and try to imitate the way of the forefathers, the people of extreme determination, in order to gain the exalted ranks.

The great Gnostic Aḥmad b. Ḥassan al-ᶜAṭṭās, may Allah make us benefit from him said:

> The amount of divine blessings a person receives depends on three traits: sincerity in seeking, approaching matters beautifully, and sound intention. If a person has these three traits they will attain their objective.

He ﵁ also explained the way to seek, and to have sincerity in seeking, he says:

> Intention is the spirit of obedience, determination is the foundation of good deeds, and upon the two are pious actions and beautiful characteristics established. Therefore, I counsel myself and my brothers to keep striving and to remove inability from oneself, as the matter requires hard work and effort because lives are short.

Imam al-Ḥaddād, may Allah make us benefit from him said:

> A person cannot cross the distance of the inward and the outward except with firm determination. One who becomes lazy, incompetent and procrastinates, hardly ever will he be able to accomplish a matter, or acquire what he desires except if Allah wills.

The great Imam and Quṭb ᶜAbdallāh b. Abī Bakr al-ᶜAydrus ﵁ said:

> When determination is weak, vision is impaired, souls are defiant, thoughts are sluggish, one will not obtain their goals and they will not reach the beloved.

# ~ Chapter 3 ~

## The Way of the People of the Right
## *Ṭarīqa Ahl al-Yamīn*

Suyūṭī narrates in '*Al-Jāmiʿ al-Kabīr*' on the authority of Umay Urāqa who said, "I prayed Fajr behind ʿAlī b. Abī Ṭālib. After finishing his prayer, he turned right but remained seated as if he was distressed. He then turned his hand over and said:

> By Allah, I have seen the companions of Muḥammad ﷺ and I have not seen in this day and age, anything that resembles them. They used to wake up in the morning, dishevelled and unkempt, their foreheads like the knees of goats, having spent the night standing in prayer and in prostration, reciting the Book of Allah, taking rest only between their prostrations and their standing. When morning arrives they would continue to remember Allah, the Blessed and Exalted, they bow like trees bow on a windy day, their eyes stream with tears until their clothes become wet. When morning arrived, by Allah, they make as if they've woken up while having slept.

I did not see him ever laughing until he was assassinated by Ibn Muljum."

The Companions, may Allah be pleased with them all, would spend their nights standing in prayer and prostrating to their Lord. They would fast the day and would be in prayer during the night so much so that because of the number of their prostrations upon hard and stony ground, their foreheads would resemble the knees of a goat. When Fajr time arrived they would recall the Majesty of Allah, and would bow out of awe and fear just as trees bend over on a windy day. They would cry because they felt that they were not doing enough for their Lord. However, anyone who saw them would think that they had spent the night in heedlessness from their Lord.

Like this, did our master ʿAlī ☙ describe them. This was despite their duties of battles, calling people to Allah and teaching, facing hardships and trials, one after another, and building the state of Islam.

It is said that the Tābiʿīn did more than the Companions in spiritual exercises and disciplining the self. This was because the state of Islam had settled during their time. During this period many scholars, judges and teachers of the Quran appeared. Therefore, within this era and following it, many of them were able to occupy themselves solely with worship. This was to such an extent that some of the Imams, who had concerned themselves with acquiring knowledge, practised such self disciplining exercises, which in our day and age baffle the mind.

It has been mentioned about Imam Abū Hanīfa ☙ that for forty years he had prayed Fajr with the ablution of his ʿIshā prayer, this is despite his occupation with teaching and learning. Likewise, Imam al-Shafiʿī ☙ used to divide a third of his night for issues of knowledge, a third for worship, and a third to take rest in. It is narrated that he once said, "I have not satiated my hunger for twenty years."

Later on, when people began preoccupying themselves with the *dunya* and turned away from the lifestyles of the Companions and those that followed them; there still remained a people who took to their way, which differentiated them from the rest, and so they were named ascetics (*zuhhād*), and later on as Sufis (*Ṣufiyya*).

The Ṣufiyya are those who have held fast to the Prophetic guidance and have been sincere with it. Neither trading nor selling has distracted them from the remembrance of Allah.

The early generation of the Ṣufiyya like Ibrāhīm b. Adham,[11] Khawwās,[12] Tāᶜī,[13] and all the others mentioned in the book '*Ar-Risāla al-Qushayriyya*' performed such spiritual exercises, and feats of self discipline, which are no longer heard of in these days and about which many books have been written.

Time passed on, and the number of people, who were on this way, gradually reduced to fewer and fewer until by the time of Imam al-Ḥaddad 🙶, the state was, as described by him, a weakness of religion and a turning away from the truth.

---

[11] Ibrāhīm ibn Adham (d. 782CE), is one of the early Sufi Saints of the 8th Century. He was renowned for his asceitism, he abdicated the the throne and chose to live life as an ascetic.

[12] Sheikh ᶜAlī al-Khawwās al Burullusī al-Ummī was from the greatest people of exclusive sainthood, who had such a level of unveiling that it would not be mistaken. He was the student of Sheikh Ibrāhīm al-Matbūlī. He was unlettered but taught by Allah. He passed away in 939AH and is buried in Cairo.

[13] Abū Sulaimān Dawūd ibn Nasir al-Tāᶜī (d.166AH): Imam Dhahabī has mentioned that he was the Imam and Juristic Scholar, and a master of many Islamic sciences. He dedicated himself to worship and solitude and became the leader of the saints of his time. May Allah be pleased with them all.

As for the masters from the ᶜAlawiyyīn, they had such spiritual exercises throughout their history, which could fill volumes. From among them were those who when they finished the Tarāwīḥ prayer, would pray another two rakᶜa, reciting the whole Quran therein. Many of them had given up sleep for more than twenty years. Others amongst them would retreat into valleys and barren places and would pray the Tahajjud prayer, reciting twenty parts of the Quran from the middle of the night until Fajr. Others of them would always sit in the position of the *tashahud* in prayer and out of prayer, maintaing their ādāb in the presence of Allah. They would reduce their intake of food until their stomachs became accustomed to eating no more than three or four morsels, as well as many other things which have been mentioned about them.

The way of the earlier generations was known as the 'Way of the Elect' (*Ṭarīqa al-Khāssa*) within which there was what is known as '*taḥkīm*.' This was when a murīd would resign all his affairs to his sheikh completely, to the extent that he would become like a corpse in the hands of one who is ritually washing him.

The ṭarīqa, as it has been described by the Imam is:

> Refining the character of the nafs and softening its denseness (*kathāfa*) with extreme exercises. These exercises cleanse away the dirt from the nafs and overpower its desires. It is then adorned with constant presence with Allah ﷻ and is described by beautiful adab seated upon a mat of lowliness and brokenness, neediness and destitution, in accordance to servitude (*ᶜubūdiyya*) and in fulfilment of the rights of the Lord.

From among the aforementioned extreme exercises is the forty day spiritual retreat, also striving against the nafs to eliminate all blameworthy characteristics completely; and also to achieve the 'stations of certainty' appropriately.

Taḥkīm is the relationship between the sheikh and the murīd in this ṭarīqa. It is when there remains with the murīd no desire or independent action. Therefore, he does nothing small or big except through the command of his sheikh, and submits himself to him completely.

As for the later times, when pre-occupation with the dunya has increased, endeavours have weakened, and the way to the life of the hereafter has diminished, the people who seek this way have reduced to a few. And those who are actually able to follow it through are even less. This led Imam al-Ḥaddād to leave this way, and led him to call people to a way which was more suitable to this time and era; it is the way of the common and he named it, '*The Way of the People of the Right.*'

The Imam once said:

> Spiritual retreats and self disciplining are no longer for these times, since their conditions are no longer met, like eating ḥalāl. However, the one who builds his affair on performing the obligations, leaving the forbidden, performing the superogatory according to his ability, enjoining good and forbidding wrong, helping the weak, favouring the needy, or helping and assisting him and the like, and remains firm upon this, he will receive that which the others received through their spiritual exercises and retreats and will receive that which he had missed from performing them.

He ﷺ also said:

> Do not ever think that we are upon the Way of the Elect (*Ṭarīqa al-Khāssa*), due to the lack of those people who truly seek it with sincerity. We are only upon the way of the common, the Way of the People of the Right.

Sufism is a way which leads to Allah; this is not complete without softening the density of the nafs until there is no veil before it. The outward means, in order to achieve this, vary from one ṭarīqa to another; however its inward action and goal is one. For this reason the Imam said:

> Even though the paths of Sufism are numerous, they are ultimately one. This is to strive against the ego, and abandon everything that it desires, and this is a hard thing to do.

He ﷺ also said:

> The path that has been mentioned is an inward path made up of beliefs and character. It has only been manifested as an outward path to be learnt and understood.

He ﷺ also said:

> The sharia is knowledge, ṭarīqa is action, and ḥaqīqa is its fruit. Each of these three can be divided further into two, and it is not upon you to investigate its branches. Therefore, if you work outwardly then your fruit is outward, and if you work inwardly then your fruit is inner. Whoever oppresses his heart, and has done works of disobedience, then that is his fruit.

He ﷺ also said:

> We do not carry people onto the ṭarīqa of the *muqarribūn*, and we are not charged to carry many of them upon it. If we do carry them, then we carry them upon the Way of the People of the Right, for people are constantly diminishing. Diminishing, firstly from the category of excellence (*iḥsān*), then from the category of faith (*imān*), and in this time most of them are almost on the verge of coming out of the circle of Islam.

It is apparent that there are very few people who have the high strength; therefore, they have travelled the way of the elect at the hands of Imam al-Ḥaddād ﵁. It has been related from him:

> Whoever comes to us, seeking the way of the common... we comfort and console him. And whoever comes to us seeking the way of the elect... we take service from him and try him, comforting the first in accordance to his nature, and testing the second to break his ego.

This indicates that the Imam did not manifest the way of the elect except for those whom were worthy of it.

## *The Way of the Common (Ṭarīqat ul-ᶜĀmma)*

The Imam ﵁ says:

> The way of the people of Allah begins with the seeker emptying his heart from the dunya, and does not engage with it except for that which is necessary. He then preoccupies all his time with remembrance and obedience. He guards himself from disobedience, and increases in that which is allowed (*mubāhāt*). He turns

> towards the life of the hereafter completely, if he does this, then he is upon the ṭarīqa.

All of that is as the Imam says:

> The path of the common is wide and open, which the salaf were upon and which encompasses the commonality of the Muslims.

## *The Way of the Elect*

Imam al-Ḥaddād ﷺ says:

> It is to be free from everything other than Allah, outwardly and inwardly, to remove blameworthy characteristics to the minutest detail, to adorn oneself with praiseworthy characteristics in all their detail.
>
> The common people are upon the Way of the People of the Right, and the elect are upon the way of the *muqarrabun*. It is not achieved, that is the way of the elect, before perfecting the first way, that is the way of the common, even though one may live as long as the age of Prophet Nūḥ عليه السلام.
>
> Whoever has not perfected his prayer, zakat or the like, then how can he ever reach the level of the elect? In fact, he will always remain behind the door, and will not reach the proximity of entrance. However, the one who perfects the way of the common, in this era will achieve what the elect have achieved even though he has not travelled upon that path.
>
> As for the one who desires the creation and is attached to them, or desires benefit from them, how can he receive

elevations in the ranks of certainty? Whoever attaches himself to them, has left certainty and is attached to desire. The action of Allah is certainty and reality (*yaqīn wa'l-ḥaqīqa*), and their actions are but delusion.

He ﷺ also says:

In this age, do works of good which are not burdensome and that which you can have consistency upon, for a little but continuous is better than a lot which is interrupted. Give thanks for the little and Allah will give you a lot. Do not wait for the states of the like of Bishr[14], Fudayl[15] and those like them. Even the Companions, may Allah be pleased with them, did not do works like theirs, but they had with them the light of prophethood.

He ﷺ also says:

It is an easy path, it brings a person, if he is consistent upon it, to reach the people of the other path, which is the path of the elect. Perhaps he has received within this path some openings and so has joined with the people of the other path. There is nothing within the path of the common from the elements of the path of the foremost

[14] Bishr ibn al-Ḥārith (d.850CE), more commonly known as Bishr al-Hāfī was one of the greatest Saints of the time. He received his *wilāya* when he found a piece of paper with *Bismillahi ir-Raḥmān ir-Raḥīm* written on it, while he was in a state of drunkenness. In this state he revered the piece of paper by perfuming it and placing it respectfully in his house. Thus, Allah gave him a great rank in sainthood, for revering the Name of Allah.
[15] Fudayl ibn ᶜIyād (d. 187AH), was a great Sufi Saint and ascetic, whose life was transformed from being a highway robber to the most devout worshipper. One day, as he was climbing the wall of a young woman's house, he heard the recitation of the Quranic verse: '*Is it not time for the hearts of the believers to become humbled by the remembrance of God...*' (Sura al-Hadīd, v.16). Thereafter his heart turned towards Allah, and he responded, 'Indeed my Lord the time has come.'

(*sabiqin*) except that which is easy. It is an easy path, there is no forty day solitude, no hardship and no danger.

As for the path of the foremost, within it is hardship and forty day solitude. However, there is danger to be feared in the affairs of the religion and a change within ones intellect and *aqida*.....' until he says, 'Change usually occurs in the forty day solitude to those who enter into it without a sheikh or without being commanded to do so.

He was asked, 'If someone comes to you, who does not know the path of the foremost, or the path of the People of the Right, then what should he do?'

He ※ replied:

He should do that which we are upon. Act upon that which he sees us doing, as he sees the establishment of prayers, recitation of the Quran, organising *dhikr*, seeking useful knowledge, and be regular with that.

The great scholar, Ḥabīb ʿAlawī b. Ṭāhir al-Ḥaddād ※ mentioned a lot regarding the path of the People of the Right, in his book '*The diamond necklace regarding the virtues of the Imam, the knower of Allah, al-Ḥabīb Aḥmad b. Ḥasan al-ʿAṭṭās.*'

From among them is what Imam Aḥmad b. Ḥasan al-ʿAṭṭās said:

Our predecessors used to say that their path is Ghazālī outwardly; they do not leave good actions, and inwardly Shādhilī, in the sense that they do not rely upon actions. They do not travel except with hope and yearning. Being obscure is their nature; it is not that they actually seek it.

As for the states (*aḥwāl*), meaning unveiling and the like, they do not seek it, nor do they turn towards it, as it interrupts them from their Lord. The practise of our predecessors was that they would bring up a student until he became a scholar and a worshipper, without him realizing it.

The statement of Imam al-ᶜAṭṭās ﵁:

> The outward of the path is Ghazālī and its inward is Shādhilī does not mean that the path of the masters of the Banī ᶜAlawī is nothing but an imitation of the way of al-Ghazālī or the way of al-Shādhilī, for these characteristics were within the path before the appearance of Imam al-Ghazālī or Imam al-Shādhilī. What it means is that the way of striving became renowned through al-Ghazālī because he wrote about it, and the way of gratitude (*shukr*) became well known through Sheikh Ibn ᶜAṭā'illāh because he wrote about it. These words were used for conciseness and understanding.

Regarding this, Ḥabīb ᶜAlawī b. Ṭāhir al-Ḥaddād ﵁ says in '*The diamond necklace*':

> Know that the Shādhilī Ṭarīqa has been summarised in their saying, 'It is seeing the favour of Allah, continually thanking Him, sincerity in servitude, being free from all things, confessing incapacity and lacking', and this is the summary of its principles.
>
> They have explained much regarding its branches and details, as can be seen from the works of Ibn ᶜAṭā'illāh, and those who came after him.
>
> These principles are indications to great meanings and high ranks. A hearer can take its words, and actualise

> them with ease, especially one who is inexperienced to the defects of the ego, the difficulty in training it, the complexity of treating it and the length of its harshness and stubbornness.
>
> Therefore, there is no doubt that one has to strive and exercise. Even if the exercise here is of the heart, for it is the hardest thing upon the ego.

He then mentions about the path of al-Ghazālī:

> It revolves around exercising, tiredness, difficulty, staying up at night, hunger and the like.
>
> This then is the ṭarīqa of the Masters of the ʿAlawiyyīn, so how does it benefit and what does it lead to?'

Imam al-Ḥaddād ﵀ says:

> A person falls below the rank of a human, meaning that he is greatly overpowered by cravings and desires to the extent that his chivalry disappears and thus becomes an animal according to the predominant characteristic that has overpowered him. Since every animal is overpowered with a certain attribute by which it is recognised. Any person who is overpowered by one of their traits is associated with that animal that best describes him. If he then wants arrive to Allah, he needs to strive, until he firstly reaches the level of a human, and that which a human is dominantly characterised by in contrast to all the other animals. He then strives more until he reaches Allah.

He ﵀ also says:

> He is not considered 'a man' with them until he has a share of every element of humanity within him, and

decreases in every element of the nafs. People are on different levels regarding this, all according to their rank and position with Allah, the Exalted.

This then is the benefit of the way of the commonality; it removes a person from base animal characteristics to the levels of humanity. As a result, everything human within him develops: his character, knowledge, and gnosis. In contrast, all the traits of his nafs which incite him towards evil decrease, such as: greed, jealousy, ostentation, vanity, arrogance and the like.

If he cuts through the dense veils, and enters into the subtle ones until he traverses to the ranks of certitude, he attains proximity to Allah, filled with His attention, receiving His inspiration.[16]

Regarding unveiling and miracles which may occur with the seeker, Imam al-Ḥaddād says:

There is nothing better for a person in this era, who desires the path, to correct his understanding of the principles of Tawḥīd, perform the obligations, refrain from the forbidden, perform the Sunna in accordance with the Quran and Sunna without disregarding them. And if these things flourish within him, he has received a lot of good.

If a seeker masters the path of the People of the Right, he ascends at the hands of his mashā'ikh to the path of the foremost.

---

[16] Imam Aḥmad has related from Abū Huraira 🙵 that the Messenger of Allah 🙳 said: 'If it were not for the devils that hover around the hearts of Banī Adam they would have seen the dominion of the heavens.'

As for the first path, in most cases the seeker only reaps its fruits of closeness and arrival in the intermediary realm (*barzakh*) that is after his death. At this time he is safe from the dangers that could affect him in the dunya due to the presence of his nafs and the defects and flaws it contains.

As for the path of the elect, its fruits are the arrival to Allah. The meaning of arrival '*wuṣūl*' has been explained by Imam al-Ḥaddād in some of his letters:

> The questioner should firstly know that the 'Arriver' (*wāṣil*) to Allah is a slave, who has arrived at a knowledge of Allah at a limit, which the knowledge of scholars ends at. The people of this level differ without number. The 'Arriver' at this rank has two states: one of them is called union (*Jamᶜa*) the other separation (*Faraq*).
>
> If he receives the state of *Jamᶜa*, he becomes extinct from his *nafs*, and from others of his kind. He is engrossed in his Lord, and he disappears completely. There is no thought there which is thought of, and no one else present who appears except the Real Presence, Majestic and High is He.
>
> In describing this grace, some of those who have achieved it have said, 'If any desire besides You occurred to me, in my mind out of negligence I would declare myself an apostate.'
>
> Another said, 'Within my heart there were scattered desires, my desires were united from the moment I saw You.'
>
> The origin of all thoughts and derivatives is due to occupations [*hum*] and the number of attachments. An Arriver to Allah does not have any knowledge of these affairs since he has made all his occupations into one, and that is Allah, the Exalted.

Union has been indicated in the saying of the Prophet ﷺ, "I have a time, within it no one encompasses me except my Lord."

It is very great if this state of union continues. In its continuation strange things appear and amazing things occur.

He ﷺ then says:

As for the state of separation; within it the 'Arriver' is protected, filled by the eye of solicitude. During it the state of mind remains lordly, it is known by the ṣufiyya as 'izn,' the state as angelic and it is called by them inspiration [*ilhām*].

# SECTION 2

## ETIQUETTE AND MANNER ON THE PATH

"I accompanied
Imam Malik for 20 years. 18 of those
were spent learning adab and 2 years
upon knowledge. O how I wish I had
spent all 20 years on learning adab"

Sheikh ᶜAbd ar-Raḥmān
b. al-Qāsim ⚅

~ Chapter 4 ~

# Adab

Amongst the Sufiyya good manner (*adab*) is a great thing, it is the main foundation within the path to Allah, hence they say, 'Adhere to adab or else await destruction!' And, 'Maintain adab even if you have ascended to the highest rank.'

This is because the soundness of the outward indicates the soundness of the inward, whatever is concealed in the inward will manifest upon the outward. The states of the outward comply with the states of the inward, whatever is upon your outward is within your inward, whatever is within the vessel will ooze out and upon the surface its effects will emerge. Therefore, refinement of the limbs indicates refinement of the hearts, and ādāb of the outward indicates ādāb of the inward.

Abū Ḥafṣ[17] ﷺ said:

[17] Abū Ḥafs ᶜUmar bin Maslama al-Ḥaddād was the first to manifest the path of tasawwuf in Naysabur. He was a blacksmith. Once, when his servant was blowing on molten metal the Sheikh's thoughts were lost in Allah, and he placed his bare hand into the fire and pulled out the metal. His hand was unburnt, witnessing this, his servant screamed. Thus the Sheikh left to seclude himself from the people.

Sufism (*Taṣawwuf*), all of it is adab, at all times it is adab, in all states it is adab, and at every level it is adab.

Therefore, whoever maintains ādāb at all times they will reach the rank of "*rijāl*",[18] one who falls short of maintaining ādāb, he is distant in spite of considering himself near, he is rejected in spite of his thinking that he is accepted.

Ibn ʿAṭā'illāh[19] ☙ said:

It is the ignorance of the murīd when he acts disrespectfully, the punishment for him is delayed, and he says, 'If this was disrespectful (*sū'al-adab*) then the blessings would be cut off from me, and I would be far away!' However, the blessing is cut off from such a person but he does not even realise, and he is very distant but he is not even aware of it, were this not the case he would not be doing as he pleases.

People do not become leaders except by ādāb towards Allah, towards His Messenger ☙ towards their shuyūkh and towards all of the Muslims.

---

[18] Rijāl: literally meaning men. In this context refers to the strong hearted men of God who have stripped from themselves every pre-occupation that averts them from God, and have annihilated their beings in His love. They firmly adhere to the sharia outwardly and inwardly. They stand in their positions witnessing the divine manifestations, not turning for an instant from their desire.

[19] Abu'l Fadl Ibn ʿAṭā'illāh al-Iskandarī (d.709AH) was amongst the great Sufi Saints. He was the student of Sheikh Abu'l-Abbās al-Mursī. He was the 3rd leader of the Shadhilli Tarīqa. The Tarīqa gained renown through his writings. He was the author of many books; his most famous composition is *Kitāb al-Ḥikam*, his book of aphorisms. This book reflects his mastery in Sufism. He passed away at the age of 60 and is buried in Cairo.

Adab with Allah is to be compliant to His commands and refrain from His prohibitions.

Adab with the Messenger of Allah ﷺ is to follow his Sunna, desire his companionship, follow his guidance, adorn oneself with his character.

Adab with the shuyūkh is to protect their honour, always serve them with excellence, and have sincere love towards them.

Adab with the Muslims is to love for them that which you love for yourself or more.

Adab of time is to occupy it with obedience. There are four aspects of time for a person, as mentioned by Sheikh Abu'l Abbās al-Mursī[20] رضي الله عنه:

> 1) The time of obedience, 2) the time of sinfulness, 3) the time of blessings, 4) and the time of tribulation.
>
> The time of obedience requires a person to witness the blessings of Allah. The time of disobedience requires a person to repent. The time of blessings requires a person to be grateful and to do shukr. The time of tribulation requires a person to be patient.

When a person fulfils all these aspects of ādāb, then they will receive complete honour and a great rank amongst the general people and the elite by the grace of Allah, exalted be He. The following pages will outline the requirements of ādāb towards oneself, the sheikh and with the brothers.

---

[20] Shihāb al-Dīn Abu'l-Abbās Aḥmad bin ʿUmar bin Muḥammad al-Ansārī al-Mursī (d.1286CE) was a Sufi Saint from Andalusia, who later moved to Alexandria and met the Great Imam Abu'l Ḥasan al-Shādhilī. He was one of the foremost students of Imam al-Shadhilli. He is also known as one of the four master saints of Egypt. He spread the teachings of Imam al-Shādhilī for 43 years, until he passed away and he is buried in Alexandria.

## ~ I ~

# ADAB OF THE SEEKER WITHIN HIMSELF

Adab is to refine the outward and the inward. When both the inward and the outward of a person are rectified and refined that is when they become a perfect Sūfī. Adab within a person is only complete with good characteristics, therefore the Messenger of Allah ﷺ said, 'Make good your character.'

When the soul (*nafs*) is cleansed, that is when a person becomes intelligent, and the inward and outward states are stable and the characteristics are refined, and good manners are formed. The most vital aspect of adab has been explained by one of the great Sufi masters, Sayyidinā ᶜAbdallāh ibn al-Mubārak[21] رضي الله عنه:

The etiquette of serving is greater than serving itself.

---

[21] ᶜAbdallāh Ibn al-Mubārak was born in Khurasan; he travelled many places in search of knowledge. He became one of the most knowledgeable and devout men of his time. There was none other like him in generosity, especially with the students of learning. Ibn Hibbān said, 'He had gathered characteristics within him which were never before gathered in any scholar in his time in the entire world.' He passed away in 181AH and is buried in Baghdad. [Cited from *The Life of Abdallah ibn Al-Mubarak*, Farhia Yahya].

Imam Junaid[22] ﷺ said:

> One who helps himself against his desires has participated in slaying his soul, because slavehood (ᶜ*ubūdiyya*) is the consequence of adab, and tyranny (or cruelty) is *sū' ul-adab*.

Sheikh Abū ᶜAlī al-Daqāq[23] ﷺ said:

> A person with his worship reaches paradise, and with adab in his worship he reaches Allah, Exalted is He.

Sayyidinā Anas b. Mālik ﷺ said:

> Adab in actions is the sign of acceptance of the actions.

The following are some aspects of ādāb that the murīd should follow, so that he may be successful in the world and hereafter and acquire the pleasure of Allah:

1. To have sincerity upon the path, and sincere love for the sheikh, visiting him frequently because of the abundant blessings and *madad* that are with him. One should acquire his praiseworthy characteristics, and remove blameworthy traits, along with acquiring the knowledge. In this there is such goodness which only Allah is aware of.

[22] Imam Junaid al-Baghdadī was one of the great Sufi Masters and Chief Qadi of Baghdad. He was the nephew of Sheikh Sarī al-Saqtī. He is a central figure in the development of tasawwuf. He passed away in 910CE and is buried in Baghdad.

[23] Sheikh Abū ᶜAlī al-Daqqāq al-Ḥasan ibn ᶜAlī ibn Muḥammad ibn Isḥāq al-Naysabūrī (d. 412AH) was amongst the greatest Sufi Saints and Ashᶜarī scholars of his time. He was both the teacher and father in-law of Imam Abu'l-Qāsim al-Qushayrī.

2. Insincerity in love towards the sheikh will turn you away from him.

3. To visit the brothers for the sake of Allah ﷻ. It is a great deed and an outstanding trait, and it is from amongst the most excellent journeys that a person undertakes. The Messenger of Allah ﷺ said, 'Allah ﷻ said: "My love is incumbent upon the people who love each other for the sake of Allah, and gather for My sake and who (strive or spend) for My sake, and who visit each other for My sake."'

4. To seek beneficial knowledge because the Messenger of Allah ﷺ said, 'Seeking knowledge is obligatory upon every Muslim.' This refers to beneficial knowledge such as the knowledge in the hadiths that will inform you about Allah, His Essence (*Dhāt*) and His Attributes (*Ṣiffāt*), His commandments and prohibitions, to learn how to perform every act of worship, to acquire knowledge of the Quran and Hadith, and about the events of the prophets and messengers, and about the pious people along with their acts of piety, and wise counsels.

5. To put an end to acts of cruelty and harshness, to solve situations where people are being mistreated.

6. To repent from all sins, outward sins and inward sins, those that people are aware of and those that people are not aware of such as backbiting, envy, harbouring any ill feelings towards fellow Muslims or despising them, ostentation (*riyā'*) and so forth.

7. To persevere with battling against the ego, Sheikh ᶜAlī al-Daqāq ﷺ said, 'One who adorns his outward by striving, Allah will adorn his inward with witnessing, and one who does not strive against his ego from the beginning, he will

not smell the fragrance of the path.' Abū ʿUthmān al-Maghribī said, 'One who thinks that they will receive the openings without striving, he is dreaming of the impossible.'

**8.** To disagree with the desires of the ego, never agree with it because the central point of the murīd is disagreement of the ego. Abū Ḥafs said, 'One who does not accuse the ego at all times, and oppose all of its desires and does not lead it towards its dislikes at all times then they are deficient in all states.' Imam Busīrī said, 'Disobey the ego and the devil; dispute with them, suspect them both even when they offer you true counsel. *Wa khālifi in-nafsa wa-shayṭāna waʿsihimā, wa in humā mahhadāka an-nuṣḥa fattihimā.*'

**9.** To only have one sheikh, Abū Yazīd al-Bistāmī said, 'One who does not have one teacher, he is a polytheist (*mushrik*) on the path, and one who associates others with his sheikh is Shayṭān.' Know that the murīd is only allowed to have one sheikh because that will assist him on the path, we have never seen a murīd that has been successful at the hands of two shuyūkh. As for the one who does not bind himself to a sheikh, then it is only *baraka* that he receives from the sheikh, if that is the case then there is no harm in him being with any other sheikh.

**10.** To remove worldly hindrances, one who has a worldly attachment will seldom be successful. Therefore, it has been said that it is one of the conditions for the repentant one to remain aloof from his wrongdoing companions, because they were his associates in sinful acts before he repented. Being associated with them may incline him to return to those acts that he has turned away from.

11. One should prepare themselves to bear the difficulties upon the path, and should not run away from them, if you are afflicted with illnesses and ailments, poverty or tribulations you should remain firm upon the path and not waver with the afflictions therein.

12. One should cleanse their inward and outward from characteristics that will prevent them from entering into the presence of Allah ﷻ, such as anger, arrogance, pride, ostentation, envy and so forth, and also control the thoughts, and rectify the characteristics, and remove heedlessness from the heart by remaining in the remembrance of Allah, Exalted is He.

13. To lower the gaze and avoid looking at pleasurable images. Looking at such images or women are like an arrow that afflicts the heart and kills it, especially the gaze of desire (*shahwa*), it is like the poisonous arrow that consumes the human body in an instant.

14. Abu'l-Qāsim al-Qushayrī رحمه الله said, 'One of the greatest hindrances for the murīd is keeping the company of gossip and women and having the heart incline towards them, whoever is afflicted with that by Allah, then it has been agreed upon that such a person has been neglected and abandoned by Allah, in spite of being a good and upright person, even if he could perform a thousand miracles because his heart is occupied with the love of a created being, Shayṭān enters it and deprives his heart of the love of Allah.

15. To maintain the etiquette of the sharia, acting upon its outward as much as possible. Elevation, all of it is in complying to the commands of the Messenger of Allah ﷺ.

**16.** To have a short term view, this is in order to strive toward performing good actions, and refrain from wrongdoing. The person that has a long term view will be slack in doing good, and will tend to fall into wrongdoing. When your death is near, you will repent to Allah for all of your previous sins, and it would be as though you have never sinned, because the one who repents for his sins is as though he has not sinned at all.

**17.** To refrain from gatherings of worldly people because of their constant neglect of Allah ﷻ and forever being occupied with worldly matters, such as food, clothes, weddings and so forth. The risk of mixing with such people for the murīd is that he may get preoccupied in worldly matters. For the murīd, his greatest concern should be to remove from his heart the attachment of worldly things and such gatherings are like poison for him.

**18.** To refrain from any act that will harden the heart, such as too much futile talk and heedlessness, for these are known to harden the heart, the Sufi should only be occupied in those things that will revive his heart.

**19.** To be constant with the remembrance of Allah ﷻ at all times. You should not abandon it until you have acquired a constant presence with Allah, at this stage one witnesses the presence in the heart without having to utter the dhikr with the tongue; dhikr should be done verbally until constant presence with Allah has been attained.

**20.** To maintain the Sunna of cleanliness and hygiene, such as removing hair from the underarm and private parts, to carry a comb, toothstick (*siwāk*) and perfume.

**21.** Beware of seeking recognition and a reputation amongst the people, for example, how the sheikh may be renowned. Sayyidī ᶜAlī Wafā ﵁ said, 'O seeker of Allah, do not be greatly concerned with making yourself known amongst the people. If you are a person of light and truth, Allah will make you manifest and Allah is sufficient as a friend and He is sufficient as a helper. However, if you are a person of wrongdoing and falsehood, then the consequence will not be your renown and the reputation of your piety because that is not what you desired. And if you seek fame, even a little bit, then beware of Allah's torment.'

**22.** To flee from those people who hurl accusations at the people of the path, such as accusing them with falsehood, slander, ostentation, hypocrisy. If anyone has the audacity to do this to the people of the path, he will be detested and loathed by Allah, and such a person will never be successful, even if his worship amounted to the whole of mankind and jinn.

**23.** One should not get bored of reciting the litanies (*awrād*) that have been instructed by the sheikh, because Allah has made every sheikh the murīd's support and secret, and the secret of the path is in its litanies that the murīd has been instructed with. Whoever abandons his litanies, he has violated the pledge with his sheikh, and it has been agreed upon that the murīd does not abandon his wird only that the spiritual blessing for that day is cut off.

**24.** One should not harbour traits such as envy, backbiting, wrongdoing, deceit, obstinacy, bitterness, dishonesty, arrogance, pride, superiority, or look down upon any of the other Muslims or argue with them, and should not criticize any of the people of the path.

**25.** Whoever claims to be sincere on the path but has any one of the traits mentioned above, then he is not sincere, neither will he receive anything on the path, because these traits prevent one from the journey, in fact they turn him away from the presence of Allah, taking him to the presence of the shayāṭīn because these are their traits.

Sheikh Abu'l-ʿAẓā'im ﵇ has mentioned this in his counsel for the people of the path:

> My brother, refrain from the characteristics of Iblīs, which are: envy, pride, greed, desire for reputation and renown, backbiting and slander, lying and deceit, and spreading gossip about your believing brothers.
>
> Desire for your brothers what you desire for yourself. Leave wrongdoing; keep away from beastly traits such as greed, miserliness, vengefulness, cunningness, slyness and deceit, committing adultery, drinking alcohol, neglecting the rights of people. Adorn yourself with angelic traits, by fulfilling the commandments, and refraining from the prohibitions, protect the mind and what it perceives, the eyes, ears, tongue and nose, protect the body and what it holds, like the hands, the heart, the stomach, the private parts, and the legs.

**26.** Increase your determination; seek more than merely the reward for actions and worship. Sayyidī ʿAlī Wafā ﵇ said, 'One who seeks reward for his actions, he is a woman, in spite of having a beard, because men have been blessed with strength and stamina, while women have been blessed with beauty. Therefore, whichever woman has a firm determination she is a *rajul* (man), and the man who is concerned with the outward matters, he is a woman.'

**27.** To be patient with any trials upon the path, as this is inevitable for the seeker who is sincere, whether he likes it or not.

**28.** One should not dwell upon their previous bad actions that were committed before entering the path. A thought might come to the mind, 'It is impossible for someone like me to succeed and become a pious person.' Thoughts such as this are one of the biggest pitfalls for the seeker, and one of the greatest tools for Iblīs to pull you down. Sheikh Abu'l-ʿAbbās al-Mursī رضي الله عنه said, 'The seeker should not think about his previous bad actions, and be in despair of receiving the opening. Many of the people of the path had previous regretful acts, but after repentance they became the friends of Allah (*awliyā*).'

**29.** The murīd should not keep waiting for the opening, rather he should worship Allah for His sake, regardless of whether he receives the opening and unveiling or not. Worship is one of the pre-requisites of slavehood (*ʿubūdiyya*). Sheikh Muḥiyy ud-dīn b. al-ʿArabī رضي الله عنه said, 'Beware of giving up your hard work and effort, for the opening will occur. However, for the opening to occur there is no specific time, therefore do not accuse your Lord, because the fruits are the consequence of your actions.'

**30.** One should not feel as though they are above the counsel of the sheikh or of the brothers. Sayyidī ʿAbdallāh al-Matbūlī رضي الله عنه said, 'One of the requirements of the sincere murīd is that he always sees himself at the level of a child, so that he can feed from the milk of his *murabbī*.'[24]

---

[24] Murabbī means one who raises, nurtures and educates.

Sayyidī ʿAlī Wafā’[25] said, ‘Beware of envying the companions that have been blessed by Allah, rather you should try to derive benefit from them and learn from them. One who envies a person that has been elevated by Allah, Allah may change the state of their heart, just as Iblīs’s heart was transformed from being elevated to the form of Shayṭān because he envied Sayyidinā Adam and became arrogant and said, “I am better than him!”

**31.** The seeker can only maintain these valuable modes of ādāb if he reads it with intellect or sees with spiritual insight that the truth of his origin is that he has been created from dust, or from earth, or from a drop of fluid, and if he sees upon himself other attributes, then these are blessings that have been bestowed upon him by Allah, Glorified and Exalted is He. Ibn ʿAṭā’illāh said, ‘Bury yourself in the earth of obscurity and the lights of arrival (*wuṣūl*) will shine upon you.’

The sincere seeker is the one who always sees the evils of his soul, and the good in his brothers, and does not look at his own good deeds, and looks down upon the faults of his brothers. Sheikh Abu’l-ʿAẓā’im said, ‘The seeker should be like the earth in humility, like the sun in usefulness, like the ocean in generosity and like the night in obscurity.’

[25] ʿAlī Wafā’ was a great sufī saint of Egypt, who took the place of his saintly father Muḥammad Wafā’. He had many followers and his litanies became widespread. He composed many supplications, prayers and poetry. He had many adversaries due to his great spiritual state. In one of his visions he was embraced by the Prophet and he said, “Truly your Lord blesses you.” He passed away on 2nd Dhu’l-Hijja 807AH, may Allah be pleased with him.

## ~ II ~

## Adab of the Seeker with His Sheikh

Know O brother that there is no seeker that can ever acquire a noble and pious state upon the path except by meeting the mashā'ikh, maintaining absolute adab, and serving them abundantly. Imam Junayd ؓ said, 'One who travels the path without a sheikh is astray and leads others astray, one who has no respect with the mashā'ikh, Allah afflicts him by making him loathsome amongst the people and he is deprived of the light of faith.'

Sayyidī ᶜAbd al-Qādir Jīlī ؓ said:

> 'One who does not believe that their sheikh is perfect, they will never succeed with him.'

Abū Jaᶜfar al-Khuldī said:

> 'One who does not maintain respect with the mashā'ikh, Allah will cause dogs to overpower him that will cause harm to him.'[26]

[26] "Dogs" is used in the metaphorical sense, referring to either harsh people or some sort of difficulty that may befall that person.

Aḥmad b. Abī al-Wardī[27] said:

> Beware of doing something that would turn your sheikh's heart away from you, for one who does such a thing, a punishment will follow, which may even occur after the passing away of the sheikh.

Sheikh Abu'l-ᶜAẓā'im has put forth the adab that is obligatory upon the seeker towards the sheikh:

1. The seeker should purify himself inwardly and outwardly from every sin in character and in action, if he desires the opening then he should observe this. The people of the path have agreed that the seeker who loves his sheikh should repent from all of his sins, and he should purify himself from all of his faults. The one who is soiled with sins and claims to love his sheikh, he is a liar.
2. The sheikh should be the seekers aim, in other words he should seek to reform his own characteristics and mould himself with the traits of his sheikh, and adorn himself with his states. The seeker's aim should not be to see miracles or to have status or worldly benefit.
3. The seeker should remove all doubts and suspicions from himself inwardly and outwardly. In order to protect himself, he should not depend upon the sheikh's state, neither should he imitate the states of the sheikh that are visible in gatherings or the private states of the sheikh when he is alone with Allah.

[27] Aḥmad bin Muhammad bin Abī al-Wardī: He was the son of Muḥammad bin Abī al-Ward and the brother of Muḥammad. From among his sayings is, 'When the status of a saint of Allah increases his humility increases, when his wealth increases, his generosity increases and when his age increases, his efforts increase.' May Allah be pleased with him.

4. Whenever Allah honours the seeker with a special position, he should never think that he is like the sheikh or equivalent to him, or that he does not need him. Such behaviour proves that he has separated from Allah, and this occurs when people are not careful with the blessings of Allah ﷻ, hence only the respectful (*ahl al-adab*) are safe upon the path.

5. Another aspect of adab is not to hide anything from the sheikh with regards to one's state. The seeker's state will be revealed to the sheikh just as Allah is aware of it. If the seeker does not reveal anything and keeps it hidden, it becomes an obstacle upon the path, and by telling the sheikh the obstacle will weaken and disappear.

Sayyidinā Abu'l ʿAbbās al-Mursī ؓ says, 'There should not be a veil between the seeker and sheikh because of the ailments that are within him. The sheikh is his doctor, and the inward state of the seeker is concealed, it is permissible for the doctor to disclose them since he has to cure them.'

6. The seeker should hold back his own choices and decisions when with the sheikh; he should only act with regards to himself or his wealth after referring the matter with his sheikh.

7. One should only visit the sheikh after informing him.

Sayyidī ʿAlī Wafā' ؓ says, 'Your guide to Allah ﷻ (i.e. the sheikh) is the eye with which Allah gazes upon you with kindness and mercy. He is the face of Allah with which you will be accepted, Allah's happiness is with the sheikh's happiness, and His anger towards you is with the sheikh's anger towards you. Know this and persevere, and be attentive of what you see.'

**8.** One should observe the thoughts of the sheikh in major and minor matters, and not overlook his dislikes. One should not rely upon the sheikh's good character, patience and compassion, being unmindful of their own behaviour.

**9.** If the seeker finds that he has not received a spiritual opening, he should not blame his sheikh, rather he should blame himself and say, 'The fault is in me.'

**10.** The seeker should not behave in any way that would distress his sheikh, because Allah angers with the anger of the sheikh, and is happy with the happiness of the sheikh. More honour is due to the sheikh than the biological father. This is because the sheikh will only command the murīd according to Allah's commands. Therefore, one who disobeys him, disobeys the one who gave us the sharia, i.e. the Messenger of Allah ﷺ, consequently he incurs the wrath of Allah, according to the sin committed.

**11.** When the seeker visits the sheikh he should enter with utmost humility and respect, and then serve the sheikh accordingly, try to do as much as possible for abundant blessings.

**12.** Sayyidī Muḥammad al-Shanāwī[28] ؓ said, 'In spite of all the blessings that Allah has bestowed upon me. I would never go to my sheikh except with a humble mind, and I

[28] Sheikh Muḥammad al-Shanāwī: He was from the saints who were immersed in knowledge. People were unable to keep up with his recitation of the Quran and dhikr and would return weakened after spending two days with him, testifying that he did not sleep at all. He would always be engaged in serving the people. Sheikh Shihāb ul-Dīn al-Subkī and Sheikh ʿAbd ul-Raḥīm al-Manāwī were from among his students. May Allah be pleased with him.

would see myself under his shoes, and I would only depart from him with madad and blessings.'

**13.** The seeker should not be content with merely having belief in the sheikh, and neglect what he has commanded or forbidden, saying: 'The gaze (*naẓar*) of my sheikh is enough for me.' This is ignorance upon the path.

One of the companions of the Messenger of Allah ﷺ said, "I ask you for your companionship in paradise." He ﷺ asked, "And anything other than that?" He replied, "Just that". The Prophet ﷺ said, "Help me, for your sake by prostrating in abundance."

The Messenger of Allah ﷺ responded by instructing him to strive with a particular action in order to gain the rank. In other words, you cannot gain a rank without striving for it.

Sayyidī ᶜAlī Wafā' رضي الله عنه says, 'Do not ask your sheikh to bless you with the spiritual secrets when you have not cleansed yourself from sinful acts. It is like inserting honey into the casing of a bitter plant, the honey will turn bitter by it.'

**14.** The seeker should never feel that he does not need the knowledge of his sheikh, even if he were to become the greatest sheikh. The knowledge that a person receives on the path is a more specific matter unlike outward knowledge received by scholars. The majority of scholars do not have the ability to remove the diseases of the heart.

Imam al-Ghazālī had a sheikh in spite of being the "Proof of Islam", likewise Sheikh ᶜIzz ul-Dīn b. ᶜAbd al-Salām[29] had a

[29] Sheikh al-ᶜIzz bin ᶜAbd ul-Salām was given the title, 'Sultan of the Scholars.' He was among the contemporaries of the great Ghawth Imam Abu'l-Ḥasan al-Shādhilī رضي الله عنه. The Prophet ﷺ once told the Imam to convey

sheikh, in spite of being known as "The Sultan of the Scholars".

The true Sufi is he who is a person of knowledge and who acts upon it with sincerity. Knowledge of Sufism is to know how to perform the act with sincerity and nothing else.

**15.** The seeker should not consider the reprimand of his sheikh insignificant. Sayyidī Muḥammad Wafā'[30] ؓ said, 'Any murīd that is not affected by the reprimand of their sheikh and does not hasten towards him to please him, he is loathed by Allah.'

**16.** Do not burden the sheikh when he is refining you. You should be attentive and compliant with everything that he instructs you with. Sheikh Abu'l-ᶜAbbās al-Mursī ؓ says, 'The murīd is not he who feels proud of his sheikh but the murīd is he of whom the sheikh feels proud of.'

Abu'l-Ḥajjāj al-Aqsarī elaborated on this saying: 'One who is sincere with his sheikh, they do not necessarily have to meet physically, in fact it suffices him to focus upon him with his

---

his salam to al-ᶜIzz bin ᶜAbd al-Salām. He passed away in 660AH. May Allah be pleased with him.

[30] Muḥammad Wafā' was born in Alexandria in 702AH. He was one of the great saints of Allah, he followed the way of Imam Abu'l-Ḥasan al-Shādhilī ؓ and people would flock to visit him. It has been related that when he was born, Ibn ᶜAṭā'illah ؓ came to visit him with his companions. When he saw the baby he kissed him, saying to his friends, "This one has come into the world with the science of our spiritual realities." Before the age of 10 he composed many books on the Sufī Way. Amongst his miracles was that one year the Nile did not rise to its level. The people of Cairo were getting prepared to flee the land in fear of famine. When Sayyidinā Muḥammad Wafā' stood at the river's edge he said, 'By the grace of Allah, rise!' The river then rose and filled the banks. And it is said that this is how he acquired his name 'Wafā'' which means fulfilment. He passed away on 11th Rabī al-Awwal, and is buried in the Qarāfa cemetery in Cairo. May Allah be pleased with him. [Cited from: Richard J.A. Mc. Gregor, '*A Study of Sainthood in Medieval Islamic Egypt: Muhammad and ᶜAlī Wafā.*']

heart. As the image is the soundness of his beliefs, if it is manifest to him, he does not need the physical form to be present. However, if the murīd is able to have the mental image and the physical presence then it is better and more complete.

The murīd should only meet the sheikh knowing that the sheikh possesses him and can deal with him as he pleases. Anyone who desires to attain the ranks without having love for his sheikh or opposing the ego, then he has mistaken the path and will not succeed.'

**17.** One who serves the sheikh without adab; it will lead him to perish. One who serves the sheikh with adab, he will receive honour in both abodes and he will acquire all of his desires and goals. Many have said that the true murīd does not attain the rank of *rijāl* until he exerts his spirit (*rūḥ*) and extinguishes his decisions, placing them all under the decisions of the sheikh, and it has been said in poetry:

*'Even if I was told to die, I would die obediently*

*And I would say to the angel of death, 'You are most welcome!'*

It has also been said, the sign of a wretched murīd is one who has companionship with the mashā'ikh but does not respect them.

**18.** One should never think that they have done enough for their sheikh, even if they have served him for 1000 years, and spent upon him thousands of pounds. And one who thinks in their mind that they have given him something that is equal to him, then they have been expelled from the path and their bond with the sheikh is nullified.

Sheikh Abu'l-Ḥasan al-Shādhillī said, 'Only accompany the mashā'ikh with sincerity and obedience, and have patience when he gets angry with you for no apparent reason, only approach them with determination and enthusiasm as that will hasten the sheikh in accepting you. The sheikh will never say to the murīd that approaches him, seeking the path, to wait a day or two, except when they see his slackness, lack of determination and disrespect. However, if they see that he is respectful, then they will hasten to form a bond with him.'

**19.** The seeker should only ever meet his sheikh with sincerity, even if he meets him several times in the day. Sayyidī $^{c}$Alī Wafā' said, 'Only when the murīd comes to the sheikh sincerely that he becomes worthy, then the sheikh is permitted to reveal the spiritual secrets to him. However if he enters the presence of the sheikh without sincerity, then the matter is reverse.'

**20.** If one of the other brothers approach the sheikh and serve him respectfully, you should be mindful not to envy him, as it will cause you to decline and you will endure harm. However, if you are obedient to the sheikh, and you adorn yourself with characteristics that are worthy of preference then it will please the sheikh. The sheikh is just and treats all the murīds equally.

Sayyidī $^{c}$Alī Wafā' said, 'There are three things that will make the murīd succeed: 1) to love his sheikh exceptionally, 2) to accept everything that he instructs you with, 3) to fulfil every matter that the sheikh desires.'

He also said, 'One who approaches his sheikh to serve him, then Allah approaches his heart and fills it with many blessings.' And, 'One who prefers his sheikh over himself, Allah reveals to him His divine manifestation. One who regards his sheikh free from any fault or imperfection then Allah bestows upon him specialities in spiritual blessings.'

**21.** One should always maintain adab with their sheikh, they should never pry into his affairs at any time, and neither incline towards it. One should not stand over the sheikh while he is sleeping or when he is eating, drinking, or in the bathroom. Any murīd that does so will be ruined. Sayyidī ᶜAlī Wafā' رضي الله عنه said, 'Beware of paying any attention to the words of any envier or enemy who speaks against the sheikh, as you will be blocked on the path of Allah.

The people have been divided into two groups: prostrating angels and the envious Shayṭān, just as has been mentioned with the event of Sayyidinā Adam عليه السلام. Therefore desire, O murīd, to be from the elite, constantly serving and submissive, whether it is to submit to the religion, to learn, or to honour and respect. But beware of bearing malice in your heart or being envious, as this will result in loss of blessings, punishment or deprivation of blessings.'

**22.** One should not be content upon the path by relying on the works of their fathers and grandfathers, as is often the case with the children of most mashā'ikh. In fact, they should have the sheikh in order to refine them. Becoming a spiritual master is not something that is inherited; rather it is acquired with hard work and striving.

**23.** One should believe that the sleep of the sheikh is better than their own worship; this is because the sheikh is free from faults and defects. The sleep of the sheikh is not a time when he is neglecting his Lord, but rather it is a time when he is experiencing *mushāhada.*[31]

**24.** The seeker, with regards to his own states should not consider any act that he has committed too grave to mention to his sheikh and he should mention it such as: adultery, pride, self-conceit, hypocrisy, love of ostentation and other acts that are forbidden in Islam. It is necessary for him to mention them all to his sheikh so that he is aware of it and can cure them.

**25.** The seeker, when he is criticised by the sheikh in front of the other brothers proves that the sheikh has extreme concern for him, and desires for him to improve and elevate. Were he not to censure and criticise him, then that would mean that he is neglecting him, just as the sheikh would neglect a person in whom he sees absolutely no good.

**26.** The seeker should never burden the sheikh to walk up to him in order to greet him, even if the seeker has returned from a journey. Neither should he trouble the sheikh to visit him when he is ill, or console him if a kin has passed away. Rather, the seeker should go to the sheikh himself on such occasions. If the seeker's heart changes towards his sheikh in a negative way, then he has committed disrespect towards him, and he would have to renew his bond with his sheikh.

**27.** The seeker should always link his heart with his sheikh and submit to him and he should believe that Allah, Exalted is He, has made all the spiritual blessings (*madad*)

---

[31] For example if the sheikh is occupied in an act that may appear like a worldly act, while the murīd is occupied in worshipping Allah. The act of the sheikh is still better than that of the murīd, due to the sheikh's purity and nearness to Allah.

only emanate from the door of his sheikh. He should also believe that his sheikh is the external being upon whom Allah focuses His blessings upon; and madad and blessings can only be received through him.

Sheikh Zayn al-Dīn al-Khawāfī ؓ said: 'The murīd should believe that he only receives madad from his sheikh, as the sheikh receives it from the Prophet ﷺ, and the Messenger of Allah ﷺ receives it from Allah ﷻ, and this is how the murīd is connected to Allah, that is through the saints (*Ahlullāh*).

He ؓ also said: 'Know that the link of the murīd's heart to the sheikh is the core principle in receiving the openings swiftly; in fact, it is the root cause. The murīd will only experience the severing of blessings and elevation when there is no link with the heart towards his sheikh, by way of submission, obedience, and sincere determination. The greatest thing that breaks the link between the sheikh and the murīd is when he opposes the sheikh in his heart.

**28.** The seeker should not turn away from the love of his sheikh or from serving him unless it is out of necessity, in which case he should seek to be excused by the sheikh. It has been said that one who turns away from the sheikh for one moment, for example even after serving him for seventy years, he loses in that moment more than he has gained in the seventy years.

Imam Sha$^{c}$rānī ؓ said, 'What a loss for the one who turns away from his sheikh, indeed his command is like the command of his Lord, it's as though he has turned away from the command of his Lord, but most murīds are ignorant of this, and for this reason they do not benefit.'

**29.** The seeker should not persist in acting disrespectfully towards the sheikh, not inwardly or outwardly. The sincere murīd, when his heart is linked with the sheikh, and he fulfils the outward forms of adab, spiritual madad flows from the heart of the sheikh to the heart of the murīd. But when the madad comes from the sheikh and finds that the heart of the murīd is soiled with disrespect, the madad returns back. It's as though the speech of the sheikh advises the heart of the sincere murīd. Therefore, whoever purifies his inward from all disobediences, and behaves respectfully with the sheikh, then all the spiritual blessings, states and knowledge that are in the heart of the sheikh will be transmitted to the heart of that murīd.

**30.** If the sheikh seeks an opinion regarding any matter from the murīd, he should refer the matter back to the sheikh, and not give his personal opinion, just as the companions of the Messenger of Allah ﷺ would do, as he was the most knowledgeable amongst them in matters of the world and the hereafter. The same applies with regards to the sheikh; he does not need the opinion of the murīd.[32]

**31.** The peak of adab with the sheikh is to have love for him. One who does not attain this level due to being affected by other desires and passions they will not succeed upon the path because love of the sheikh is the rank upon which the path relies upon in order to ascend to the ranks of nearness to Allah ﷻ.

We will end this section by a beautiful quotation from Sheikh Muḥiyyuddīn Ibn al-ᶜArabī ؓ cited from his book *'Futuḥāt al-Makiyya'* that describes the nature of a devoted murīd:

[32] On occasions when the Messenger of Allah ﷺ would ask for the opinion of the Companions they would respond by saying: "Allah and His Messenger know best."

'The traits of the lovers: to be slain in devotion to his beloved, running to his presence constantly, suffering from sleeplessness, concealing his grief, desiring to leave everything which pre-occupies him from him, such as the desires of the world and the hereafter, for he is distant in his companionship which will veil him from his beloved.

He is abundantly sighing, resting only in the speech of his beloved, and the mentioning of his name, always in agreement to the love of his beloved, fearful of offending his sanctity. He deems great that which is from his beloved even if it is little. He embraces the obedience of his beloved, and avoids disobedience.

He has habituated his soul to the love of everything that his beloved wants. He does not have a soul, for all of it belongs to his beloved. He rebukes himself regarding the rights of his beloved and he never rebukes his beloved. He is jealous over his beloved more than he is over himself. He therefore yearns that his beloved is not seen, despite his own desire to see him.

His love does not accept an increase because of the favour of his beloved. He is characterised with anonymity as though he is a beggar, but he is not a beggar. He does not sober up from his drunkenness, and is between unification (*wuṣūl*) and separateness (*hajar*). He never says to his beloved; 'why did you do that?' or 'why did you say that?' He shows happiness, yet he is sad. His rank is voiceless, but his state translates itself, due to his drunkenness in love. He chooses the pleasures of his beloved over all the preferences of himself.'

~ III ~

# ADAB OF THE SEEKER WITH HIS BROTHERS

The sincere seekers are the pioneers of their era, together forming a noble community. The first example of this can be seen at the time of the Messenger of Allah ﷺ when the blessed community was formed in the enlightened city, Madīna, and Allah described them as: "*Muḥammad the Messenger of Allah and those that are with him...*"[33]

Allah described the companions of the Messenger of Allah ﷺ as having mercy and compassion amongst them: "*ruḥamā'u baynahum*", this is the essential meaning of being brothers in faith. Sheikh Abu'l-ᶜAẓā'im ﷺ has elaborated on this:

> Brothers are made of various physical bodies with one spirit flowing through them. Like one body, they are one with many limbs, so if one of the members experiences pain the whole body should feel pain.' Therefore, all the brothers sense pain when one of them is in pain. The wealthy amongst them are poor because they sense what the poor ones amongst them experience, and the poor are wealthy because of their extreme confidence in their Lord. These inward traits of the heart adorn their outward.

[33] Sura al-Fatḥ 48:29

Each brother spends for his brother in whichever way he can. One brother will provide the other with knowledge, while the other will provide him with sustenance. It is certain that when they meet in this way, the doors of heaven will be opened and blessings, sustenance and spiritual blessings will pour forth, and Allah will remove the malice and greed from their hearts because they love Allah more than themselves.

Let us consider the two that meet for their desire and love of Allah, wishing to spend for His sake, Glorified and Exalted is He. One of them employs himself for his brother intending the hereafter, educating him with his knowledge and meeting him with good character, while the other spends upon him with his wealth, giving him food, drink and money, such people have been described in the Hadith Qudsi on the authority of Sayyidinā ʿUbāda b.Sāmit ☙, in which Allah says:

"My love is obligatory upon those who love each other for My sake, My love is obligatory upon those who give each other good counsel for My sake, My love is obligatory upon those who visit each other for My sake, and My love is obligatory upon those who spend upon each other for My sake, and they will be upon pillars made of light. The prophets and saints will be envious of their station."

Such a description is only evident amongst the saints, the abdāl and the Messengers, may peace be upon them all. Therefore, every brother that behaves in this way will be from among the saints, the abdāl and the messengers. This brotherhood for the sake of Allah amongst the believers is necessary to support one another and to help them towards piety and taqwa, goodness and excellence, especially if it is for the sake of the world and the hereafter, and not only for the world.

The following is a guideline of the manner that should be maintained towards our brothers:

1. You should look upon your brother as though he is better than yourself, in any aspect that you can think of. If you see one elder, you should believe that he is better because he has been worshipping Allah before you. If you see one younger, they are better than you because they have fewer sins. If you see one of equal age and more knowledgeable, you should consider him to be better; on the other hand, if he is less knowledgeable, you should deem him better as his reckoning on the day of judgement will be easier, since a man is judged according to his knowledge and so forth.

2. You must not look down upon the faults of your brothers as they are not infallible Messengers, or angels made of light without any human (*basharī*) traits. Instead, be occupied with purification and eliminate your own faults. Perceive yourself with censure and rebuke, and recognise the virtues of your brother, so that you may acquire them. The Messenger of Allah ﷺ said, 'Do not harm the Muslims, or insult them, and do not look for their faults, one who looks for the faults of their Muslim brother, Allah will look for his faults, and the one whose faults Allah searches for, he will expose them even if it is in the privacy of his house.'

3. Restrain yourself from desiring the possessions of your brother, and do not enquire about them, instead be accustomed to preferring your brother over yourself. The

greatest of men have not elevated except by preferring others to themselves and having a sound heart, free from malice, envy and resentment.

4. If you are in the company of one or more of the brothers, you must strive together in acquiring beneficial knowledge, good deeds, be active in increasing each others determination, so that you benefit from your brother and he benefits from you.

5. To cover the faults of your brother which only you are aware of and none other. If the need arises to discuss the matter with him, you must address him with compassion and kindness, and it should remain confidential between you and him.

6. On visiting your brother, you must not burden him by occupying too much of his time, as the Messenger of Allah ﷺ said, 'Visit at intervals and the love will increase.' Also be wary of the time when you visit, it should not be too late in the evening or too early in the morning, or at a time when you know he will be occupied with his family.

7. One should be eager to fulfil any promise that is made to his brother. If he requires you to do something for him, you must try to fulfil it whenever possible without making excuses.

8. One must not desire esteem or veneration over the other brothers. There should be humility in those who are elevated, either by knowledge, action, status, and so forth out of reverence for Allah, the One who has raised him. The mashā'ikh have agreed that to desire esteem amongst the people is one of the swiftest ways to failure.

9. When counselling your brother in religious matters or when encouraging him towards acts of worship, you must

speak to him with kindness and compassion and not adopt a manner that is demeaning or humiliating, whereby he is offended and does not comply.

**10.** One must not consider themselves better than any of the brothers due to their obedience in acts of worship or because of any spiritual blessings that they may have received. Sayyidī ᶜAbd al-ᶜAzīz Darini رضي الله عنه said, ‘One who desires that their whole existence be filled with goodness, they should regard themselves beneath the whole of creation in rank. The likeness of madad that is with the people is like water. Water only flows downwards to low-lying places, it does not flow upwards. Therefore one who thinks that they are equal to their companion, then the madad will cease to flow towards him, and if he thinks that he is better than him, then not even an atom’s worth of it will flow towards him.’

**11.** One should refrain from the desire of leadership. If one sees this desire within himself he should censure himself, and adorn himself with ādāb. The goal of the seeker is to remain concealed amongst the people and present with Allah.

**12.** One should not seek *maqām* (rank) or *hāl* (spiritual state) through their worship. One who does seek this, they are very far from the paths of *maᶜrifa* (gnosis). In fact they should seek Allah through their worship and in all matters.

One should not forget to counsel themselves and their brothers. They should not desire the things that other people have, or accompany an innovator, or a woman. One should not see fault in the sheikh, or be heedless in remembering Allah, and not refrain from the gatherings of dhikr or from serving the ṣāliḥīn and honouring them. If one does refrain from these, Allah will afflict them by being detested amongst the people.

# Section 3

# Keeping Good Company

*"A man is upon the religion of his friend, therefore let one of you look at the one whom he takes as a friend"*

The Prophet ﷺ

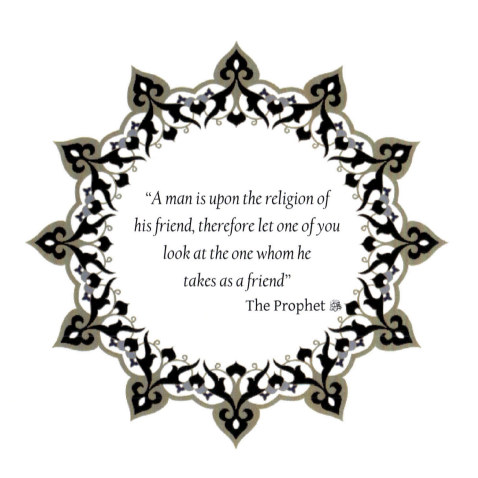

# KEEPING GOOD COMPANY

Imam al-Ghazālī ﷺ said, 'Know that not everyone is suitable to keep as company. The Prophet ﷺ said, 'A man is upon the religion of his friend, therefore let one of you look at the one whom he takes as a friend.' Hence, there is no doubt that a number of characteristics must be taken into consideration. A companion must be:

1. Intelligent
2. Of good character and not corrupt.
3. Not an innovator
4. Not greedy for the world.

As for intelligence it is the capital.

The commander of the believers, Sayyidinā ᶜAlī ﷺ said:

> Do not accompany an ignorant brother, woe to you and woe to him, for how many of the ignorant are clothed in forbearance! They have been taken as brothers; a man is measured according to his companion, an object with another object has its measurements and likenesses, and a heart compared to a heart is a guide when it is met.

How can it not be with an idiot who harms you while having the intention of benefitting you!

Allah, Exalted is He has said, "*And do not obey one whose heart we have made heedless from Our remembrance, and follows his own desires.*"'[34]

Imam $^{c}$Abd ul-Wahhāb Sha$^{c}$rānī said:

> A covenant was taken with us from the Messenger of Allah ﷺ that we will choose to keep righteous company. They are those by whose company we do not fall into sin. This is either through repentance of a sin that may have occurred. Therefore, if one of us falls into a sin due to the company we associate with, then repentance should be made immediately, and we must be determined not to persist in the wrong. On the other hand, it may be due to the company we keep that we do not fall into sin at all.
>
> The one who wants to perform this covenant requires astuteness (*siyāsa*) and insight (*firāsa*) in order to know who is worthy of companionship and who is not. Whoever does not posses such astuteness then he will keep the company of anyone that he sees; and then after such a companionship he may break off that relationship, and so will now have an enemy.

It has been said that the intelligent person is the one who employs a reference before companionship (*tajrīb qabla taqrīb*). I swear by Allah, the sin a person commits in isolation is enough for him in this day than to add more sins to it by associating with people. A person can hardly find one gathering in these days, which is without sin at all: backbiting,

[34] Sura al-Kahf 18:28

rumours, heedlessness of Allah the Exalted, or an encouragement to acquire the world, or something other than that.[35] Therefore, being alone is better than keeping the company of people in present times, unless the sharia specifies for such a person to be in company.

For this reason, search my brother, for the company of the righteous. If you do not find them then sit on your own. It has been said, 'Be alone rather than with bad company.' And also, 'The company of a dog has more priority over the company of one who will lead you to sins.' Know my brother that whosoever has become a means by their companionship for you to commit a sin then they are an evil companion.

The two sheikhs (Bukhārī and Muslim) and others have related: 'The likeness of a good and bad companion compares with a perfume seller and a blacksmith. The perfume seller will either offer you (some perfume), sell it to you or (at least) you will find from him a good fragrance. However, a blacksmith will either burn your clothes, or you will find from him a foul smell.'

Related in Abū Dawūd and Nasā'ī: 'The likeness of a good companion and a bad companion is like a perfume seller, if you do not receive something from him then you will (at least) receive his fragrance. And the likeness of bad company is like a blacksmith, if you are not blackened by him then you will be harmed by his smoke.' And Allah, the Exalted and Glorified knows best.'[36]

Ḥabīb Abū Bakr al-ᶜAṭṭās b. ᶜAbdallāh b. ᶜAlawī b. Zain al-Habshī ﷺ said:

> It has been related from the Prophet ﷺ, "Zuhd in our time is abstinence from dinars and dirhams. However, there will come a time upon people when abstinence from

[35] This is over four hundred years ago in the blessed city of Cairo.
[36] Imam ᶜAbd ul-Wahhāb Shaᶜrānī, *ᶜUhūd al-Muḥammadiyya.*

people will be more beneficial for them then abstinence from dinars and dirhams."

Likewise, take assistance my children and brothers in the correction of your hearts and limbs by distancing yourselves from associating with opposites, and they are those people who are contrary from the way of the great predecessors. For the heart of a man is like a mirror which reflects everything which is before it, whether pretty or ugly. It has also been said, that associating with low people for just one day, infects its companion with evil from his association which he cannot remove even through the companionship of scholars for a whole year.[37]

[37] Sayyid Abū Bakr al-ᶜAṭṭās, *Tadhkīr al-Muṣṭafā,*

## An Encouragement to Sit with the Awliyā and to Accompany the Righteous

It is related from Sayyidinā Ibn Abbas ﷺ who said, 'I said, O Messenger of Allah, which of our companions are the best?' He ﷺ replied, "He whose sight reminds you of Allah, whose speech increases you in knowledge, and whose knowledge reminds of the Hereafter.'[38]

Habīb Aḥmad b. Umar b. Sumait ﷺ said:

> Good and evil are seeded within a human; it does not appear until one mingles with others. So if he mingles with the good, then good actions will appear from him, and if he mingles with evil, then evil actions appear from him.

Imam ᶜAbdallāh b. ᶜAlawī al-Ḥaddād ﷺ said:

> Know that to mix with the people of good and to sit with them, grows the love of good in your heart, and helps with good works, just as mixing with the people of evil and sitting with them, plants the love of evil and its works in the heart. Whoever mixes with a people and lives amongst them, he will love them implicitly, whether they

[38] Related on the authority of Abū Yaᶜlā

> are good or evil. A man is with the one he loves in the world and the Hereafter.

Our master Imam Muḥammad b. Zain b. Sumait said:

> Sit with those whose vision reminds you of Allah, whose states and energy motivate you towards Allah. Stick to him if you find him, and cling on to him tightly if you meet him. There is nothing more beneficial to the heart and nothing more in paying dividends than the company of the righteous and the good. There is nothing more harmful than accompanying their opposite from the people of heedlessness and evil.
>
> It has been related in a hadith, 'A man is upon the religion of his friend.'[39] It has also been said, 'Whoever accompanies the good, Allah will make him from the good even though he is from the evil, and whoever accompanies the evil, Allah will make him from the evil even though he is from the good. If you are unable to see them - as it is common in our time - then there is nothing better than perusing through their biographies, narrations, virtues, and traces.'[40]

It has been related from our master the Imam, the Gnostic, Sayyidinā Aḥmad b. Zain al-Ḥabshī, may Allah make us benefit from him:

> Understanding is a light which shines upon the heart. It is not given except to he who sits with the righteous, or reads their books.' He also said, 'Sitting with the righteous is more beneficial than a hundred or a thousand

[39] Related by Aḥmad, Abū Dawūd, Tirmidhī

[40] *Majma ʿal-Baḥrayn*

> seclusions.' He also said, 'It could be that sitting with one person is more beneficial than sitting with seventy thousand others.

Our master Imam Aḥmad b. Ḥasan al-ᶜAṭṭās said:

> If there was only one virtue in sitting with righteous, it would have been enough. That is pulling people's endeavours, hearts, and intention; raising them to high ranks, or to save them from dirty thoughts. If this isn't achieved then it would be enough for you that you are saved from disobedience, as long as you are in their presence.

It is related from Imam al-Shāfiᶜī:

> There are four characterisitics which increase you in intellect: Leaving useless speech, the siwāk, sitting with the righteous, and sitting with the scholars.

Some of the righteous have said:

> Whoever prays behind someone who is forgiven is also forgiven, and whoever eats with someone who is forgiven is also forgiven. Whoever sits with the righteous, his desire for obedience increases. Whoever sits with the scholars increases in knowledge and action.

Sheikh Ibrāhīm al-Khawwās[41] said:

[41] Abū Isḥāq Ibrāhīm bin Isma'īl al-Khawwās: He was from the greatest of those who travelled the path through reliance upon Allah. He was from among the contemporaries of Imam Junaid. He passed away in the year 291AH. May Allah be pleased with him.

> Medication of the hearts is in five: reciting the Quran with reflection, emptying the stomach, praying at night, pleading in the early hours, and sitting with the righteous.

From the stories that have been related: It has been mentioned regarding the great sheikh, Abū Sulaymān Darini رضي الله عنه:

> I once attended the gathering of a storyteller, and his speech affected my heart. When I stood up, there was nothing of his sermon left in my heart. I returned a second time, and I heard him speak and the affect of his speech remained in my heart up until the street, it then disappeared. Then I returned a third time, and the affect of his speech remained in my heart, until I got to my house, and so I broke all the things which were contrary to the shariah and I adhered to the path.[42]

It is related that once a slave, who was owned by some business men passed by the gathering of Manṣūr b. ᶜAmmār, may Allah have mercy upon him. He heard him say, 'Whosoever gives this faqīr four dirhams, I will make four supplications for him. The slave had four dirhams which his master had given to him for an errand, so he gave it to the faqīr, who then supplicated for him. He then returned to his master with nothing. His master asked him about the supplications the faqīr had made for him. The slave said, 'Firstly that I'm freed from bondage,' so his master freed him.

'Secondly, that Allah returns the dirhams to me.' The master replied, 'You can have four thousand dirhams.'

[42] Imam ᶜAlī b. Ḥasan al-ᶜAṭṭās, *Al-Qirṭās*

'Thirdly, that Allah relents towards me and to you.' The master then said, 'I repent to Allah.'

'Fourthly, that Allah forgives me, you and him and all the people.' The man said, 'As for this, it is beyond me.' That night when the man went to sleep, he saw Allah who said, 'Do you think that you are able to fulfil that which is due from you and I would not fulfil that which is due from me? I have forgiven you, the slave, the faqīr and all the people.'[43]

He also said, may Allah make us benefit from him:

> You should accompany the good and adopt their manners. Benefit yourself from their speech and actions. Visit them both the living and the deceased, along with extreme reverence, having a true good opinion regarding them, and by this will a visitor be able to benefit from them. You will receive from their madad. The only reason why the people of this time benefit little from the righteous is because of the lack of their reverence for them and the weakness of their good opinion of them. So they have been deprived from their blessings because of this and they have not witnessed their miracles; to the extent that people now think that the times are deprived of the awliyā'. However, they are - by the praise of Allah - many and abundant, apparent and hidden. Only those whose hearts Allah has illuminated with the lights of reverence, and granted good opinion regarding them recognise them.

Some of the Gnostics have said:

> Whoever desires to achieve all good within the gatherings of the awliyā then he should have three traits:

[43] Imam ᶜAbdallāh al-Ḥaddād, *Fuṣūl al-ᶜIlmiyya.*

i) He should never divert his attention away from them, for they look into the heart just as you look into water through a glass.

ii) Do not expect from them infallibility, for they are protected.

iii) Do not listen to them being criticised in comparison to others. A wali is able to speak regarding others who are less than him.

Sheikh Abu'l Ḥasan al-Shādhilī ﷺ has said:

If one of you attend the gathering of any of the scholars, or the righteous, and you do not understand anything from their speech, then resign the matter to him. Do not say, 'There is no benefit in this speech!' For the angels and the jinn also attend the gatherings of the scholars and the righteous. Perhaps that scholar of righteous person gives his speech in accordance to the understanding of those angels, or jinn alone and not to those attending from the deficient humans.

Our master the Imam and Gnostic, Sheikh ᶜAydarūs b. ᶜUmar al-Ḥabshī ﷺ said:

The blessings of sitting with the righteous returns upon one even though it may be after some time. A person should not say, 'I cannot see that I have acquired or received anything.' For the one who strives will find, whoever walks on a path will reach. Very often, it is the case that whatever the seeker on the path to Allah receives is hidden.

The example is like the increase in the growth of trees or animals. For you see a child everyday just as he was the

> day before, and there is no apparent growth. The palm tree is similar, but without a doubt there is growth occurring, but it is hidden. As for apparent increase which is manifest, this is rare, and is only in the sense of a miracle. So let a slave adhere and await the bounty of Allah. For it has been related, 'Your Lord has in the days of time and moments, so present yourself to them.'[44] Presenting yourself is in working hard for the pleasure of the High, the Great.[45]

Our master, the Imam, Sheikh $^{c}$Alī b. Abī Bakr as-Sakrān Bā $^{c}$Alawī, may Allah make us benefit from them, mentioned in his book *Ma$^{c}$ārij al-Hidāya*:

> It has been related that the great sheikh Muḥammad b. Ḥusayn al-Bajalī, may Allah the Exalted have mercy upon him, said, 'I saw the Messenger of Allah ﷺ in a dream, and I asked, 'O Messenger of Allah, which actions are the best?' He ﷺ replied, 'To stand before a friend of Allah for the time it takes to milk a goat or for something white to appear is better than to worship Allah until all of your limbs fall off in worship.' I asked, 'O Messenger of Allah, alive or deceased?' He ﷺ replied, 'Whether he is alive or deceased.
>
> Some have said, 'This is because the standing before a saint (*walī*) you come under him and enter into his supervision, and so the saint then becomes a means towards Allah ﷻ. You receive that which you cannot receive through your worship. In fact, one receives in accordance to the capacity of that saint. For help is in accordance to capacity.'[46]

---

[44] Tabarānī

[45] *Nahr al-Mawrūd*

[46] Aḥmad b. Ḥasan al- Ḥaddād, *Al-Fawā'id as-Saniya*

The Gnostic, our master, Sheikh ʿAbdallāh b. Muḥsin al-ʿAṭṭās, may Allah make us benefit from him, mentioned regarding the meaning of their saying: "Standing before a friend of Allah, whether he is alive or deceased is better than worshipping until limbs fall off." He replied:

> This bounty is not received except by one who stands before a walī, recognising that he is a walī of Allah, in that Allah has shown him his *wilāya.* It was then said to him that this is difficult. He replied, 'It is not difficult, did not Sayyidinā Abū Bakr as-Ṣiddīq and Abū Lahab both sit with the Prophet ﷺ and eat with him? But Sayyidinā Abū Bakr sat with him recognising that he is the Prophet of Allah and His Messenger, knowing this truly. Thus he received that which he received, until he became the best of people. Abū Lahab saw the Prophet not as a prophet but as the orphan of Abū Ṭālib and a man from Quraysh, so he received nothing of that which Sayyidina Abū Bakr received.
>
> Therefore, if sitting with the Prophet ﷺ does not give one this distinction except through recognition then how is it with others? As for sitting with a walī of Allah then there is always a benefit, if it is with belief. Help is in the way you perceive. Therefore, one receives according to his perception.

Imam al Ḥaddād said:

> The blessings of a righteous person are not manifest upon those who accompany him until after he dies. The attention of a walī upon his relatives, and those who are with him, is greater after his death, than during his life.

> During his life, he is pre-occupied with the burden of sharia but after his death this is cast off.

Sheikh Aḥmad b. $^{c}$Uqba was asked, 'Is the help of the alive greater or those who are deceased?' He replied, 'The help of the deceased for they are upon the spread of al-Ḥaqq.'

When Sheikh $^{c}$Alī al-Muttaqī was about to pass away, his student Sheikh $^{c}$Abd ul-Wahhāb began to grieve, and so he said to him, 'Do not be sad, for we are a people who help our murīds after death just as we helped them in life, and even more.'

It has been related that the one who writes the biography of a walī of Allah the Exalted will be with him in Paradise. Whoever looks up his name in a book, out of love for him it is as though he has visited him. Whoever visits a walī, his sins are forgiven, as long as he does not harm him or any Muslim in his path.

# SECTION 4

# SUMMARISED BIOGRAPHIES OF SOME OF THE EMINENT FIGURES AMONGST THE SĀDA BĀ ᶜALAWĪ

*"Mercy descends with the remembrance of the Righteous"*

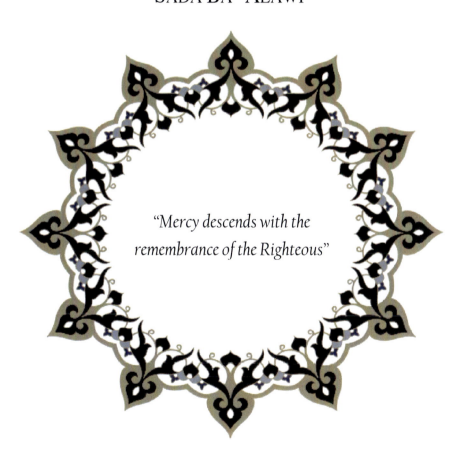

# Summarised Biographies of some of the Eminent Figures amongst the Sāda Bā ᶜAlawī

One of the people asked about the mercy that descends on remembering the righteous. Ḥabīb ᶜAydrūs b. ᶜUmar ﷺ replied:

"It is the recognition of your faults that you find in yourself when they are mentioned, and the reverence you feel for them when they are mentioned, and it is when you find within yourself the desire to be like them, and it is the expansion that you feel within yourself, and so forth. It may be that their remembrance will lead you to act like them. All of these are the different types of mercies that descend with their remembrance."

~ I ~

# Sayyidinā al-Faqīh al-Muqaddam Muḥammad ibn $^{c}$Alī رضي الله عنه

Sayyidinā al-Faqīh al-Muqaddam, may Allah be pleased with him and make us benefit from his rank, is also known as *Abū Tarīm*, 'The Father of Tarīm'. He was born in 574AH (1178CE) and passed away in 653AH (1255CE). His full name was Muḥammad b. $^{c}$Alī Khāli$^{c}$ Qasam b. $^{c}$Alawī b. Muḥammad Ṣāḥib al-Mırbāṭ b. $^{c}$Alawī b. $^{c}$Abdallāh b. al-Muhājir Aḥmad b. $^{c}$Īsā b. Muḥammad b. $^{c}$Alī al-Murtaḍā b. Imam Ja$^{c}$far as-Ṣādiq b. Imām Muḥammad al-Bāqir b. Imām $^{c}$Alī Zain al-$^{c}$Ābidīn, b. Imām Ḥusain b. Imām $^{c}$Alī and b. al-Sayyidā Fāṭima, the blessed daughter of the Messenger of Allah, may the blessings and peace of Allah be upon him and upon them all.

He is known as the Greatest Teacher (*Al-Ustādh al-A$^{c}$ẓam*), and was titled: 'Al-Faqīh al-Muqaddam' (The Foremost Faqīh), 'The Father of the $^{c}$Alawiyya' (Abū $^{c}$Alawī), 'The Adornment of the Muslims and Islam'. He was most certainly the Sheikh of sheikhs in sharia, and by consensus the Imam of the people of *Ḥaqīqa*; he was the Ghazālī of his time and the Junaid of his era, the Master of the people of tassawuf. He was the essence of the circle of *wilāya*, the model for all lordly scholars and the crown of the leading gnostics.

He was born as a saint by the grace of Allah, protected during his childhood. From an early age he had a great thirst for knowledge, and would seek to please Allah with every form of worship possible, with this he had constant steadfastness, and would subject himself to intense spiritual exercise. He was resolute and regular in following the Book of Allah and the Sunnah of the Messenger of Allah ﷺ. He took the Companions and the Pious Predecessors as his role models, and constantly strove in perfecting his character. He would conform himself to the adāb of the sharia and endeavoured assiduously in gaining the knowledge of the sharia both its intellectual (*ᶜaqliya*) and transmitted (*naqliya*) sciences. His quest for knowledge was proverbial, day and night, in contemplation and revision, learning and teaching. Always researching and verifying, examining and investigating. He delved into secrets of the sharia, and penetrated into the oceans of its realities until he reached the level of *Mujtahid Muṭlaq*; fulfilling all of its criteria, and rising to the level of perfection.

The Sheikh and Gnostic, the Quṭb ᶜAbd ar-Raḥmān b. Muḥammad b. ᶜAlī ᶜAlawī ؓ said, 'We do not prefer any of the awliyā above al-Faqīh al-Muqaddam Muḥammad b. ᶜAlī, except that they be a Companion of the Prophet or someone whose virtue has been specifically stated by a Prophetic Tradition, such as Owais al-Qarnī ؓ or others.' This was a spiritual vision (*mushāhada*) of his when he was entering into his prayer.

Others amongst the mashā'ikh have said, 'The people of the time were amazed and baffled with the speeches of al-Faqīh, with the level of his spiritual states (*aḥwāl*), the power of his *kashf* and the number of his miracles but they did not value him as he deserved.'

He was once asked three hundred questions in various sciences, he answered them all in a way which expanded the breast and removed all doubt, and showed the depth and breadth of his knowledge both outwardly and inwardly.

The greatest of scholars during that time all conceded that he was the most knowledgeable person at that time, as did all the awliyā who agreed that he was certainly the Quṭb and Ghawth of his era.

Sheikh Aḥmad b. Abī al-Ja[c]ad, and Sheikh Sufyān at-Taymī, came to Ḥaḍramawt to visit Prophet Hūd, peace and blessings upon our Prophet and him. Sayyidinā al-Faqīh sent Sheikh Sufyān a letter containing many subtle issues, rare secrets taken from the depths of ḥaqīqa. When he read the letter he said, 'This is a level where our spiritual state has not reached O Faqīh, I cannot reply to your letter, he agreed to the level of his perfection regarding esoteric knowledge (*[c]ilm al-ladunnī*).

It is also related that he would receive many unveilings *(mukāshafāt),* thus his wisdom from esoteric knowledge and divine openings would be expressed upon his tongue. His initial stage of kashf and spiritual knowledge was like the end states of the perfected mashā'ikh. He once sent a couple of letters to the Great Sheikh and famous scholar Sa[c]ad b. [c]Alī at-Tafāzī. Upon which Sheikh Sa[c]d was astonished at the level of subtleties and secrets contained therein, and so he wanted to become from among his murīds. Among the things that he mentioned regarding him was: 'And you, O Faqīh are advanced in guidance than requiring a guide yourself and are more knowledgeable of the sharia and ḥaqīqa, both its outward and inward.' He acknowledged the perfection and greatness of his rank.

Some of the scholars have recorded over two hundred of his miracles.

## Worship

His worship was like an ocean without shores; he would be occupied with teaching and fasting throughout the day; and would remain in vigil throughout the night, reciting the Quran inaudibly and audibly. He would restart the recitation upon every completion.

One night his son decided to follow him into the valley of Na'ir the place where the Imam would worship. When the Imam got to the valley, he made dhikr of Allah verbally and everything in the valley, including the trees and the rocks began to perform dhikr too. Upon hearing this, his son fainted until his father took him back home.

He was a complete ascetic and could only be compared with Ibrāhīm b. Adham 🙵. He was extremely humble, never claiming to posses a special rank or state, although he was entitled to in every respect. The greatest sufis and scholars of the time all concurred that no one had attained his rank. Such was his humility that he did not compose any works except for a few treatises which contain a reflection of the depth and breadth of his knowledge on subtleties which astound the minds and impress the soul.

When he was asked: who will teach after you? He replied, 'The Mother of the Poor' (*Umm al-Fuqarā*); that is the Imam's own noble wife whose name was Zainab bint Aḥmad b. Muḥammad b. Ṣāḥib al-Mīrbāṭ 🙵. She was known as the 'Mother of the Poor', as she was beyond compare in giving charity. She would take care of the Imam's students, guests and all of the poor people that would approach or she was aware of. He made her his successor (*khalīfata*) and she assumed the role of advice and guidance after he passed away.

His house was a refuge for orphans, widows and the poor. Whenever the guests arrived, he would arrange large dishes for them, and would feed them abundantly, more than they were able to consume.

## *The khirqa of Sheikh Abū Madyan al-Ghawth* رضي الله عنه

The Imam and Gnostic Shuᶜayb Abū Madyan b. Abī Ḥasan al-Tilmisānī رضي الله عنه guided one of his greatest students, the grand sheikh ᶜAbd ar-Raḥmān b. Muḥammad, more famously known as al-Maqad. He said to him, 'We have in Ḥaḍramawt companions, go to them and take from them the pledge of *taḥkīm* and bestow upon them the *khirqa*.' He then gave him the khirqa and told him to give it to Imam al-Faqīh al-Muqaddam, he also said to him; 'I see that you will die on your journey there, so pass this on to someone who is worthy of it. He then left Tilmisān and when he arrived at the noble city of Makka, he passed away, but before his passing away he instructed another person who was from amongst the sheikh's students, the great sheikh ᶜAbdallah Ṣāliḥ al-Maghribī and entrusted him with the khirqa. He said to him, 'You will enter into the town of Tarīm and you will find the Sayyid: Muḥammad b. ᶜAlī, known as al-Faqīh, reading to the Faqīh will be ᶜAlī b. Aḥmad Bā Marwān. Give him the khirqa and taḥkīm. Then go to the town of Qaydūn to Sheikh Saᶜīd b. ᶜĪsā al-ᶜAmūdī and do the taḥkīm with him.

When the Imam knew that Sheikh ᶜAbd ar-Raḥmān al-Maqad had left, he came out to meet him, but when he learnt that he had passed away, he returned. When Sheikh ᶜAbdallāh as-Ṣāliḥ arrived in the city of Tarīm, he found the great teacher as the sheikh had described him, so he sat with him. He then informed him of his purpose and everything that had occurred. So the Imam welcomed him warmly with love and he received the khirqa and took the pledge of taḥkīm.

## *His legacy*

As was the custom of the people of that time, due to the harsh environment that they were living in; al-Faqīh al Muqaddam would carry a sword with him. But then he broke his sword and handed it to the great righteous scholar Sheikh Saʿīd b. ʿĪsā al-ʿAmūdī, and others followed him.

Traditionally, the people of Ḥaḍramawt preoccupied themselves with Fiqh and Hadith and were not learned in the ways of Tassawuf. Sayyidinā Faqīh al-Muqaddam ؓ revealed these sciences to them and masses of scholars, saints and everyday people received from him. He was an all encompassing spiritual and scholarly university, churning out great scholars, ascetics, awliyā and ʿārifīn. Constantly giving, and outpouring his *baraka* to the ummah of the Prophet ﷺ. People from all backgrounds and from all continents came to visit and receive from him.

Sufyān ath-Thawrī has said that whoever combines two of the following characteristics, no one from their era will surpass him. A Sayyid who is a Sunni, a jurist who is a sufi, a scholar who is an ascetic, a rich person who is humble, a *faqīr* who is grateful. The scholars have said that all of these characteristics were combined in the Greatest Teacher that is Sayyidinā Faqīh al-Muqaddam ؓ.

Some of the Gnostics have also said that Sayyidinā al-Faqīh al-Muqaddam was able to reflect the Divine Attributes upon the mashā'ikh who had spiritual power after they had passed away, like they had when they were in this world, and they are the lordly qutb, Sheikh Abd al- Qadir Jīlānī, Sheikh Maʿrūf al-Karkhī, Sheikh Aqīl al-Minhi, Hayyu b. Qais, may Allah be pleased with them all.

The greatest legacy that the Imam left behind was that he established and propagated the Path of the Gnostics in Ḥaḍramawt. Similar to Imam Abu'l Ḥasan al-Shādhilī ﵁, who when he was asked about any books that he was to leave behind for the ummah to benefit from, he replied: 'My companions are my books.'

The children and students of the Imam, al-Faqīh al-Muqaddam are his books and are a reflection of a path that he made manifest and established for them. For how many aqṭāb, awliyā, ṣālihīn, ṣiddīqīn, lordly scholars have come from his lineage! He made three supplications to Allah for his lineage: firstly that they have beautiful conduct, secondly that Allah will not subjugate them to an oppressor who will harm them, and thirdly that none of them will die except that their state will remain veiled from others.

## *Imam al-Ḥaddād and Sayyidinā al-Faqīh al-Muqaddam* ﵁

In the original Rāṭib of Imām al-Ḥaddād (d.1132AH) ﵁, there is only one person that is mentioned in his fātiḥa: Sayyidinā Faqīh al-Muqaddam. Despite there being around 400 years between Imām al-Ḥaddād and al-Faqīh al-Muqaddam, Imām al-Ḥaddād always considered him as one of his foremost mashā'ikh. He was once heard saying; 'We are indebted in this matter to four people from the intermediary world (*barzakh*): al-Faqīh al-Muqaddam, Sheikh ᶜAbd ar-Raḥmān as-Saqqāf, Sheikh ᶜUmar al-Mihdār, and Sheikh ᶜAbdallah b. Abī Bakr al-ᶜAydrūs...'

Dr Mostafa al-Badawī mentions in his book: '*Sufi Sage of Arabia*' the following:

Imam al-Ḥaddād's relationship with al-Faqīh al-Muqaddam was extremely intimate and he was once heard saying, "I never do anything until I receive a sign from the Real, Exalted is He, or the Prophet ﷺ or Sayyidina al-Faqīh al-Muqaddam Muḥammad ibn ᶜAlī Bā ᶜAlawī ﷺ."'

Also: 'It was said by many of his companions that Imam al-Ḥaddād in his young days frequently came under the sway of spiritual states during sessions of remembrance. He sometimes became lost in ecstasy and the only way to return him to ordinary consciousness was to carry him to the tomb of al- Faqīh al-Muqaddam and lay him there for a while. He was also frequently seen sitting before the grave for so long that his clothes became thoroughly soaked with sweat, he would be so engrossed that he would not feel it at all.'

And that Imam al-Ḥaddād mentioned in one of his letters: "Both al- Faqīh al-Muqaddam and Sheikh ᶜAbd al-Qādir were great Imams: they were all encompassing poles and Sunni Sharīfs. Both are among the foremost and the drawn near. We benefit and depend more on al-Faqīh, since he is the father and the sheikh whom everything in this region revolves, both as concerns us and as others. They are equal in station, however Sheikh ᶜAbd al-Qādir is better known in this world and al-Faqīh in the intermediary world (*barzakh*)."

## *His passing away*

He passed away on Thursday night, in the month of Dhu'l-Hijja in the year 653AH. He was 79 years of age. His resting place is well known in Zanbal. It is famous, for it is a place where supplications are answered, with an outpouring of blessings, and the acquisition of mercy. The mashā'ikh have said that when visiting those who have passed away one should not visit anyone before al-Faqīh Muḥammad b. ᶜAlī, even though it may be there own father, but rather they should visit him first and then whomever they wish.

The faqīh and great scholar Muḥammad b. ᶜAlawī said, 'The most beloved spot to me on the Earth is the grave of al-Faqīh Muḥammad b. ᶜAlī.' He would sit there for hours on end, people would travel to another town by the name of al-Qara which is six miles away and return and he would not have moved from his place. Many of the awliyā and scholars have spoken about visiting Sayyidinā al-Faqīh. Some of the ulema would kiss his grave and would be questioned but they would reply, 'We do not have the patience to hold back!' The states of the Gnostics would surpass into annihilation, they would be elevated and honoured. Others would go during the heat of summer, saying that they find at Sayyidinā al-Faqīh that which they cannot find at the resting place of any other walī.

It has been related from ᶜAlī b. ᶜAlawī Khird that he saw one of the ṣāliḥīn in a dream and he asked, 'Who do the deceased seek refuge in when they are suffering in their graves? They replied, 'Al-Faqīh Muḥammad b. ᶜAlī ᶜAlawī.' And so he asked about others of the awliyā and they replied, 'O ᶜAlī, all of them have blessings!' Another pious person saw a man who had passed away. He enquired regarding his state, he replied: 'Al-Faqīh Muḥammad b. ᶜAlī came to me and Allah granted me firmness. All those who have died go to him.'

He رضي الله عنه left behind five children: Sheikh ᶜAlawī, Sheikh ᶜAbd ar-Raḥmān, Sheikh ᶜAbdallāh, Sheikh ᶜAlī, and Sheikh Aḥmad all of them fulfilling the meanings and criteria of a sheikh. May Allah increase him in the beauty of his rank and may He make us benefit from the rank of his beauty, *āmīn.*

~ II ~

# ᶜAbdallāh ibn ᶜAlawī Ibn al-Faqīh al-Muqaddam

Abdallāh b. ᶜAlawī b. Faqīh al-Muqaddam was the Imam of the scholars of his time, the leader of the Gnostics, no one denied the rank of his place. There is consensus that he was Sheikh al-Islam, and the Renewer of the 7th century. People flocked to him from all directions. He possessed the most noble and sublime rank, he ascended to the highest rank of praise. He was a man of many virtues, favours and perfections. He had immense determination and was acquainted with many sciences. His divine knowledge was like that of Imam al-Ghazālī. After Sayyidinā al-Faqīh al-Muqaddam, there was none other like him; no one else exceeded the perfection of his knowledge and action to the extent that he became the focal point of reference for all regions and communities.

He ﵁ was born in 638AH, raised amongst the eminent ones, with Allah's favour and felicity. He had been prepared for the bounties when he was in the cradle. He studied with his grandfather when he was young. He honoured him with his gaze, prayed for him and raised him. His father also took care of him and raised him with praiseworthy qualities until he grew up and reached an exalted rank.

He sought his knowledge one by one; he never rested not even for a moment. First he sought the knowledge of Fiqh, which informs people of the lawful and the prohibited. He studied it to the extent of gaining knowledge of the ambiguous and their rulings. The people of his time acknowledged that he had the highest position. He studied Fiqh with the great scholar Ba'l-Faqīh Aḥmad b. ᶜAbd al-Raḥmān b. ᶜAlawī b. Muḥammad Ṣāhib Mīrbāṭ and the great sheikh ᶜAbdallāh b. Ibrāhīm Bā Qushayr رضي الله عنهما. He studied Tafsīr, Fiqh, Hadīth and Tasawwuf with his distinguished grandfather and father. He also studied the sciences of Arabic until he was very proficient in it. He received the investiture from the aforementioned shuyūkh, who also transmitted litanies (*adhkār*) to him. He travelled to Yemen, to the city of Ahwar. There he studied with Sheikh ᶜUmar b. Maymūn, who was one of the students of Sheikh Aḥmad b. al-Jaᶜd.

He performed the Hajj in 670AH, and went to visit his noble grandfather, the Messenger of Allah ﷺ. He stayed in Madina for approximately one year, then returned to Makka and remained there for eight years. On his arrival, Makka was one of the driest lands, as there had been no rain, and the prices of commodities were extremely high. By the blessings of his presence, Allah poured down His bounties upon the people. It rained in Makka, they received rain in every region, and all the valleys were filled. By the favour of Allah, the barren lands were replaced with prosperity and abundance. He رضي الله عنه was renowned for this from a very young age. Any place that he stayed in the people received rain.

Thereafter, he set out to study the Prophetic Hadiths and acquired splendour from its lights. Then he dedicated himself to studying the sciences of Sharia, and literature and drank from their vast oceans especially the ocean of Realities. He extracted its gems and pearls as he did from the other sciences. He became proficient in the different branches of knowledge. He had over a thousand shuyūkh, and he acquired from all of them tremendously to a level that is beyond description. He received *ijāzāt* to give legal opinion (*fatwa*) and to teach in every field of knowledge.

Then he went to visit his noble grandfather, the Messenger of Allah ﷺ for a second time and stayed in Madina for many days. He went back to Makka and he received what he had been hoping for, after the forgiveness of sins. The people of Makka adhered to him as they sought rain for the second time. With his *baraka* Allah relieved their distress and with his prayers their wishes were fulfilled and their prayers were answered.

Eventually word of him spread throughout the regions and he was also described in the newspapers. His praise was also expressed in their poems. The people of Makka and Madina studied with him, both local residents and visitors too. They particularly made use of his knowledge of Aqīda and Tasawwuf. The renown of his teachings gave him the title 'Imam al-Haramayn.'

He was gifted with a talent whereby he knew the inner thoughts of all of those who came and went. In argumentation (*munāzara*) he was unique, and never referred to the lexicons while teaching. In addition to this he was dilligent in worship and action, adherent to the path that leads to felicity. He was steadfast with fasting; his eyes always remained awake and never savoured sleep.

In Makka, he would often go to the mosque during the night and remain there after the Fajr prayer until mid morning (Duhā). During this time he would recite half of the Quran, then pray eight *rak'ahs* for the Duhā prayer. He would sit in the mosque after ᶜAṣr until the Ishā prayer. In Ramadān after Tarāwīh he would perform two rakᶜa in which he would recite the whole Quran.

His brother, $^{c}$Alī ibn $^{c}$Alawī, who stayed in Makka moved to Tarīm. That is when the scholars of Ḥaḍramawt wrote to him requesting him to return to Tarīm as they needed him there. So he travelled to the city of Zabid, where he met many great scholars, and men of eminence and studied with them. He related to them the knowledge that he had acquired, and gave benefit to them with his teachings. Then he went to the city of Ta'iz and he studied with the scholars and they studied with him and many of them received the khirqa from him. Then he went to the city of Ahwar to visit his Sheikh Imam $^{c}$Umar ibn Maymūn and he found that he had passed away, they had performed his *ghusl* and shrouded him.

During his lifetime Sheikh $^{c}$Umar ﵁ asked one of his followers to take his place after him; he said, 'When I die, wash me and shroud me and a sheikh will come forth...' and he described him, '...he will be the sheikh after me, let him lead my funeral prayer.' When Sayyidinā $^{c}$Abdallāh b. $^{c}$Alawī came, they found that he fit the description, and they informed him of the Sheikh's request. So he led the funeral prayer, and they insisted that he stay with them as he was to be their sheikh. But he apologised and declined the offer, and when he saw the son of Sheikh $^{c}$Umar worthy of being a sheikh he appointed him and bestowed him with the blessed khirqa and he was established as the sheikh amongst them.

After further travel he went to Tarīm, upon his arrival, the people of Tarīm received immense blessings, and his secret prevailed. The city became revived and the people rejoiced. They came towards him shining with happiness and his words filled the earth with radiance and light. He began to teach the madhhab of Imam Muḥammad ibn Idrīs al-Shāfi$^{c}$ī ﵁. He taught about conduct on the spiritual path and spoke about the sciences of Ḥaqīqa, people came to him from all regions.

Amongst them were his three children: $^{c}$Alī, Muḥammad and Aḥmad and his brother Mawlā al-Dawīla and Abū Bakr and $^{c}$Alawī, and the two sons of his uncle: Aḥmad and Muḥammad b. $^{c}$Alawī, and al-Sheikh $^{c}$Abdallāh the son of his Sheikh al-Faqīh Aḥmad b. $^{c}$Abd al-Raḥmān, who carried both knowledge and forbearance, al-Sheikh $^{c}$Alī b. Sālim the spring of divine knowledge, Sheikh Faḍl b. Muḥammad Bā Faḍl, Sheikh $^{c}$Abdallāh b. Faqīh al-Faḍl, the Gnostic Muḥammad b. Abū Bakr Bā $^{c}$Abbād, the great Imam Sheikh Muḥammad b. $^{c}$Alī Bā Shu$^{c}$ayb al-Ansārī, Sheikh Muḥammad b. $^{c}$Alī al-Khaṭīb, Sheikh Aḥmad b. $^{c}$Alī al-Khaṭīb, the great Sheikh $^{c}$Umar Bā Wazīr, Sheikh Mufliḥ b. $^{c}$Abdallāh ibn Fahd, Sheikh al-Jalīl the son of his Sheikh $^{c}$Umar ibn Maymūn Ṣāḥib Ahwar, Sheikh Bā Hamrān. These are the shuyūkh, whose lives and works became well known, and they all emerged from that ocean and they derived from that river. He endowed them with the khirqa and he extended them with his sublime *madad*. Men with dense veils would approach him and they would attain their goals by his noble gaze.

A great Gnostic said that most of the openings that Allah bestowed upon the children of $^{c}$Abdallāh Bā $^{c}$Alawī were in relation to the recitation of Quran. The greatest opening that was bestowed upon the children of his brother $^{c}$Alī b. $^{c}$Alawī was dhikr.

He رضي الله عنه would weep during the night with fear of Allah, especially when reciting the Quran to the extent that he lost his physical sight. At times, he would spend most of the night crying feeling that he has neglected. It was one of his noble habits to go to the mosque during the night, perform the witr and then recite the Quran until sunrise. He would then go home, sit for a while and return back to the mosque and start teaching until the afternoon, when he would take a nap. He would stay at home studying and researching from the books between the time of Ẓuhr and ʿAṣr. He would perform ʿAṣr with the people and remain with those that kept his company until Maghrib. From Maghrib to ʿIshā he would recite the Quran. After ʿIshā he would continue to pray as much as he willed, thereafter he would go home. As for Ramaḍān he would stay in the mosque and pray the Tarawīh prayer then he would perform two rakʿā and recite the whole Quran in them. Then he would go home eat for *suhūr* then go back to the mosque. He would pray Ẓuhr in congregation and then teach until ʿAṣr. After ʿAṣr he would sit to perform dhikr, and this was his noble habit that became famous, and his worship that manifested. This conduct of his was renowned amongst his followers, and mentioned in the books of the scholars.

Sayyidinā Sheikh Mawlā Dawīla would say, 'I have not seen anyone like my uncle ʿAbdallāh when traveling and when at home.' The Gnostic Sheikh ʿAbd al-Raḥmān al-Saqqāf would say, 'All the Gnostics agree that Sheikh ʿAbdallāh b. ʿAlawī has miracles that are continuous and manifest.' In spite of having the most miracles, he was the most discreet, he would only make his miracles manifest when necessary. He disliked his miracles being attributed to him, and he did not like the general masses to see this side of him. Some of these have been related in *'Jawhar al-Shafāf'*, in *'Munahhal al-Saf'* and *'Kitāb al-Ghurar'* and have become known. Similarly al-Faqīh ʿAbd al-Raḥmān b. ʿAlī b. Ḥasan has mentioned it in his book, which is about the virtues of the Banī ʿAlawī and their history and it is called, *'Al-Bahā kathīran min karāmātihi al-shahīra wa aḥwālihi munīra.'* I will mention some of the miracles for the blessings.

It has been related that he prohibited a man in Makka from drinking wine. The man replied, 'I am a tailor and I need this to help me in my work.' He said, 'If Allah suffices you without it, do you promise that you will not return to it?' He said, ‘Yes.’ Then he ﵁ prayed to Allah that he may repent to Him and help him without it. Then he repented, and Allah accepted his repentance and helped him to live without it.

Sheikh ᶜAbdallāh b. ᶜAlawī once saw in his dream that there was a person saying, ‘Dig, look there is a person in such and such a place, whoever prays his funeral prayer will be forgiven.’ Then he awoke, and inquired about that man and was informed that he had died, so he ﵁ prayed his funeral prayer. May Allah be pleased with him and make us benefit from him.

## ~ III ~

# ᶜAbd al-Raḥmān ibn Muḥammad Mawlā al-Dawīla ibn ᶜAlī ibn ᶜAlawī ibn al-Faqīh al-Muqaddam ﵁

He was renowned by the name al-Saqqāf, the master of the Sādāt al-Ashrāf, the prime of the Banī ᶜAbd al-Manāf. All the eminent scholars go back to him; he reached a rank that no other has perceived of reaching. With his knowledge, he dispelled the clouds of ignorance and arrogance. He was matchless in his time; he had acquired the glories of his noble fathers. He was an ocean and there was no other ocean that possessed the jewels of gnosis and knowledge that he did.

He was born in the year 739AH in Tarīm. He memorised the noble Quran under the great scholar Aḥmad b. Muḥammad al-Khaṭīb, he mastered the science of Tajwīd and occupied himself with learning the sciences under the scholars. With his determination he excelled in these to a great level. He paid much attention to the books of the former scholars especially the books of the two great imams, the eminent Muḥammad al-Ghazālī, and the imam of the madhhab, Sheikh Abū Isḥāq. He read their books '*al-Wajīz*' and '*Muhadhdhab*' a lot, to the extent that he almost memorised them. He studied these books with ᶜAllāma Muḥammad b.

ʿAlawī Aḥmad b. al-Faqīh al-Muqaddam in Tarīm. Then he travelled to al-Nil and he studied them with Sheikh al-Islam, Muḥammad b. Abū Bakr Bā ʿAbād, he remained close to him until he benefitted from him immensely.

Then he رضي الله عنه travelled to Aden and studied Grammar, Morphology and other sciences of the Arabic language with Qādī Muḥammad b. Saʿīd. He excelled in Theology, the sciences of Theology and also in Rhetoric (*ʿilm al-maʿānī* and *bayān*). He was consolidated in Tafsīr and in Hadith, not an area remained in this field that he was unacquainted with. On the path, he accompanied many upright scholars, the most famous of these: Imam Abū Bakr b. ʿĪsā Bā Yazīd, who lived in Wādī Amad, Sheikh ʿUmar ibn Saʿīd Bā Jabir and the Gnostic Mazahim b. Aḥmad Bā Jabir, the saintly imam ʿAbdallāh b. Ṭāhir al-Dawʿanī and others.

He always seemed to surpass every rank until he reached a rank that had no end. He reached a level beyond the shining stars, and surpassed all the great mashā'ikh of the time. His striving exceeded the striving of all others; he was the prime of his time. He used to perform his worship in Sha'b al-Na'ir during the last third of the night. Throughout the night he completed the recitation of two Qurans, and two during the day. Then he started completing four in the night and four in the day. For thirty years he lived without sleeping, he did not sleep in the day or the night. He would say, “How can one sleep, when they lie down on the right side, they see Paradise and when they lie on the left they see the Fire."

He would visit the blessed grave of Prophet Hūd عليه السلام. He would stay there for a month without eating except for a very small amount. Everyday he would visit them and also pray in all the mosques of Tarīm. When he stood for prayer, people would think that he was a pillar because of his long standing. He would say, “We have not prepared any outward deeds.” He was often seen at the Hajj in the different places, and one of his special students asked him "Have you performed the Hajj?" He replied, "As for externally, no I have not." Many of his mashā'ikh permitted him to benefit the people, instruct them and bestow them with the khirqa.

He taught Fiqh and Usūl al-Fiqh, he was established and excelled in many sciences to a level that could not be reached. As a result of his reputation, people travelled from far, students would travel from the East and the West and people would travel such distances for fatwas, by land and sea. Many people benefitted from him with the knowledge of haqā'iq, which shone upon their hearts and they radiated its light. The light of its secrets illuminated from them. Amongst them were his children, his nephews, the Gnostic Abū Bakr b. $^{c}$Alawī al-Shayba, and his brother the famous Imam Muḥammad b. $^{c}$Alawī, the Gnostic Muḥammad b. Ḥasan, renowned by the name Jamal al-Layl, the great imam Muḥammad Ṣāḥib $^{c}$Īd$^{c}$īd b. $^{c}$Alī, the Gnostic Aḥmad b. $^{c}$Umar, Imam Sa$^{c}$d b. $^{c}$Alī Madhaj, Sheikh Muḥammad b. $^{c}$Abd al-Raḥmān al-Khaṭīb, his son Sheikh $^{c}$Abd al-Raḥmān, who was the author of *'al-Jawhar'*, Sheikh $^{c}$Abd al-Raḥīm b. $^{c}$Alī al-Khaṭīb, Sheikh $^{c}$Alī b. Muḥammad al-Khaṭīb, Sheikh Shu$^{c}$ayb b. $^{c}$Abdallāh al-Khaṭīb, Sheikh Aḥmad b. Abī Bakr Bā Harmī, Sheikh $^{c}$Abdallāh b. al-Faqīh, Ibrāhīm Bā Harmī, Sheikh $^{c}$Abdallāh b. Aḥmad al-$^{c}$Amūdī, Sheikh $^{c}$Alī ibn Aḥmad ibn $^{c}$Alī ibn Muslim, Sheikh $^{c}$Abdallāh b. Muḥammad Bā Sharāhīl al-Mu$^{c}$allim, Faqīh b. Muḥammad al-Mu$^{c}$āfa, the gnostic $^{c}$Abdallāh b. Nāfi$^{c}$ Bā Mundhir, the Gnostic $^{c}$Īsā b. $^{c}$Umar b. Bahlūl, Imam Aḥmad $^{c}$Alī al-Habānī, Faqīh Sa$^{c}$d b. $^{c}$Abdallāh Bā Antar, Sheikh Muḥammad b. Sa$^{c}$īd al-Maghribī, Ṣāliḥ Muḥammad b. Aḥmad al-$^{c}$Umrī and others.

The ones mentioned above are the most famous, those who excelled inwardly and outwardly. They were able to see the intrinsic meanings, the gems and the pearls that lay therein. Sometimes they would recite from the book 'al-Wajīz,' and they were able to see the treasures that it contained, which all the other fuqahā were unable to perceive.

He would teach each person according to that which was appropriate for him. And for each matter they would receive according to their level. How pleased those souls must have been travelling on that path and being distinguished by him amongst the deep oceans until they arrived at the station of Truth. Each one of those that had received the khirqa by the Sheikh, informed those who desired the world, that when they came under the Sheikh, Allah the Exalted removed from their hearts the love for the world immediately, and Allah the Exalted removed their blameworthy characteristics, and replaced them with praiseworthy ones. He would say to them, "Strive with the actions of the heart, surely an ounce of inward action is equivalent to a seaful of outward action."

On some days, in his lessons he would mention the excellence of Fiqh. He encouraged his son, ᶜUmar to spend his life in the science of Fiqh and leave all the other sciences. At the end of the lesson he would call him, and say, "O ᶜUmar, strive with the deeds of the heart, an ounce of inward action is equivalent to an ocean full of outward action."

One day he mentioned the Imam and Gnostic Abū Mansūr al-Hallāj ⬥ in his praise, and he elaborated in his praise. His son ᶜUmar was present at this time and he wished in his heart that Allah the Exalted would give him the state of Hallāj. Then his father turned towards him and said, "Al-Hallāj, how astonishing was his fate! As for consolidated piety, and travelling the path of the pious forefathers, this is more illustrious than being famous, and more manifest than being mentioned."

Whenever anyone gave him some dates in charity, he would touch it with his hand and he would not take it to his mouth due to his scrupulousness. As for his abstinence (*zuhd*), he was the foremost in his community and his heart never turned to the dunya. As for his generosity, he would give away thousands, in money and in items.

He planted many trees in Tarīm, and he would recite Sūra Yāsīn at every tree. When he planted the big tree, which is commonly known as Bā Habshī, all those present recited Sūra Yāsīn while it was being planted. After it had been planted, he recited a Quran at every tree and he left it as a continual sadaqa for all of his children, who were alive. They were at this time, eight boys and six girls. Every son would recite seventy thousand *tahlīl* a month and every daughter would recite thirty five thousand *tahlīl* a month. And they would pass on the reward of this to their father. He had built ten mosques and his children built three mosques. He would spend money on them, and stop off at every mosque of theirs and perform that which was required. He would say, "These trees are not mine at all, and it was said to me, 'All of your trees that produce fruit become shy out of joy.'"

It has been related that he had a gathering, it was a famous gathering in which the awliyā also attended. It has been said that he saw a man saying to him, "Why do you not preach to the people?" He said, "My heart admonishes as long as the clouds of revelation pour down upon it and divine wisdom sails." Then his student, Imam Abū Bakr b. ᶜAlawī al-Shayba said to him, "What did this man look like?" Then he described him, the student said, "This was the description of Imam al-Ghazālī, who was allowing you to preach to the people." And many of the people of spiritual insight and the awliyā saw this.

His brother, the ᶜĀrif billāh said, "My brother and I had an argument over one of the trees. I said to myself, 'What deed does he perform that is greater than mine? He fasts and I fast, he prays and I pray, we both have the same father, the number of my guests exceed his.' Then I saw a man in my dream saying to me, "You have said such and such?" I said, "Yes", then he said, "Come with me," and he took me to my brother, ᶜAbd al-Raḥmān, and we found that his body was light and Sura Ikhlās and '*Lā ilāha illa Allāh Muḥammad ur-Rasūl Allāh*' were written on his limbs, with light. Then he said to me, "When you have reached this rank then talk." Then I apologised to him."

He ﷺ disliked the gatherings of poetry (*samā'*) during his earlier days, then he started to attend them and eventually he became fond of them. He would teach it in his mosque and during the *samā'*, spiritual inspiration (*wāridāt*) would overtake him. At such times his face would become exalted, and a great awe would manifest on all those present.

He was saddened when his brother passed away, and he left the *samā'* for a while then he returned to it. He said, "I wanted to leave it but it would not leave us."

The scholars (*ulama al-muḥaqqiqūn*), the awliyā and gnostics named him Saqqāf to conceal his state from the people of the time. Since he had not left behind a state or rank, neither was there an aspect of knowledge or action that was not attributed to him. He absolutely detested any kind of fame. Since he had outstripped (*saqafa*) all of the awliyā, that is, surpassed them and ascended above them like a rooftop (*saqaf*) over a house, because he was the Ghawth. He would say, "We were informed about Hallāj and we thought that his glass had broken, but we found it leaking and it had not been broken. We were informed about Abu'l-Gayth b. Jamīl and we found his state. We were informed about Aḥmad b. al-Jaᶜd and we found that his speech went beyond his state." Muḥammad b. Jassan b. Abī Bakr said, "In my dream I saw someone saying,

"The jewels are Muḥammad b. ᶜAlī, his son ᶜAlawī, his son ᶜAlī and his son Muḥammad", then I said, "And ᶜAbd al-Raḥmān al-Saqqāf. Then he said, "He is the essence of the jewels."

He would say, "I do not have a heart that turns to anything other than Allah, not towards family, children, money, paradise, or hell." He would also say, "By Allah I have not built a house or mosque nor have I planted a tree but that I was instructed to do so." He would also say, "We strove, but we did not receive a great opening until we returned to acknowledging the soul (*nafs*)."

He had many sayings:

> "One who does not have a litany is a monkey."
> (*man laysa lahū wird wa huwa qird*).
>
> "One who does not read *Muhadhdhab* does not
> know the principles of the religion."
>
> "One who does not have manners is a bear."
>
> "The medicine of the heart is to abandon all hindrances"
>
> "Success is by taking every good companion. These include the fuqahā and the ṣūfiyyā of the time, as they are involved with beseeching and imploring with Allah."
>
> "All people are in need of knowledge, and knowledge is in need of action, and action is in need of intellect, and intellect is in need of success (*tawfīq*). Every kind of knowledge without action is void. Every kind of knowledge and action without intention is dust. Every knowledge, action and intention without Sunna is rejected. Every knowledge action, intention and Sunna without piety (*wara'*) is a waste. Be according to your time, if you see that the people are like wolves, do not be

a sheep, so that they may devour you. If you see that they are sheep then do not be a wolf and devour them."

He ﷺ was fragrant. When he would enter a house, his pleasant fragrance would spread, and the people knew that he had entered. Or when he passed by a street it would be known that he had walked upon it, and ᶜAbd al-Raḥmān al-Khaṭīb has illustrated this by saying:

*Lo, his fragrance makes sweet the earth,*

*By it, amber and perfume received their fragrance,*

*As it flows it shines with light, together,*

*And it makes all dust (earth) turn green,*

*And they benefit, all those who pass by it,*

*And by it they are healed, all those who are sick,*

*And it erases from them their grave sins.*

Towards the end of his life, when he was not physically strong enough to exert himself, he had a Quranic reciter who would recite the Quran to him and he would listen, sometimes he would recite it with him. In spite of his physical weakness, he would be at the mosque, purified, ready and prepared before the time of prayer had even begun. When he stood for prayer, he stood as though he was a young boy, at times he would only perform the fard.

His actions were inward, and most of his obedience was hidden. The remembrance of Allah did not escape his heart, neither in the night or the day. The trembling of his heart with dhikr and istighfār could be heard. Many of the great mashā'ikh could hear all of his limbs, his hair and skin doing the dhikr of Allah. One of the seekers objected to this thinking that he was an ordinary person. Then, during a conversation with him, he heard his heart doing the dhikr of Allah. So he repented for what had crossed his mind.

He had miracles that Allah exposed through him, such as knowing about the unseen, matters of the future, curing the sick, making things abundant, helping those who were eager, and many more. There was no one like him; he did not like his miracles to be mentioned. His student, Sheikh ᶜAbd al-Raḥmān ibn al-Khaṭīb related approximately one hundred miracles and his extraordinary states in the book *'Jawhar al-Shafāf'*. Here I will mention some of them in short, to benefit the people of understanding.

One of his saintly students said, "It crossed my mind that I have spent quite some time with the Sheikh but he has not given me an opening." Then he said to him, "The Sheikh guards over the seeker in a way that they do not perceive."

His student Sheikh ᶜAbd al-Raḥīm b. ᶜAlī al-Khaṭīb said, "Nothing has ever crossed my mind only that our Sheikh, ᶜAbd al-Raḥmān would fulfil it in the best way, as necessary. He would pray for all the requests of the people and they would receive it. He would pray that they perform good deeds and they would do it. For a woman, he would ask for a son and she would give birth to a son, he would pray for a man who is unable to get married, and he would get married. He would pray for a widow and she would get married, he would pray for the poor that they become enriched and they would be enriched. He would pray for the people that have exceeded in sins, that they seek repentance and that their state becomes better, and they would seek repentance. He would pray for the ignorant that they are endowed with knowledge and Allah would give them openings in this and much more."

Someone related, "I travelled with him from the village of Izz. When we arrived at Kahlān, we stopped to pray the mid-morning prayer. I went to relieve myself, on my return I found that he had some ripe dates with him, and during this time they were not in season. So I asked him about that and he said, "Eat and do not ask."

His student the Gnostic Muḥammad b. Ḥasan, known by the name Jamal al-Layl said, "I was in the mosque of our Sheikh, ᶜAbd al-Raḥmān, while he was upstairs. I was feeling very hungry, so he called me. I found that he had with him some expensive food and I was amazed. So I asked him who had brought it for him, and he said a woman had brought it for him. But I had not seen anyone enter the mosque, I searched around the mosque and I did not find anyone there."

As for what has been related regarding his knowledge of the unseen and future events. It has been related that he said to his wife, who was pregnant at the time and in the village of 'Izz, "You will give birth to a son and he will die on such and such a day." He gave her a garment and said, "Wrap him in this, as a shroud and travel." And thus it happened, he was in Shibām at the time, and he said to the person that was with him, "My son has passed away in Tarīm at this time." And it was as he had said.

He ﷺ had told his son, Abū Bakr, to sell some dates. He sold it and hid some of the money. Then his father said to him, "I have been informed that it was such and such." He said, no one else knew of this, before me." He said, "Taqwa is the discernment of the believer, and they see with the light of Allah." Then Abū Bakr said, "I felt that the money I hid away was openly crawling on my stomach, so I threw it away and I intended never to depend on it again." A similar thing occurred with Sayyidina ᶜUmar al-Miḥḍār ﷺ except that he was afflicted with a pain in his leg, and when his father came he prayed for him and it was cured.

One of his wives said, "My father has been ill for a very long time so pray that he becomes better or that he may die with ease." He said to her, "Your father will pass away on such and such a day." And so it happened.

One of his students said, "I wish I could meet al-Khidr." He رضي الله عنه said, "You will receive this". He said, "And I met al-Khidr in the form of a bedouin, there was an acknowledgement between me and him. Then he disappeared and I smelt a beautiful fragrance, I was amazed by this and I told the Sheikh about it. He said, "That was al-Khidr", then I met the Bedouin again and I asked the Sheikh about him and he said you have not seen him again until this day."

He رضي الله عنه said to one who was travelling to his city, "The valley of your town will flood on such and such a day." He travelled and he found one of his friends irrigating the land for him. He said to him, "The valley will flood on such and such a day", so he stopped, and what he had said came true.

His student ʿAbd al-Raḥīm b. ʿAlī al-Khaṭīb and others related that the Sheikh used to keep some money with them, so that they could take care of the expenses of his family and children. Outwardly the money was not enough; it would suffice them for a short while. They said, "Then we saw it increase".

Shuʿayb ibn ʿAbdallāh al-Khaṭīb said the Sheikh entrusted me with the money for food and other such things. So I went up to him and said that only a very small amount has remained, he did not say anything to me for a while. Then he said, "Go and spend on them." So I went and I spent on them all and a small amount still remained. He gave ʿAbd al-Raḥīm and Shuʿayb a bundle and said "Go and make three garments for your children." Shuʿayb said, "The tailor will not be able to make more than two with this." He said, "Just get it made with the Name of Allah." He went and three were made.

A woman asked him for some money for some clothes. He said, “In such and such a place there are fifteen dinars.” She said, “I looked in that place and there was nothing there”. He said, “Go and you will find it there.” So I went and found fifteen dinars there.

Once he was travelling with a group of people, they stopped at a place where there was no water and they were tired. He said to them, “Lift this stone and you will find water under it.” So they lifted it and they found fresh water there.

He travelled with one of his wives to Tarīm at midday. She said to him, “Wait here, until it gets a bit cooler and we can rest and eat a bit.” He refused and travelled, then he found a blind man on the ground, who had become tired because of his intense thirst. The Sheikh said, “There is some water by the reef” and he told one of his companions to bring some water and help the man. He went to the reef and found some water there, he gave it to him and they all drank from it. Then they travelled and they came across an old man, who asked them for some water. The blind man said, “Water is near.” And the man said, “This blind man talks about that which he has no knowledge of.”

He ﵁ had a tree. The dogs would eat its fruit as it was not so tall. One of the Sheikh’s companions used to guard it every night, one night he became tired, and fell asleep. Then the Sheikh came to him in the dream and said, "“Keep them away by placing the leaves around the tree, and then sleep.” So he did that and in the morning he found the footprints of the dogs around him and they were unable to go past him.

There is no end to the collections of virtues, miracles, states and characteristics of the Sheikh ﵁. Nonetheless, this much is enough for the one who reflects. And all of it falls within the realm of veneration for those who seek insight. In short, his virtues are well known, his miracles are numerous, and his excellence is higher than the sun at its peak.

He رضي الله عنه passed away by Allah's mercy on Thursday $7^{th}$ Sha'ban in the year 819AH. He was buried at the time of *Duhā*, on Friday. Many, many people attended his funeral and countless people performed the funeral prayer. It was a scene that the eyes had not witnessed before. He rests in Zanbal, beside the gardens of Bishar. His blessed grave stands out more than the light of the day, his thirteen sons rest behind him, whose virtues are countless and too many to be mentioned here. Many miracles occurred at the hands of all of them, may Allah make us benefit by them all in this world and the next.

~ IV ~

# Aḥmad ibn ᶜAbd al-Raḥmān ibn ᶜAlī ibn Abī Bakr ibn ᶜAbd al-Raḥmān al-Saqqāf ﷺ

He ﷺ was famous by the name Shihāb al-Dīn. He was an upright scholar, eminent amongst the mujtahidīn, the awliyā and the ᶜārifīn. He was one with tremendous kashf, and possessed an exalted rank. He was the greatest murshid of his time, exceeding his peers and associates. He spoke by the tongue of divine knowledge, and all of those that heard him would listen attentively.

He was born in 887AH, in Tarīm, he had memorised the Quran and adopted the way of his forefathers. He ascended with tremendous blessings by the favour of Allah. He progressed in acquiring knowledge and becoming consolidated as an exalted man of eminence. The imam of that time, his grandfather Ḥabīb ᶜAlī b. Abī Bakr perceived this. Ḥabīb Aḥmad b. ᶜAbd al-Raḥmān said, "I came to my grandfather Ḥabīb ᶜAlī when I was seven years old, he stretched his tongue out towards me and said, "Absorb this." So I sucked it for a long time. He then said, "You are the inheritor of my secret." Thereafter, he acquired his spiritual learning from his father, from whom he received the khirqa. He learnt Sharia from his father, Fiqh from Qāḍī Aḥmad al-Sharīf, the science of Hadith from the muḥaddith Muḥammad b. ᶜAlī Khird and the Faqīh Muḥammad b. ᶜAbd al-Raḥmān and Sheikh ᶜAbdallāh b. ᶜAbd al-Raḥmān Bā Faḍl. He studied with all of these eminent scholars and others in Ḥaḍramawt. He also studied in Yemen, Makka and Madina under Sheikh Abu'l-Ḥasan al-Bikrī, Sheikh b. Ḥajar al-Makkī and others. By the time he returned to Tarīm, he possessed knowledge of every science. He began to teach the seekers of knowledge, and guided the seekers of guidance.

Generation after generation acquired knowledge from him in Sharia, Ṭarīqa and Ḥaqīqa. As a result many *muḥaqqiqīn* emerged and upright scholars, such as Sheikh b. ᶜAbdallāh b. Sheikh b. ᶜAbdallāh al-ᶜAydrūs and Qādī Muḥammad b. Husayn b. Sheikh ᶜAlī, Sheikh Yaḥyā al-Khaṭīb. Also the Muḥaddith Muḥammad b. ᶜAlī Khird, the author of *Al-Gurar* acquired his knowledge from him.

He was distinguished and incomparable in generosity, he was a refuge in the year of drought, and the destitute would seek rain from his bounty. He would give them from the oceans of his generosity and bounty. Strangers would seek refuge and protection at his door and they would also receive from his knowledge and gnosis.

It has been related that there was once a time of inflation and during this time the Sheikh possessed many dates. One of his servants considered selling those dates so that he may earn a good price. So he ﷺ said to him, "This is the way the envious think, not the truthful and generous. If you do this then do not give in charity with these dates but give with the eye because of the abundance that will manifest to those with evil eye. He then said, "How repulsive is the nature of those who possess such a trait, and what an unprofitable transaction it is for those with this intention." Then he immediately gave all the dates that he possessed in charity, and he did not incur any loss.

Amongst his miracles it has been related that he asked a man for a large amount of wood so that he could use it to make doors for his house. That man said to him that I seek something from you too, I would like to memorise the Quran. So the Sheikh said to him, "Open your mouth", and he opened it, and he spat in it three times. Then the man memorised the Quran in a short period of time.

Another miracle is that he said to his student Imam Sheikh b. ᶜAbdallāh al-ᶜAydrūs, "People from distant places will seek your attention, and the people of Ḥaḍramawt will wish for your gaze (*naẓr*)." And thus it happened; he travelled to India and stayed in Ahmadabad until he passed away.

Another miracle is that he selected a group of his companions and gave them a blessing whereby they would benefit the Muslims. Amongst these people were the Āl ibn Sharf, who received *barqiyat ul-ḥayāt.*

Many other similar accounts have been related on the miracles. He ﷺ would say that one who looks at the mashā'ikh with restraint, they are deprived of their baraka. One who looks at them with veneration, they receive from their baraka and they remain attached to that sheikh even if they do not perform actions like theirs.

He ﷺ was one whose intercession was accepted amongst the kings and others. His intercession was not rejected even if it was repeated many times in a day. His character was like a gentle breeze, his speech was composed like a string of pearls, his virtues were many, his states most exalted. It has been mentioned in *al-Nūr al-Ṣafir* that his student, the walī Ṣāliḥ al-Shahīr Yaḥyā b. al-Khaṭīb has a compilation of his virtues. His praiseworthy attributes continually manifested until the All-Forgiving called him, and he left this world in the year

946AH. He is buried in Zanbal, where his noble grave is very well known, may Allah make us benefit from him.

~ V ~

# Sheikh ibn ᶜAbdallāh ibn Sheikh ibn ᶜAbdallāh al-ᶜAydarūs ﵁

He was the Ṣāḥib of Ahmadabād, the Sheikh of his time in knowledge and state. He was the Imam of the time officially and in reality. He wrote with the pen of eloquence and was the most eloquent in speech. He was the foremost in his studying of all the sciences. He relieved people of their problems, and he would solve problematic situations. He would extract the fruits from the teachings of his teachers.

He ﵁ was born in 919AH, in Tarım, he memorised the Quran and other books and occupied himself with seeking knowledge. He was the foremost in sailing through the oceans of knowledge. He was the first one to learn from his father and was adorned with noble manners with his virtuous and praiseworthy qualities. He also studied with Imam Shihāb al-Dīn ᶜAbd al-Raḥmān, Sheikh ᶜAbdallāh b. Muḥammad Bā Qushayr, the author of *'Al-Qalā'id.'* He travelled to Bandar Aden in Yemen, where he studied with Sheikh ᶜUmar Bā Qudām and others. Then he travelled to the Hijaz, where he achieved all of his aims. He performed the Hajj, and this Hajj took place on a Friday in the year 938AH. During this year, he was with his father, and they met Sheikh al-Islam Abu'l-Ḥasan al-Bikrī. He was with his son, the Crown of the Gnostics and all of those that accompanied them asked them to pray for their child.

He also studied with Abū Ḥusayn ﷺ, and studied with the father of Sheikh b. ᶜAbdallāh. Allah answered their prayer and made each one of them the leader of their time, and the imam of their locality. Then he travelled with his father to the blessed sanctuary of Madina, and they visited the Master of all creation ﷺ. Each one of them received everything that they had wished and aspired for. They entered into the noble presence and a great state overcame Sheikh b. ᶜAbdallāh, he was unaware of his physical senses and he fell down unconscious. Then his father pleaded with the holy Prophet ﷺ. He then regained his consciousness and he received that which he had never thought of before.

They returned to Tarīm, in the year 941AH. During the lifetime of his father, he went to perform the Hajj for a second time, but this time on his own. Once again his Hajj occurred on Friday and he stayed in Makka for three years. His manner was like the pious (*ṣāliḥīn*), seeking knowledge, worship, travelling the path that would take him to felicity. He studied with Sheikh al-Islam Aḥmad b. Ḥajar al-Ḥaythamī, the great scholar ᶜAbdallāh b. Aḥmad al-Fākihi, his brother ᶜAbd al-Qadir al-Fākihi, the learned ᶜAbd al-Ra'ūf b. Yaḥyā and Muḥammad al-Khaṭṭāb al-Mālikī. He remained with them until he excelled in the sciences: Tafsīr, Hadīth, Fiqh, Arabic, Tasawwuf, along with many other subjects. He performed many *Ṭawāfs* and Umrahs while he resided there.

It has been related by Mujāhid that in Ramaḍān he would often perform four Umrahs in the night and four in the day. The great scholar Hamid b. ᶜAbdallāh al-Sanadī said, "Being able to do this is one of the extraordinary miracles. This practice has not been related from anyone in the previous generations. It has been related in a sound hadith that the

Messenger of Allah ﷺ said, "Umrah in Ramaḍān is equivalent to Hajj." In another version, "It is equivalent to performing a Hajj with me." The eloquent ᶜAbd al-Muᶜtī b. Ḥasan Bā Kathīr alluded to this in his praise of the Sheikh:

*You lived in Umm al-Qurā[47] for a time,*

*To acquire knowledge, then studied the Quran,*

*Worship, and zuhd was in seclusion,*

*Concealed from all the brothers.*

*The qiyām al-layl with fasting rewarded,*

*As you held fast to the Ka'ba and the rites.*

*You were written down as one of the Hujjāj,*

*the Ummār and the Returning from the radiant Makka to*

*the noble sanctuary of the Prophet, al-Musṭafā al-Adnān*

*You did not receive wilāya, O son of ᶜAydrūs, the gift and the rank of Sultan,*

*Except by your kindness, diligence, worship*

*and striving for the pleasure of al-Raḥmān.*

*Sublimity is not just by wishing for it O young one,*

*It is but through hardship*

*You are a walī, the son of a walī, and the father of a walī to pure pleasure,*

*Al-ᶜAydrūs is your father and Saqqāf is your grandfather,*
*And Muqaddam is the third of this pride.*
*You are included amongst the pride, you, your fathers and your brothers.*

[47] Umm al-Qurā is another name for Makka

During his stay at Makka, he would visit the blessed Prophet ﷺ. His Sheikh, Sheikh Ibn Ḥajar would ask him to convey his greetings to the holy Prophet ﷺ. He would also ask him to pray for him in the presence of the holy Prophet ﷺ that Allah cure his haemorrhoids, and accept his books. And Allah answered his prayer.

Then Sheikh b. ᶜAbdallāh travelled to Zabid and he studied with great Ḥāfiẓ ᶜAbd al-Raḥmān al-Dibāᶜī. In Shahr he studied with the great Sheikh, Ahmad b. ᶜAbdallāh Bā Faḍl. He received *ijāzāt* from all of his shuyūkh for all of their books and narrations. He received the noble investiture (*khirqa*) from many shuyūkh, and many of them gave him *ijāza* for *taḥkīm* and allowed him to bestow the khirqa to others.

He stayed in Tarīm for approximately 13 years then he travelled to India in 958AH. He received Ahmadabad from the great wazir ᶜImād al-Mulk and people complied to his commands. People from the city and the country devoted themselves to him, they came to him from all places, and students travelled to him from different regions. He devoted himself to teaching and benefitting others. He taught every valuable science, and countless people studied with him. Many completed all of their studies with him, such as his son, Imam al-ᶜĀrif billāh ᶜAbdallāh, the great sheikh ᶜAbd al-Qādir, his grandson, the Imam, Sheikh Muḥammad b. ᶜAbdallāh, the great walī Sayyid ᶜAbdallāh b. ᶜAlī, Sheikh Aḥmad b. ᶜAlī al-Yashkarī, the learned ᶜAbdallāh b. Ahmad ibn Falāh, Sheikh Abū Saᶜādat Muḥammad b. Ahmad al-Fākihi, Sheikh Hamid b. ᶜAbdallāh al-Sanadī.

He also wrote many beneficial books, such as *Kitāb al-ᶜAqd al-Nabawiyy* and *Sirr al-Muṣṭafawiyy*, this book has been translated into many languages, and *Kitāb al-Fawz wa'l-Bushrā.* He wrote commentaries for books on Aqīda called *Tuhfat ul-Murīd*, which has two extensive commentaries called,

*Ḥaqā'iq al-Tawḥīd* and *Sirāj al-Tawḥīd.* He also had two short mawlids, a *Risāla* on *ᶜAdl,* he also had a wird called *Hizb ul-Nafīs,* and a book on Tasawwuf. His compositions were for everyone to see, as he was diligent and persevered with his striving.

He had been endowed with much bounty (*faḍl*), understanding, plenty of knowledge and the ability to research. He had a diwān, a collection of poems, in which his words were enchanting. Most of his sayings were about aims (*maqāsid*), the eminent and learned ones memorised his sayings, and all those that heard his words liked them. Amongst his compositions is this *wasīla* which goes back to the noble Prophet ﷺ:

*Intercession with Muḥammad, the seal of the Prophets,*

*And Fāṭima, and the Commander of the believers ᶜAlī,*

*Then Ḥasan and Ḥusain with Zain al-ᶜĀbidīn ᶜAlī,*

*Muḥammad al-Bāqir, the prostrator, Jafar ᶜAlī,*

*This ᶜUraydī Imam Muḥammad is his offspring,*

*ᶜĪsā, the brave lion, the blessed heroic Aḥmad with ᶜUbaydillāh,*

*Then the ᶜAlawī's, Muḥammad ᶜAlawī, Khāli' Qasam, ᶜAlī Muḥammad Ṣāḥib al-Mirbāt,*

*Then ᶜAlī and Ba'l-Faqīh Muḥammad ᶜAlawī and ᶜAlī Mawlā Dawīla Muḥammad,*

*Then the Saqqāf's, Fakhr, ᶜAydrūs, Sheikh al-ᶜAfīf walī,*

*These sons of Zahrā made true their lineage and manner,*

*With the Chosen One is connected the quality of the descendants of Fāṭima,*

*A lineage like the sun of the morn,*

*The noble lineage clearly radiates its lamp,*

*From the Master of the Messengers, Zahrā and descending from ᶜAlī,*

*Continuously like a chain of pearly stars,*

*The beginning and the end is Muḥammad the Seal of the Messengers.*

The commentary of this qasīda is called *ᶜAqd al-Nabawiyy wa'l-Sirr al-Muṣṭafawiyy* as mentioned earlier. Many mashā'ikh and great saints of his time have praised it, such as Sheikh Abū Bakr b. ᶜAbdallāh al-ᶜAydrūs. He said to his son ᶜAbdallāh, you will have children called so and so, mentioning their names. Sheikh b. ᶜAbdallāh was included amongst them. He praised him and indicated that he will behold a secret that will be hidden in him. He said, "He is my son and the possessor of my secret." On the authority of Sheikh ᶜAlī b. Abī Bakr, who said, "I hope to marry ᶜAbdallāh b. Sheikh to one of my daughters or to one of the daughters of my children, and from them will emerge upright offspring." At this time he was young, when he was older he married Sharīfa the daughter of Muḥammad Bā ᶜUmar. Her mother was ᶜAlawiyya the daughter of Sheikh ᶜAlī and she gave birth to Sheikh ibn ᶜAbdallāh and his brothers Abū Bakr, Husain and Muḥammad. The desire of their grandfather was fulfilled.

The Gnostic Sheikh Abū Bakr b. Sālim ﷺ said, "I was not given one like him from the Āl Bā ᶜAlawī." The righteous scholar, ᶜAbdallāh Bā Harūn al-Nahwī said, "He is but a precious sign and a warner for his era. When he read his works he thoroughly approved of them and said, "He has produced that which has not been written before." One of the scholars said, "He is praised as the Sheikh of his time by consensus of the scholars of his time." Allah has inspired him and his family, thus they call him a sheikh due to his widely circulated expertise that he had achieved and this name proved true to him in four ways. The first, that his name is knowledge, the second that at a young age he acquired the wisdom of a sheikh, the third that he was the sheikh of the people of Sharia, the fourth that he was the sheikh of the people of Ḥaqīqa. Thus he was a sheikh by quality, name, and imam of the sciences of Realities (*Ḥaqīqa*) and of the outward. Regarding this, the adept ᶜAbd al-Laṭīf al-Dibar ﵁ composed:

*Sheikh, whose demeanour is the path to guidance,*

*on his path of knowledge there is nothing that remained unknown (to him)*

*Sheikh, with his excellent conduct and articulation, the most greatest of problems are made easy,*

*Sheikh, a master in the sciences, who has seen an ocean that is so accessible when one desires water from it*

*Sheikh, upon him solemnity, and splendour like the full moon, and his face shines with radiance*

*Sheikh, who has students with questions of sufism, if you come you can ask*

*Sheikh, the foremost on the Path, the masters of miracles consider that the first scholar ᶜAydrūs is the exemplar of his time, one who possessed great determination and hope*

*The Qutb and Gawth of his time and his help is for those who hope for it, they are not at loss nor are they neglected*

*Ibn al-ᶜAfīf, Abū Shihāb al-Murtaḍā, an ocean of the realities and generosity is their way*

*A spring of sweet water for the one who comes to drink from it, with his bounties he cleanses without any strictness*

*What is said about one whose soul is perfect,*

*Only that I say al-Sheikh is more perfect than him,*

*The bounties (fayḍ) of his perfections still continue as long as Sheikh is a part of the ṭarīqa.*

His virtues are many, his qualities renowned, his lights radiant. Many other scholars have written about him in their works and he has been mentioned in the *Ṭabaqāt* and other works. Amongst those who wrote about him are the brilliant Hāmid b. ᶜAbdallāh al-Sanadī and Sheikh Shihāb Ahmad b. ᶜAlī al-Baskarī al-Makkī, who wrote a treatise about him called '*Nuzhat ul-Ikhwān wa'l-Nufūs fi manāqib Sheikh ibn ᶜAbdallāh al-ᶜAydrūs.*' His son ᶜAbd al-Qādir has mentioned a lot about him in the introduction of his book *Al-Futuḥāt al-Quddūsiyya fi'l-khirqāt il-ᶜAydrūsiyya.*

# ~ VI ~

# Sayyidinā Imam ᶜAbdallāh ibn ᶜAlawī al-Ḥaddād ﵁

Imam ᶜAbdallāh b. ᶜAlawī b. Muḥammad al-Ḥaddād ﵁, renowned by the name Imam al-Ḥaddād was born, raised and spent most of his life in Tarīm. He was born on Sunday night, 5th Safar, in the year 1044AH/ 1632CE. He came from a family of saintly scholars, who had surpassed in excellence with the outward sciences of the sharia and the inward sciences of ḥaqīqa. His father, Sayyid ᶜAlawī b. Muḥammad al-Ḥaddād was one of the most virtuous and upright of men, whose mother, Salma possessed the ranks of sainthood and gnosis.[48] Likewise the mother of Imam al-Ḥaddād was called Salma and possessed the nobility and virtues of her forefathers.

The signs of sainthood upon Sayyidinā Imam al-Ḥaddād were manifest and recognised from the time of his birth, and became even more obvious at the age of three, when the Imam was afflicted with a serious illness, whereby he lost his physical sight.[49] It was assumed that the loss of sight would

[48] Imam al-Ḥaddād had noted approximately forty to fifty miracles of the noble Salma's father, Sayyid ᶜUmar ibn Ahmad al-Munaffar Bā ᶜAlawī, who was one of the great *ᶜārifin* and upright scholars ﵁.
[49] Cf. *Ghāyat al-Qaṣd wa'l-Murād*, other reports state the age as being four.

render him deficient and incompetent in many aspects; instead the scholars of the time were amazed to witness the various talents that emerged from him. They witnessed his eagerness to memorise the Quran and from a very young age he was completely focused towards Allah, he had no interest in playing with the other children; rather he preferred to occupy himself with memorisation and seeking knowledge. Hence, the children acknowledged that he had been created for Allah, since he did not seek any other or turn to any other than his Lord.

His childhood friend, Sayyid ʿAbdallāh Ba'l-Faqīh would often say, "Although our performance of worship was together, ʿAbdallāh would always surpass us." He also said, "Allah had endowed him with spiritual openings from a very young age. During the recital of Sūra Yāsīn, we would see the effects upon him and he would weep incessantly. Sayyid Aḥmad b. ʿUmar al-Hindawān, also amongst his companions, describes, "We would gather for dhikr and an ecstatic state would overcome Sayyidinā ʿAbdallāh to the extent that he would faint."

After his session of Quranic recitation, Imam al-Ḥaddād was accustomed to hasten towards the mosque, at the time of Duḥā, with his friend, Sayyid Ba'l-Faqīh, and together they would perform one hundred to two hundred rakats of prayer. As Sayyid Ba'l-Faqīh describes, "The children would approach us to play but we would hasten towards one of the blessed places or one of the mosques and perform supererogatory prayers." Thereafter, Imam al-Ḥaddād would ask Allah for the rank of Sheikh ʿAbdallāh b. Abū Bakr al-ʿAydrūs,[50] and Sayyid Ba'l-Faqīh would seek the rank of his grandfather, the great

---

[50] Some reports relate that he would seek the rank of Sheikh ʿAbdallāh ibn ʿAlawī Bā ʿAlawī.

Gnostic, Sayyid ᶜAbdallāh ibn Muḥammad, may Allah be pleased with them all.

By the age of fifteen, Imam al-Ḥaddād رضي الله عنه had studied every discipline under many scholars. In addition to the teachings of the scholars and the guidance of his father, his intellectual sphere was shaped by his extreme enthusiasm towards acquiring knowledge. He had the desire to undertake and memorise texts such as Imam al-Ghazālī's *Bidāyat al-Hidāya* and *al-Irshād*, the manual of Shafiᶜī fiqh by Ibn al-Muqrī, despite being discouraged by his father, who directed him towards easier texts appropriate for his age. Imam al-Ḥaddād would study the books of useful knowledge with his close friend, Sayyid ᶜAlī b. ᶜUmar b. al-Ḥusayn, together they would spend days and nights narrating from them. Imam al-Ḥaddād said, "Sometimes he would recite to me as we walked through the streets, and at times the day passed into the night and we would still be studying."

Imam al-Ḥaddād loved to remain in seclusion. At the age of seventeen he stayed in the mosque al-Hajīra. He, رضي الله عنه relates, "After the Friday prayer in the Jāmiᶜa mosque, I would hasten back to al-Hajīra, lock the door and sit in seclusion. At times, people would knock at the door but I would not respond to it." During this seclusion he received countless spiritual openings and lights. After his period of seclusion at the mosque, people started to approach him in order to seek knowledge. He had no desire to teach, it was only when a man from the family of Bā Faḍl sought to acquire blessings from him in his learning of *Riyādh al-Ṣālihīn*, followed by Sayyid Ḥasan al-Jifrī who wanted to learn *Al-ᶜAwārif wa'l-Maᶜārif* that the Imam allocated a time for teaching.

Thus, the love of knowledge and learning increased and advanced to an unfathomable degree. He had gained profundity in both the outward disciplines and in Divine knowledge to the extent that he was unrivalled and unique. When the faqīh, Bā Jubayr returned from India, he found that the Imam was established in all the sciences, and that his knowledge was immeasurable. Hence, he felt no shame in seeking knowledge from a man who was once his student. Not only the Faqīh Bā Jubayr, but also many shuyūkh sought knowledge with the great Imam.

It was recitation from the sound books of knowledge and the learning of religious sciences that occupied the gatherings of Imam al-Ḥaddād. He loved the seekers of knowledge and those aspiring for the Hereafter. He disliked any form of worldly discourse in his gatherings, he would say, "No one has sat with me and been diverted from the remembrance of Allah." He was known for his Prophetic character, he was gentle, kind, compassionate and extremely generous. He would accept any excuses that were made to him, and his eyes would gaze upon the pious and the sinful with complete compassion and mercy.

He was never annoyed at those who harmed him and never did he curse them; likewise he prevented those who had been treated unjustly from cursing their adversaries. He said, "If anyone harms us we do not curse them nor do we dislike them but we speak to them in a kind and friendly manner so that when Allah takes them to account for it they will be impressed with a good opinion in mind. As we have seen and experienced the nature of Allah, that anyone who harms us Allah takes him to account for it." He was extremely kind to the servant, the poor, the widow and the orphan. Whenever his servant caused annoyance to him, the Imam would give him a present to abate his anger. Then the servant would say, "If only he could be annoyed with me at all times."

He had great concern for the welfare of the Muslims, he was very patient with them, lowering his wing to them, he was very mild, easy going, with a soft temperament. Those in his gathering would feel that they were dearest to him; they received intimacy and special attention from him the likes of which they would not experience in any other gathering. He would say, "If all the people approached us, the old and the young, the men and the women, they would all derive benefit from us, in religious and worldly matters, outwardly and inwardly, immediately and with time; even if they dwell physically in the West and their spirits are with us..."

At the age of 26, Imam al-Ḥaddād ﷺ said, "We are now included amongst the dead, as all the worldly desires within us have perished. I do not find within myself an inclination whatsoever, or desire for anything of the *dunya,* nor do I find any delight therein. But if food comes to us then we eat from it."

Imam al-Ḥaddād experienced much distress at the hands of the government and by others who were envious and harboured enmity towards him. But he was a man of forbearance and nothing dissuaded him from upholding the religion and truth. He would often utter the noble words of his grandfather, al-Muṣtafā ﷺ, "The believer who interacts with the people and forebears when they cause harm to him is better than he who does not interact with the people and is not patient when they harm him."

All of his actions were in complete emulation of the Messenger of Allah ﷺ his standing throughout the night, his worship, devotions, determination and characteristics. He was described as 'extremely fearful of Allah, always in reverence and awe of Him, and readily inclined to tears.' He would say, "In all of our affairs we rely on Allah, His generosity and His bounties. By the praise of Allah, we spend from the treasuries of His generosity and spending from it does not worry us, rather keeping it does." He desired to keep secret his charitable works. Hence most of the money that he spent in charity was spent in secrecy; his family and those most close to him were unable to know about it.

Every aspect of the Imam's life was inviting to Allah. He would invite with his speech, his books, his teachings, his character, his actions, his worship and his striving. This came as a result of his extensive knowledge and his complete firmness and embodiment of what he knew. Every action and speech of his was solely for the sake of Allah, they were not tainted with any other motive or desire, and he had no concern for matters that did not involve his Lord. On one occasion when he was speaking about the blessings of Allah, he said, "Allah the Exalted has honoured me with two blessings, the gratitude of which cannot be fulfilled. The first is knowledge that is so extensive that we do not require any other knowledge on the face of the earth. The second is that Allah has bestowed me with an intellect that is so complete we do not require the mind of any other." The Imam would never utter such statements only that they would be coupled with the utmost humility. He did not see these as his own qualities but he saw it as an act of Divine Will.

As for his shuyūkh, Imam al-Ḥaddād received the openings of knowledge and received spiritual transmissions in two ways, that is, outwardly with the physical guidance of the shuyūkh of his time and spiritually by transmissions from the great masters in the *barzakh.* He had studied with approximately 140 shuyūkh, amongst them, one of the most significant in the Imam's life was Ḥabīb ᶜUmar b. ᶜAbd al-Raḥmān al-ᶜAṭṭās رضي الله عنه. He had also received the khirqa from many of the Sādāt Bā ᶜAlawī, most of them went back to Sayyidinā *Quṭb al-Aqṭāb* ᶜAbdallāh ibn Abī Bakr al-ᶜAydrūs رضي الله عنه. He received many spiritual transmissions from the latter and from Sheikh ᶜAbd al-Qādir Jīlānī, may Allah be pleased with them all. He رضي الله عنه said, "I have been favoured by four people through the *barzakh*, Sayyidinā Faqīh al-Muqaddam, Sheikh ʿAbd al-Raḥmān al-Saqqāf, Sheikh ʿUmar al-Miḥḍār, and Sheikh ʿAbdallāh ibn Abī Bakr al-ʿAydrūs. Now I receive directly through the Messenger of Allah ﷺ."

Imam al-Ḥaddād's great concern for the people of his age and the ensuing generations, as expressed in his counsels and books, indicates that he was the Imam of the end of times. His works gave expression to the indispensable teachings of Imam al-Ghazālī in a concise and simplified manner, so that it could be readily accepted by the masses. Hence the wisdom and practices of the elite and assiduous were made accessible to the imperceptive and feeble.

He saw that one of the greatest tribulations of the end of time was an extreme occupation with worldly matters, lack of desire and time to study useful knowledge and lack of determination to embody it. Therefore he said, "This is not an age for spiritual retreat (*khalwa*) and spiritual exercises (*riyāda*) as people would not be able to fulfil the conditions, rather it is an age in which the obligatory forms of worship should be maintained and sins should be abandoned...." Thus, the Imam introduced a path called: "*Ṭarīqat Ahl al-Yamīn*", that is, 'the path for the people of the right' to facilitate the path to Allah for the people of the end of times. He would say, "Do not ever think that we are on the path of the elite, as there are very few that seek it sincerely, but we certainly say that we are on the common path, the path of the people of the right."

Imam Aḥmad b. Zayn al-Ḥabshī, may Allah make us benefit by him, mentions of his beloved master, "One thing that really stood out about our sheikh, may Allah make us benefit by him, was his ability to benefit the common and the elite. He did not aim at a particular group of people, rather he called everyone to Allah: the awliyā, the scholars, all the believers and the Muslims, including the leaders and the rulers benefitting them inwardly and outwardly. This was due to the great capacity he had received from Allah and his firm footing in the Sharᶜīa, Ṭarīqa and Ḥaqīqa."

The signs of the approach of his passing away were indicative from about the year 1128AH. Towards the end of his life he was not physically strong enough to attend the mosque for every prayer and eventually he did not allow any visitors. On 8th Dhu'l-Qaᶜada, Sheikh Shajjār visited him and found that he had no flesh on his body and face. In the past he would often say to his son, Hasan ﵁, "I wish that on the day that I pass away, I do so without a shred of flesh on my body." During his last days he would repeat the Hadith of the noble Prophet ﷺ: "Two phrases are light on the tongue, heavy in the Scale and beloved to al-Raḥmān: *Subḥān Allāh wa bi ḥamdihī, Subḥān Allāh il-Aẓīm.*" He remained unwell for forty days and on the fortieth day on Monday night 7th Dhu'l-Qaᶜada, 1132AH/ 1720CE, the great Imam passed away to the heavenly abode, may Allah be pleased with him and make us benefit by him.

## *Literary works*

Imam al-Ḥaddād's books are distinctive by their conciseness and brevity, they convey the essence of the inward and outward teachings of the Quran and Prophetic Sunna. He ﵁ particularly aimed at keeping the chapters of his book as short and simple as possible, without omitting any essential details. Amongst his works, many of which have been translated into English are, *Risālat al-Mudhākara maᶜa al-ikhwān wa'l-muhibbīn min ahl al-khayr wa'l-dīn*, which he wrote in 1069AH. It is a simple treatise describing the meaning of *taqwa* and illustrating the benefits of the path, purifying the soul and illuminating the heart. *Risālat al-ādāb wa'l-sulūk*, which has been translated into English as *The book of the Murīd* was written in the month of Ramadan in 1071AH, it is an indispensable guide for the seeker on the path. *Ittiḥāf al-sā'il bi ajūbāt il-masā'il,* or *'Gifts of the Seeker'* was written in 1072AH, when the Imam was 28 years of age. It is a collection of answers that were written in response to some constructive questions, put forth to him in writing by Sheikh ᶜAbd al-Raḥmān Bā ᶜAbād. *Al-Nasā'ih al-Dīniyya wa'l-Wasāya al-Īmāniyya*, written in 1079AH, is one of his greatest works. It is a practical, beneficial and simple guide for every Muslim, explaining the practical aspects to the tenets of faith. The first half was written before he travelled to perform the Hajj, and he recited it to the Messenger of Allah ﷺ at his noble sanctuary. Some people have called this book the "*Ha al-Iḥyā*", and the Imam ؓ said, "One of the scholars of the *Haramayn* said to us, "This is the essence of the *Iḥyā*." We replied, "The matter is as you see it." It has been related that when the mufti of Syria went to perform the Hajj, on his arrival a crowd gathered around him and he said, "There is not on the face of this earth, one more learned than Sayyid ᶜAbdallāh al-Ḥaddād, to him belongs the book *al-Nasā'iḥ*, which is of great worth. There is no seeker of knowledge that remains in our region except that he has a copy of it."

*Risālat al-Muᶜāwana* or *'The Book of Assistance'* was written in 1069AH; it is a practical guide for the Muslim that leads them to perfecting their obligatory and supererogatory acts of worship and conduct. *Sabīl al-iddikār wa'l-Iᶜtibār bi mā yamurrū bi'l-insān* or *The Lives of Man* was written in the year 1110AH, when Imam al-Ḥaddād was 67 years of age. It is a short treatise that illustrates the five stages that one passes through their life from pre-birth to their final abode. *Al-Da'wat al-Tāmma wa Tadhkirat al-ᶜĀmma*, which was written in 1114AH is a compilation that explains all the modes and techniques of calling people to Allah. *Fusūl al-ᶜilmiyya wa al-usūl al-ḥikmiyya* or *Knowledge and Wisdom* was written in 1130AH. Made up of forty extremely short and profound chapters that are a vital aid to the seeker on the path.

Imam al-Ḥaddād also has a collection of over 150 poems compiled in a diwan entitled: *Al-Durr al-Manẓūm li Dhaw il-ᶜUqūl wa'l-Fuhūm.* Regarding these poems, ᶜAbd al-Qadir Jīlānī b. Sālim Khird has mentioned that every verse in each poem contains an amazing secret that cannot be commented upon by the masters of rhetoric. The spiritual effects of these that enlighten the soul cannot be expressed in words. Therefore, he concludes that the poetry of Imam al-Ḥaddād is connected to the heavens more than it is connected to the earth. Accordingly, Imam al-Ḥaddād رضي الله عنه said, "One who possesses this diwan needs no other."

## ~ VII ~

# IMAM $^{c}$ALĪ IBN MUḤAMMAD AL-ḤABSHĪ رضي الله عنه

He is our master al-Ḥabīb $^{c}$Alī b. Muḥammad b Ḥusain b. $^{c}$Abdallāh b. Sheikh b $^{c}$Abdallāh b. Muḥammad b. Ḥusain, b. Aḥmad Ṣāḥib ash-Shi$^{c}$ab b. Muḥammad b. $^{c}$Alawī b. Abī Bakr al-Ḥabshī b. $^{c}$Alī b. Aḥmad, who was known as the lion of Allah, b. Ḥasan at-Turabī b. $^{c}$Alī, b. al-Faqīh al-Muqaddam Muḥammad b. $^{c}$Alī b. Muḥammad the Ṣāḥib of Mirbāt b. $^{c}$Alī Khāli$^{c}$ Qasam b. $^{c}$Alawī b. $^{c}$Ubaidillāh b. *al-Muhājir illallah* Aḥmad b. $^{c}$Īsā b. Muḥammad al-Naqīb b. $^{c}$Alī al-$^{c}$Uraidī b. Imam Ja$^{c}$far as-Ṣādiq b. Muḥammad al-Bāqir b. Imam $^{c}$Alī Zain al-$^{c}$Ābidīn b. Imam Ḥusain, the grandson of the Messenger of Allah ﷺ, and the son of Sayyida Fāṭima al-Zahrā', the pure one and daughter of our master the Messenger of Allah ﷺ and the son of our master $^{c}$Alī b. Abī Ṭālib, may Allah ennoble his face, and may Allah be pleased with them all.

He رضي الله عنه was born on Friday 24$^{th}$ of Shawwāl 1259AH (1843CE), in the village of Qasam in Ḥaḍramawt which lies on the road to the valley of the Prophet Hūd عليه السلام. His mother was the blessed, pious and saintly Sharīfa, Al-Sayyida $^{c}$Alawiyya bint Ḥusain al-Jifrī, who served the religion by calling people to Allah. His father Ḥabīb Muḥammad was the Mufti of the Shāfi$^{c}$ī school of thought, for this role he had to move to

Makka in the year 1266AH, while Ḥabīb ᶜAlī stayed behind with his mother in Qasam and received much of his early instruction at her hands.

In 1271AH, they moved to Seyūn and studied with Ḥabīb ᶜAbd al-Raḥmān b. ᶜAlī al-Saqqāf and Ḥabīb Muḥsin b. ᶜAlawī al-Saqqāf. In 1276AH he travelled to Makka and studied with his father, alongside other great scholars of Makka such as Sayyid Aḥmad Zaynī Daḥlān and others.

Two years later he returned to Seyūn and established himself there. Soon his fame spread and many people from all over the world came to seek knowledge from him. People from all levels of society benefitted from him, the learned and the unlearned. He established a centre of learning (*Ribāṭ*), a place of study to spread religious teachings. It was the first Ribāt that had been established, this was around 1878CE.

It has been said that his sermons resembled the sermons of Sheikh ᶜAbd al-Qādir Jilānī رضي الله عنه, regarding the powerful impact that his words would have upon the hearts, and would make tears flow from the eyes. Thus, it was said that he received a share of the blessings that had been bestowed upon Sheikh ᶜAbd al-Qādir Jilānī رضي الله عنه.

His heart was filled with immense mercy for the ummah; he would always seek forgiveness for them and sought from Allah to avert punishment away from them. He was compassionate, especially with the poor, eager to help them and students of learning. He provided food and accommodation for those who attended the annual mawlid. Many people attended; at times the numbers would amount to 40,000, not one person remained without food or a place to stay, he took care of everybody that attended.

It has been related that the Imam absolutely loved to teach Arabic grammar, and would begin the day's lessons, after praying Fajr with teaching grammar. Sheikh Tayyib b. Aḥmad Bā Bahir was leaning against a pillar when a moment of sleep overtook him. He saw three people with faces like the moon. The first of them was the greatest and grandest. He said, "The first and the second passed by me, and so I grabbed the hem of the third and I asked, "Who are you?" The man replied, "As for the first person you saw that was the Prophet ﷺ, and the second was ʿAlī b. Abī Ṭālib." I asked, "And you are? "He replied, "I am Ḥasan, the son of ʿAlī." I asked, "What is it that you came for?" He replied, "We came to attend the lesson of our son, ʿAlī." Some people were guided to the ribāṭ by the Prophet's ﷺ recommendation in their dream.

Every year they would have a grand mawlid on the last Thursday of the month of Rabīʿ al-Awwal. In the mawlid gatherings of Imam ʿAlī b. Muhmmad al-Ḥabshī, it is reported that people would see the light of the Prophet ﷺ like the sun which when Imam ʿAlī would sit down it would land before him.

Many others would see the Prophet ﷺ enter into the mawlid saying to them, '*maqbūlīn, maqbūlīn, maqbūlīn,*' '(accepted, accepted, accepted)'.

He wrote the mawlid, *Simṭ ad-Durr* (Stringed Pearls) in the year 1328AH. The mawlid itself was an inspiration upon the heart (*ilhām*). Imam ʿAlī b. Muḥammad said regarding it, "Within the mawlid is a great secret. Every time I recite it or hear it, I receive new spiritual openings; it's as though it did not actually emanate from my tongue."

He رضي الله عنه said, "If one is consistent with the recitation, or memorises it and makes it from among his litanies, then something of the secret of al-Ḥabīb رضي الله عنه will be revealed to him." Every time it was recited before me, a door of connection was opened to the Prophet ﷺ.

One of his students, one of saintly rank, Sayyid ʿUmar b. ʿAydrūs had a dream in which he was complaining to the Imam about the lack of intelligence within his children. He was told, "Get them to write out my mawlid." It was as if he was indicating that the opening to intelligence was in the writing out of the mawlid. The Imam replied that whoever wants an opening, they should memorise or write out the mawlid.

Ḥabīb ᶜAlī ﷺ said that one should, for every action of good, make an abundance of intentions, so that he may be rewarded for them all. He gave an example for a person who may want to attend a lesson. They should say, "I intend to attend a lesson, I intend to undergo seclusion in the mosque, I intend to increase the number of students, I intend to hear the hadith of the Messenger of Allah ﷺ, I intend to hear the speech of Allah ﷻ, I intend to hear the speech of scholars of Allah ﷻ, I intend to look at the faces of the scholars of Allah ﷻ."

He also said that those who do not know how to make intentions, they should intend to enter their intentions into the intention of their Sheikh and say, "I intend what my Sheikh so and so has intended." And also say, "I intend all good actions", and thus continuously renew their righteous intentions. It is related from the Prophet ﷺ, "The intention of a believer is better than his actions."

Ḥabīb ᶜAlī ﷺ was known for the great love he had for the Prophet ﷺ and for the strength of his connection with him. He was in this rank of being annihilated in the Prophet ﷺ. This annihilation (*fanā*) is reflected in his mawlid. It is because of his attachment to the Prophet ﷺ that he would receive abundant spiritual aid (*madad*), and was under the Prophet's protection and care.

In fact, in one vision he saw the Prophet ﷺ who said to him, "My son, I have placed a wall around you and your companions."

Many gnostics during his time would see him praying his obligatory prayers at the noble *rawda* of the Messenger of Allah ﷺ and that he would meet the Prophet ﷺ in abundance.

There was not a single gathering of Ḥabīb ʿAlī except that the Prophet ﷺ was mentioned in it, including his virtues and characteristics, in addition to many poems of this nature.

People around him would see the Prophet ﷺ abundantly in his gatherings, and would very often see the Messenger of Allah ﷺ in the form of Ḥabīb ʿAlī b. Muḥammad al-Ḥabshī رضي الله عنه.

He took from many mashā'ikh, ten of whom are specifically mentioned. The first was his father Ḥabīb Muḥammad b. Ḥusain al-Ḥabshī رضي الله عنه who was the mufi of the Shafiʿī school of thought in Makka.

Ḥabīb ʿAlī would praise the great quṭb and caller to Allah, Ḥabīb Aḥmad b. ʿUmar b. Sumait رضي الله عنه abundantly, and would spend the whole of a lesson just talking about him. Ḥabīb Jaʿfar b. Muḥammad al-ʿAṭṭās once saw the Prophet ﷺ in a wakeful state and asked him for the great spiritual opening (*al-fatḥ al-kabīr*) the Prophet ﷺ said that the great opening is with Ḥabīb Aḥmad b. ʿUmar b. Sumait رضي الله عنه.

The third is Ḥabīb Ḥasan b. Ṣāliḥ al-Bahr رضي الله عنه, who was the great quṭb, the imam and leader of the ʿAlawiyyīn. He was Ḥabīb ʿAlī's Sheikh al-Fatḥ. He relates that once Ḥabīb Abū Bakr al-ʿAṭṭās saw Paradise, the *ḥūrs*, and its palaces all under the house of Ḥabīb Ḥasan b. Ṣāliḥ. Ḥabīb Ḥasan b. Ṣāliḥ رضي الله عنه said, "My intention is not the *hūr* or the palaces, but my intention is the removal of veils."

He also said, 'Ḥabīb Ḥasan b. Ṣāliḥ رضي الله عنه would recite the whole Quran in one rakʿah, and in the second rakʿah ninety thousand Sūrah Ikhlās. One of the scholars of Makka, who himself had a daily wird of a thousand rakʿahs, on hearing that Ḥabīb Ḥasan b. Ṣāliḥ was coming, desired to see something of his miracles. When he came to see him in the

Haram, Ḥabīb Ṣāliḥ knew, through his spiritual perception that which he desired. So he began to recite the Quran at Bāb as-Salām, with the sheikh who walked alongside him, listening. By the time they reached Maqām Ibrāhīm he had heard him recite the whole of the Quran, in spite of the fact that Ḥabīb Ḥasan b. Ṣāliḥ had not even memorised the Quran.'

The fourth teacher was Ḥabīb ᶜAbdallāh b. Ḥusain b. Ṭāhir ﵁, the great imam, and scholar, who had combined both outward and inward knowledge. From among his daily litanies was the invocation "*Yā Allah*" 25,000 times, "*Lā ilāha illallāh*" and invoking blessings upon the Prophet ﷺ 25,000 times.

The fifth was the great imam, the quṭb and caller to Allah, Abū Bakr b. ᶜAbdallāh al-ᶜAṭṭās ﵁, who was his Sheikh al-Fatḥ, and the one who filled him light and secrets. He had the greatest impact on Ḥabīb ᶜAlī who received from him in abundance. In fact, the Imam once said to Ḥabīb ᶜAlī b. Muḥammad, "I have presented you to the Prophet ﷺ twenty times".

From among his miracles was that he was from *ahl-al-khatwa*, which means that he would often be seen by many different people in different places at the same time. He also had the knowledge to recognise the wretched from the felicitous, by reading the signs from people's foreheads.

Also amongst his mashā'ikh was the great scholar Aḥmad Zainī Dahlān ﵁, the Mufti of Makka.

There was also Ḥabīb Muḥsin b. ᶜAlawī as-Saqqāf ﵁, who was a great imam, scholar and saint, he had the ability to see from behind just as he could see in front of him.

There was also Ḥabīb ᶜAbd ar-Raḥmān b. ᶜAlī as-Saqqāf ﵁, the imam and quṭb. And Ḥabīb b. Muḥammad al-Miḥḍār ﵁, the great imam, and saint. He would recite one Quran every morning and one in the evening, and had a strong connection with Sayyidā Khadīja ﵂.

Ḥabīb $^{c}$Aydrūs b. $^{c}$Umar al-Ḥabshī, the great scholar, and muḥaddith would say, "Upon recitation of the Quran, I would be able to feel the meanings of the Quran pouring upon my heart like clouds." From the age of eight he was seeing the Prophet ﷺ.

Ḥabīb $^{c}$Alī ؓ passed away on 20$^{th}$ Rabī al-Thānī 1333AH (1915CE). He is celebrated and remembered till this day for his tremendous connection with the Messenger of Allah ﷺ. He had many children, the most famous amongst his sons, who followed in his footsteps was Ḥabīb Muḥammad. And his daughter Ḥabāba Khadīja was renowned for her piety. May Allah be pleased with them all, and make us benefit from their secret.

~ VIII ~

# Sayyidinā Ḥabīb ᶜUmar bin Aḥmad bin Sumait ﷺ

## *A short introduction by Ḥabīb Aḥmad Mashhūr Al-Ḥaddād* ﷺ

Sayyidinā Ḥabīb ᶜUmar b. Aḥmad b. Abī Bakr b. Sumait ﷺ is the firmly established scholar with taqwa, knowledge, humility and submission before Allah, with perfection, firmness, uppermost in generosity and guiding towards the right way. He spread the call of the Prophet ﷺ and directed upon the path of the ancestors around the country verbally, physically and in writing.

Sayyidinā Ḥabīb ᶜUmar b. Sumait ﷺ was born in 1303AH in the Comoro Islands. He grew up in an environment of knowledge and right conduct, and was raised under the care of his father, the master and great scholar Ḥabīb Aḥmad b. Abī Bakr b. Sumait ﷺ. Signs of nobility were manifest upon him from a very young age. He accompanied his father to Ḥaḍramawt to the dwelling of his family in the city of Shibām, wherefrom great scholars emerged that encompassed both knowledge and action together. The foremost amongst them was Ḥabīb ᶜAydrūs b. ᶜUmar al-Habshī, Ḥabīb ᶜAlī b.

Muḥammad al-Habshī, Ḥabīb Aḥmad b. Hasan al-ᶜAṭṭās, Ḥabīb Muḥammad b. Ṭāhir al-Ḥaddād, and his uncle Ḥabīb ᶜAbdallāh b. Ṭāhir b. Sumait and his father Ḥabīb Ṭāhir amongst others.

Their characteristics were impressed upon him, and their gaze was upon him. He strove with sincerity, seeking knowledge and worship with his attraction (*jazb*) and under their protection. He arrived at the levels of nearness (*qurb*) and felicity (*saᶜādah*) until he was amongst the exalted ones. Then he returned to Zanzibar to see his father, and he had fulfilled all of his requirements, and those of the extremely knowledgeable: Sheikh Ṣāliḥ ᶜAbdallāh b. Muḥammad Bā Kathīr, in relation to his spiritual knowledge and sciences of the religion.

Then he went to Maruni, the capital of Comoro and spread guidance and knowledge. He spent all of his time in calling people to Allah in the cities and the villages, striving on his feet, day and night. Many would call him in order to see him, and on gazing upon him they would be amazed. In those distant regions the people would be marked with the signs of piety, going back to the roots of their religion and enhancing their Islamic sentiment, despite being surrounded with misguidance and corruption of various kinds. This can only be through excellent and sincere daᶜwah, which penetrates into the depths of the hearts.

May Allah be pleased with this imam, who had great concern for calling people to Allah. There was no religious leader in those regions only that they were with him, both inwardly and outwardly. How many accepted Islam at his hands! And Allah had guided many people amongst the ummah through him.

When I was in Uganda with a group of people calling people to Allah, he extended great protection and attention towards us and drew up a programme of daᶜwah and said,

"Give glad tidings and do not flee, make things easy and do not make them difficult." He also said, "There is nothing more beloved and closer to Allah and His Messenger than calling people to His path." And these were the steps of his family and his grandfather the Qutb Ḥabīb Ahmad b. Abī Bakr b. Sumait رضي الله عنه.

Sayyidinā Ḥabīb ʿUmar b. Sumait رضي الله عنه was a man of uprightness (*ṣalāḥ*), conveyer of guidance and a light to whom the rich would resort to and all others would adhere to, he perfected and refined them by removing their deficiencies. We saw upon him the marks of our pious predecessors, with their splendour, consolidation on their guidance, and their noble qualities. We would almost feel as though we were living in the time of our great predecessors, we could witness them upon him and find the gems of their wisdom upon his lips. He had encompassed traits of nobility and perfection that would bring together the hearts towards loving him, and encourage the tongues to praise him. Whoever saw him cherished him and loved him, and you could see his gaze and concern upon all of those that were attached to him.

Sayyidinā Ḥabīb ʿUmar b. Sumait رضي الله عنه spent four years in seclusion in Madagascar, this was during the early part of his life, following the instruction of his sheikh. In 1936 he returned to Zanzibar and was called upon by the colonial authorities, who desired that he take his father's place, Ḥabīb Aḥmad, who was a distinguished and revered judge. After the passing away of his noble father in 1925, Judge Tomlinson, his father's former colleague, pointed out that finding a good qādī was not easy, and now the authorities looked to the son of the former Chief Qādī to take over. Ḥabīb ʿUmar rose rapidly in the Zanzibar court system and held the same title as his father.[51] In 1975, (two years after his passing away), Ḥabīb ᶜUmar b. Sumait's portrait was printed on the 1000 franc-bill, which is still in circulation.[52]

Many miracles have been related about Ḥabīb ᶜUmar ﷺ. Amongst them was that during his youth, while he was studying his father would ask him to turn out the lamp and rest. After obeying his father's instruction, the room remained illuminated and his father saw that he was using the light that glowed from his finger to see in the dark.

It has been related that once he desired for his chair to be moved to another position. Once the chair had been moved his eyes were filled with tears. One of his students asked him regarding this. He ﷺ said that when the chair was moved, the position of the heavens moved with it.

In the year 1393AH (1973CE), on 9th Safar, Ḥabīb ᶜUmar b. Sumait ﷺ passed away, at the age of 87. On the Comoro Islands, he lies to rest next to his exalted grandfather Ḥabīb Abū Bakr ﷺ. May Allah sanctify his secret and make us benefit from him in both abodes.

---

[51] Anne K Bang, *Sufis and Scholars of the Sea*, London 2003

[52] Ibid.

~ IX ~

# Sayyidinā Ḥabīb Aḥmad Mashhūr al-Ḥaddād ﵁

He is al-Sayyid Aḥmad Mashhūr b. Ṭāhā b. ᶜAlī b. ᶜAbdallāh b. Ṭāhā b. ᶜAbdallāh b. Ṭāhā b. ᶜUmar[53] b. ᶜAlawī b. Muḥammad b. Aḥmad b. ᶜAbdallāh b. Muḥammad b. ᶜAlawī b. Aḥmad[54] b. Abī Bakr b. Aḥmad b. Muḥammad b. ᶜAbdallāh b. al-Faqīh Aḥmad b. ᶜAbd al-Raḥmān b. ᶜAlawī[55] b. Muḥammad Ṣāḥib Mirbāt b. ᶜAlī Khāliᶜ Qasam b. ᶜAlawī b. Muḥammad b. ᶜAlawī b. ᶜUbaydillāh b. Sayyidinā *Muhājir illa Allah* Aḥmad b. ᶜĪsā b. Muḥammad al-Naqīb b. Imam ᶜAlī al-ᶜUraydī b. Imam Jaᶜfar al-Ṣādiq b. Imam Muḥammad al-Bāqir b. Imam Zain ul-ᶜĀbidīn ᶜAlī b. Imam Hussain (grandson of the Messenger of Allah ﷺ), b. Sayyidinā ᶜAlī and Sayyida Zahrā, may Allah be pleased with them all, daughter of the Messenger of Allah ﷺ.

He ﵁ was born in Qaydūn a town in Ḥaḍramawt, in the year 1325AH. He grew up and was raised in an environment of piety and knowledge, under the attention of his blessed, pious

[53] ᶜUmar was the brother Of Sayyidinā Imam ᶜAbdallāh b. ᶜAlawī al-Ḥaddād ﵁.
[54] Aḥmad was the first to be entitled with the name al-Ḥaddād.
[55] ᶜAlawī was the uncle of Sayyidinā Faqīh al-Muqaddam, renowned by the name ᶜAmm Faqīh al-Maqaddam ﵁.

and saintly mother Ṣafiyya, the daughter of Ḥabīb Ṭāhir b. ᶜUmar al-Ḥaddād, and his father, Ḥabīb Ṭāhā, who was from amongst the *Abdāl.*[56] During his childhood he was taught by his two distinguished and learned uncles ᶜAbdallāh and ᶜAlawī, the sons of Ṭāhir b. ᶜAbdallāh al-Ḥaddād.

## *His shuyūkh*

Ḥabīb Aḥmad would accompany his Sheikh, Ḥabīb ᶜAlawī b. Ṭāhir on some of his travels. On his visit to Tarīm, he was taught by some of the great masters such as Ḥabīb ᶜAbdallāh b. ᶜUmar al-Shātirī and Ḥabīb ᶜAbd al-Bārī b. Sheikh al-ᶜAydarūs. When he travelled to Indonesia, by this time he was not even twenty years old, he was under the care and teachings of his sheikh and uncle, the great Ḥabīb ᶜAlawī b. Ṭāhir Al-Ḥaddād رضي الله عنه. He also learned from all of the scholars of the Sāda Bā ᶜAlawī such as Ḥabīb Muḥammad b. Aḥmad al-Mihdār, Ḥabīb ᶜAlī b. ᶜAbd al-Raḥmān al-Habshī, Ḥabīb *ᶜĀrif billāh* ᶜAbdallāh b. Muḥsin al-ᶜAṭṭās and Ḥabīb ᶜAlawī b. Muḥammad al-Ḥaddād.

After returning to Qaydūn, he remained under the instruction of Ḥabīb ᶜAbdallāh b. Ṭāhir and also taught in the ribāt benefitting the other students. The Great Quṭb, Ḥabīb ᶜUmar b. Aḥmad b. Sumait was the last of his teachers, who he remained with until the end, may Allah have mercy upon them all.

---

[56] Abdāl are a category of saints who according to sound Prohetic Traditions number forty at any one time. It is through the blessings of their presence amongst the ummah that the earth is given sustenance and calamities are averted.

## *His character and practise*

Ḥabīb Aḥmad ﷺ was recognised for spreading knowledge, teaching and giving guidance wherever it was required. Neither did trade or any worldly necessities deter him from his mission. His preoccupation with knowledge and learning was a trait that he was distinguished with. Anyone who came to him seeking knowledge would know that they have come upon a unique personality, he was the key to knowledge and learning with which the soiled hearts would become illuminated, and souls that have gone astray would be guided, and those with no insight would begin to perceive. He established many centres of learning (*madāris*) and mosques, in order to increase the remembrance of Allah and to circulate sound teachings according to the way of the Messenger of Allah ﷺ and have ignorance removed.

He was an upright scholar (*muḥaqqiq*), he turned away from giving legal opinions but he would respond to questions, giving clear answers, leaving the questioner feeling content. He was averse to judicial positions, which were offered to him. His speech was eloquent, and his sermons effective, he was an outstanding intellectual and his poetry was excellent, he commanded the good and forbade wrongdoing, he did not fear any censurer for the sake of Allah.

He ﷺ surpassed every difficulty with utmost excellence. He travelled great distances, reaching Indonesia and East Africa, carrying with him all the teachings that he had received through his sheikh and uncle, the great Ḥabīb ᶜAbdallāh b. Ṭāhir al-Ḥaddād ﷺ in Qaydūn.

His focus and attention was in calling people to Allah. His time was occupied in teaching and spreading knowledge, and this was the distinguishing mark of his personality. Thus, he had love for knowledge and the desire to attend every gathering of knowledge, regardless of the difficulties and obstacles that came his way.

He ﷺ travelled between Kenya, Tanzania and Uganda. He was living in an environment that was filled with confusion, life that was corrupt in knowledge, literature, culture and society. This did not restrict him in carrying out his goal, which was tiresome and hard work. He would come across people who were influenced by the society that they were living in. He strove with his *daʿwah*, calling people to Allah, and people were influenced through his speech and the gatherings of learning increased. The gatherings were held regularly especially in the month of Ramadan. His speech was not aimed at any specific group or class of people; rather he would address all the people according to their capacity of knowledge and understanding.

During this period there was also much commotion with the spread of deviated beliefs that had found a place in society from sects such as the Qādiyānīs, the Shias and the Wahhabis. Sayyidinā Ḥabīb Aḥmad strove hard to protect the religion from being corrupted with such beliefs.

He ﷺ knew rulers and governors and he acknowledged their rights; he honoured them for their position but did not accommodate them in any special way with compliments and praise. He knew many people of worldly prestige and rank, but he was not inclined towards them.

Sayyidinā Ḥabīb Aḥmad - may Allah make us benefit from him - was averse to fame and recognition, worldly embellishments, and luxuries, in spite of having the means before him. In fact, he was always surrounded by people who loved and venerated him and honoured him at home and during his travels.

By the grace of Allah, he inherited the Prophetic way, and he walked the path of his pious forefathers, in knowledge, wisdom, character and practice. He رضي الله عنه had embodied the Sunna inwardly and outwardly. He had utmost humility, in spite of being the Quṭb of the time he would come across as an ordinary person. His devoted murīd, Sheikh Muḥammad Ṣādiq, describes his beloved sheikh:

> 'Ḥabīb's *maqām* (status) was great, but his path was humility. His path was the royal and the sacred path of self-sacrifice and self-denial. He was totally humble before his Lord. His prayers were always full of *khushūᶜ* (pleading) with Allah, the Exalted.
>
> Through his entire life, his character reminded one of the blessed Prophet ﷺ. Ḥabīb was absolute love. He will be remembered because of his character. People remember pious people because of their miracles; we remember Ḥabīb because of his character, which was an absolute reflection of the Holy Prophet ﷺ.
>
> He was born with *Lā ilāha ill Allāh*, he breathed *Lā ilāha ill Allāh*, he propogated *Lā ilāha ill Allāh*, he departed this world with *Lā ilāha ill Allāh,* his maqām was *Lā ilāha ill Allāh* and his *janāzah* was lifted, under the canopy of the Kaᶜba, with *Lā ilāha ill Allāh.*'

A student of Sheikh Muḥammad Ṣādiq writes about Ḥabīb Aḥmed رضي الله عنه in the following description:

> 'Everybody knows that Ḥabīb was an *ᶜālim*, a scholar, but very few are aware that he رضي الله عنه was from the men of Allah (*rijālullāh*), he was no different to Sheikh ᶜAbd al-Qādir Jīlānī رضي الله عنه, the only difference is that contrary to his blessed name "*Mashhūr*", which means famous, he was "*mastūr*", i.e. hidden, this was due to his extreme humility, he desired to remain hidden just like his pious predecessors, since this is the way of the Sādāt, and this is their trait.

Ḥabīb Aḥmad - may Allah make us benefit from him - embodied the actions of his ancestors, the Sāda Bā ᶜAlawī, inwardly and outwardly.

He reflected the qualities and attributes, morals and manners of his noble grandfather, the Messenger of Allah ﷺ. His compliance of the Quran and Sunnna was absolute.

Many people know of Ḥabīb Aḥmad's scholarly capacity, which was indeed great, along with his zest and energy in calling people to Allah. Very few are aware that he was, and still is an alchemist, one who purifies the hearts, removing the darkness and replacing it with light.

Simply with his blessed gaze he could turn the sinful into a saint, he could change the hearts of the worldly people (*ahl al-dunya*) and make them into the men of Allah (*ahlullāh*).

The greatness of a saint is not by the amount of miracles that he performs, but by the great people that he produces, and a prime and excellent example is manifest in our lives.

Sheikh Muḥammad Ṣādiq is the product of this great quṭb, he has been reared and nurtured at his hands for forty years during Ḥabīb's lifetime, and is still being nurtured, because the ability of a saint only increases in the intermediary world (*barzakh*). For this reason, the murīd should always remain hopeful, and should not slack in his actions just because his sheikh has passed away. Although the sheikh is not always in the murīd's vision, the murīd is always under the gaze of his sheikh. The more the murīd is mindful of this the firmer is his grasp that connects him to his sheikh. Imam al-Ḥaddād describes this as the "*ᶜurwat ul-wuthqā*" (the rope of Allah).

> For the murīd, Ḥabīb is the "Ark of Noah" (*Safīnat un-Nūh*), and he is a protection. Ḥabīb is the lighthouse, the reviver of the hearts. Ḥabīb is like a diamond, priceless, pure, full of clarity and light, flawless and rare, and his dear murīd, Sheikh Muḥammad Ṣādiq is a facet of this diamond.
>
> The reason for being this facet is having spent 40 years in the service of Ḥabīb Aḥmad with absolute love and absolute *adab*, which made him a perfect traveller on the path (*sālik*). For Sheikh Muḥammad Ṣādiq, Ḥabīb was like a loving mother and a compassionate father, and also a physician of the heart.
>
> Sheikh Muḥammad Ṣādiq's love for his master is so pure and absolute that it manifests in his actions and words, and he emanates the fragrance of Ḥabīb Aḥmad, hence the *baraka* of Ḥabīb Aḥmad can be felt in the presence of Sheikh Muḥammad Ṣādiq. It is as though Ḥabīb Aḥmad, with his gaze has formed a precious gem and kept him hidden away, revealing him only to a few, who have realised that he has great worth and is very rare.'

Muḥammad ᶜAlī al-Bār, who spent more than twenty years in the company of Ḥabīb Aḥmad Mashhūr relates:

> 'Ḥabīb Aḥmad - may Allah have mercy upon him - informed me of how he would call people to Allah in the jungles, approaching idolatrous tribes. Ḥabīb Aḥmad would go into jungles that contained wild beasts and snakes, but he was not perturbed by them. He would take with him a couple of oxes and slaughter them for the tribes and their families. He would also take with him someone who knew their language to translate. Ḥabīb would go to the tribes

> distribute food and clothes, and then gradually start talking about Islam, making it really easy for them. With the blessing of his sincerity, Allah opened their hearts towards Islam. Tens of thousands accepted Islam at the hands of Ḥabīb Aḥmad Mashhūr رضي الله عنه.
>
> When it came to calling people to Allah, Ḥabīb Aḥmad remained strong and very courageous. Fatigue and hardship did not stop him or slow him down in any way. He would travel from one place to another, crossing rivers and jungles, with a small number of companions and sincere students. He even travelled as far as the Congo, Rawanda and other neighbouring countries. He called them to Allah, and guided them with wisdom and kindness. He united communities and peoples hearts with good character. His patience and humility was immeasureable. He forgave when he was harmed, but when it came to the rights of Allah, there was no one more firm than him, just like al-Mustafa ﷺ.'[57]

Ḥabīb Aḥmad was very self-sufficient, he did not accept favours from people. His students and close companions would help out with his business, to give him more time to teach and spread Islam. Many people would come to him from all over the world: America, Spain and Britain. However the majority were from Kenya Tanzania, Uganda, Singapore and Indonesia. Ḥabīb Aḥmad's house was always open and welcoming for all, visitors would stay with him for days and nights and his household were always very hospitable.[58]

In spite of being engaged in teaching and calling people to Allah, Ḥabīb Aḥmad wrote a book entitled *Miftāḥ ul-Jannah*

---

[57] Ḥāmid b. Aḥmad Mashhūr al-Ḥaddād, *Aḥmad Mashhūr al-Ḥaddād, Ṣafaḥāt min Ḥayātihi wa Daʿwatihi*, Jordan 2003.
[58] Ibid.

(Key to the Garden), which is also available in English. It is a concise and profound book on the phrase of Tawḥīd: '*Lā ilāha illa Allāh.*' He - may Allah make us benefit from him – also has many poems that have been compiled into a *diwān*, but is yet to be published.

Ḥabīb Aḥmad Mashhūr ﷺ departed from this world on 14th Rajab 1416AH, (6th Dec 1995CE). After the funeral prayer in the *Ḥaram* in Makka, hundreds of people desired to touch and get a glimpse of the pure and blessed body of Ḥabīb Aḥmad, as it travelled through the Noble Sanctuary towards al-Maᶜlā, where many Companions of the Prophet ﷺ and awliyā lie to rest, including the Mother of the Believers Sayyidā Khadīja, may Allah be pleased with them all.

## ~ X ~

# AL-ḤABĪB ᶜABD AL-QĀDIR AL-SAQQĀF ﵁

He is the noble Sayyid, from the pure and glorious lineage, the Imam and erudite scholar, the embodiment of noble and great characteristics, the Caller to Allah and His Messenger, al-Ḥabīb ᶜAbd al-Qādir b. Aḥmad b. ᶜAbd al-Raḥmān b. ᶜAlī b. ᶜUmar b. Saqqāf b. Muḥammad b. ᶜUmar b. Ṭāhā b. ᶜUmar b. Ṭāha b. ᶜUmar b. ᶜAbd ul- Raḥmān b. Muḥammad b. ᶜAlī b. ᶜAbd ul-ᶜRaḥmān al-Saqqāf b. Muḥammad the *Mawla of Dawīla* b. ᶜAlī b. ᶜAlawī b. al-Faqīh al-Muqaddam Muḥammad b. ᶜAlī b. Muḥammad, *the Ṣāḥib of Mirbāṭ* b. ᶜAlī Khāliᶜ al-Qasam b. ᶜAlawī b. Muḥammad the Mawlā of al-Sauma'a b. ᶜAlawī al-Mubtakir b. ᶜUbaydillāh b. *al-Muhājir ila Allah* Aḥmad b. ᶜĪsā b. Muḥammad b. ᶜAlī al-ᶜUraydī b. Jaᶜfar al-Ṣādiq b. Muḥammad al-Bāqir b. ᶜAlī Zain al-ᶜĀbidīn b. al-Ḥusaīn b. ᶜAlī b. Abī Ṭālib and Fātima al-Zahra, the daughter of the Messenger of Allah, may Allah bless him and his family and grant them peace.

## *His birth and Upbringing*

Al-Ḥabīb ᶜAbd al-Qādir b. Aḥmad al-Saqqāf ﵁ was born in the city of Seyun in the month of Jumād ul-Ākhir in the year

1331AH. He grew up in a household of guidance and piety. His father Ḥabīb Aḥmad b. ᶜAbd al-Raḥmān was a renowned Imam of his time, his fame required no introduction. He was the noble Sayyid, the generous scholar and worshipper who had excelled in the ranks of the spiritual path and ascended to the highest levels.

He would speak regarding the ocean of realities without any hesitation, as the great scholars and saints of the time all attested that he was a slave who knew his Lord. His Lord taught him, honoured him, granted him proximity, purified him, and adorned him. Therefore, there is no surprise that his son would speak wisdom at such an early age when he was filled with such knowledge, forbearance and light.

His mother was the noble Sayyida ᶜAlawiyya, the daughter of Ḥabīb Aḥmad b. Muḥammad al-Jifrī. She - may Allah be pleased with her - was from the noble family of al-Ḥaddād, a righteous woman who loved good and its people. Ḥabīb Aḥmad b. ᶜAbd al-Raḥmān had been married to a number of women previously, when one of the *muḥibbīn* suggested this match he pondered over it, not wanting it to end wrongly until Allah expanded his breast to the matter and he married her. She became pregnant with a child whom Ḥabīb ᶜAlī b. al-Habshī named ᶜAbd al-Qādir. However this child passed away.

When the second child was born Ḥabīb ᶜAlī b. Muḥammad al-Habshī named him ᶜAbd al- Qādir once again, and gave glad tidings regarding his future rank. The child opened his blessed eyes to divine secrets, lights, worship, and obedience in his environment. There was nothing that surrounded him but the signs of His Lord, remembrance, prayer, fasting, recitation of Quran, guidance, piety, belief, knowledge, action and excellence.

His heart was nurtured on the natural inclination of *Tawhid.* Day after day he would yearn for ascensions. And he was surrounded by all the means to fulfil that which was brimming in his heart. He grew up taking to those means in all earnest, seeing his father, the Imam either in prayer, fasting, in knowledge or action, in night prayers, in gatherings, or teaching, or in the veneration of the masters; and watching his pure pious and blessed mother in remembrance and worship throughout the day and night.

Such an environment had an impact on the heart of the child. He witnessed the fruits of striving, in a household that knew no laziness or boredom. This is the way of the people of the righteous predecessors, those who knew the preciousness of time and so they filled it with openings and bestowals.

## *Early Childhood*

The early childhood of Ḥabīb ᶜAbd al-Qādir al-Saqqāf was under the supervision of his parents, who gave him an educational upbringing and fine manners. For early education in Ḥadramawt was at the peak of fine manners and in engaging the limbs in worship, with sincerity and perfection of the heart. According to the Bā ᶜAlawī tradition, he received from his father, who inherited the secrets of his forefathers. Whenever Ḥabīb ᶜAbd al-Qādir went to learn about his forefathers, his inward would overflow with a strange motivation over his outward. His sheikh during this early phase was Sheikh Ṭāhā b. ᶜAbdallāh Bā Ḥamid, who was in charge of education and instruction.

## *Education in Madrasa an-Nahda ʿIlmiyya (The School for reviving knowledge)*

Ḥabīb ᶜAbd al-Qādir ﷺ received a great portion in this madrasa. He learnt the various Islamic sciences, literature, Sirah, history and many other subjects. He was amongst the most outstanding students. His father opened up a section of the school just for the memorisation of the Quran. Ḥabīb ᶜAbd al-Qādir with all earnestness memorised the Quran in a very short amount of time.

Ḥabīb ᶜAbd al-Qādir mentioned that Sheikh ᶜAlī Bā Kathīr would encourage them to visit him when they were not studying. He would give them something to eat and drink and would read from books of literature and wisdom to them. On their return home, Ḥabīb's father would enquire what he had read with his teacher and if he found any exaggeration therein, he would correct it and guide him towards the couplets of Imam al-Ḥaddād, and Ḥabīb ᶜUmar b. Saqqāf and Ibn al-Muqrī.

Ḥabīb ᶜAbd al-Qādir was not accustomed to mixing with other youngsters and neither was he interested in what they did. Instead he would spend his time studying everything that he had memorised. Very soon he had mastered the seven various recitations of the Quran with Sheikh Ḥasan ᶜAbdallāh Bā Raja and then soon after, when his teacher returned from Makka he had mastered all of them.

Despite all these lessons of Quran, Language and Fiqh he continually studied with his father, sometimes completing an entire book in one day. He learnt from his father about the secret and the blessings of time. With such determination, the mind of Ḥabīb grew in understanding and knowledge from the outpouring of the One, the Everlasting Lord.

## *Teaching in the Madrasa Nahda ʿIlmiyya.*

This madrasa was distinguished for producing geniuses who would go on to teach in the school. Ḥabīb ᶜAbd al-Qādir was amongst the most outstanding students who started teaching. He - may Allah be pleased with him - excelled in teaching in such a competitive environment, where knowledge was at its peak. His students and murīds still remember and honour those days.

Alongside teaching at the Madrasa, Ḥabīb ᶜAbd al-Qādir ﷺ took his father's place teaching in public and private gatherings, which used to be held in Masjid Ṭāhā b. ᶜUmar as-Safi. He would teach all of the students that came to the city. Manifest within his teaching was the depth of his understanding and soundness of knowledge. He was the delight of his father's eye and the inheritor of his forefather's secret. He was able to solve the most complex problems in the easiest of ways. Many students emerged grateful, and would always remember him and testify to the greatness of his wisdom.

## *The passing away of his father*

Ḥabīb ᶜAbd al-Qādir, may Allah make us benefit from him said:

> 'My father's illness, may Allah have mercy upon him, began as a light fever on the eve of 18th Ramadan 1356AH. He ordered me to lead the people in prayer and so I did. Thereafter, my father was in and out of consciousness, and he was suffering from a very sever fever. He would say at such a time: 'Imam al-Haddad endured a fever for 15 years and would say this is the rank of the Quṭb.'

> He remained in this state of weakness and bearing the fever until moments before the sunset on Saturday 4th of Muharram 1357AH when his noble spirit poured out to his Lord. Throughout he remained steadfast with utmost patience and forbearance, with a sound state of mind, always asking the timings of the prayer. His noble spirit did not leave him until he had completed his ʿAṣr prayer on that day. He prayed upon his bed, as he had done so throughout the whole of his illness.'

After the passing away of his father, the burden of responsibility grew upon the shoulders of the inheritor Ḥabīb ʿAbd al-Qādir al-Saqqāf. The great responsibility of teaching and calling to Allah, looking after the needy, the impoverished and their problems; all fell upon him. It was his responsibility to ensure their happiness, to tend to the affairs of his family and relatives and all of those around him. All of the great masters and noble contemporaries agreed that Ḥabīb ʿAbd al-Qādir had indeed inherited his father's secret.

He, may Allah be pleased with him said:

> I witnessed 21 years of my father's life. These were years in which I was conscious. He passed away at the age of 79 and my age was 25. He took great care of me and made me accompany him to Tarīm, ʿAynāt, Huta, Shibām and would present me to the Mashā'ikh.

## *His character*

Everyone who knew Ḥabīb ʿAbd al-Qādir or had an affiliation with him, would feel the depth of kindness and proximity that he had towards them, each one would feel that they were the most privileged in his company. This was because of the beautiful way he would receive them, his cheerfulness, kindness, perfection and compassion towards people. He would never show any harshness, a frown, or rebuke, even if it was over a matter that displeased him. His kindness with people was to such an extent that their heart would become attached to this blessed role model, and as a result of this, the filth of their *nafs* would be cleansed away. Such a person would soon repent, become upright and begin to follow him. Many of his close companions witnessed this and saw many people impacted by his virtuous character.

He disliked any talk of the world and its events in his gathering and would only mention things in passing, or for an important reason, or to warn of a dangerous situation regarding the Muslims or Islam. You would see that a minimal amount of news was enough for him. He would then call the Muslims to that which is good for the matter of their religion and world.

There were many of his lovers and well wishers in Jeddah, Makka, Madina and other places, who would ardently desire his presence in their houses. He would answer their invitation with pleasure and happiness. At times, there were several invites in one day and he would attend each invitation or gathering even if it was just for a few minutes in order to comfort the host. He would then leave to attend another gathering.

In his sermons and in calling people to Allah, he was always more cheerful and kind to the people of Tawḥīd. He did not like to rebuke people directly, and would unite hearts and attract them towards their Lord, their Prophet, their righteous ancestors, in ways which were inviting and attractive. He would present sayings and stories which were inviting to the hearts to the point that the listener would feel the rank of those men and would be encouraged by their states. A person would feel his shortcomings and his heart would be moved to repentance and seeking Allah.

In many of his gatherings and reminders he would emphasise the importance of the Quran, Hadith, Tafsir, the books of the righteous Salaf, preserving time, and arranging one's duties. He would use the example of his father and the lives of the righteous predecessors.

Al-Ḥabīb ﷺ would always emphasise in his gatherings the importance of having a connection with the Mashā'ikh, and the impact that this would have upon the inward and the outward of a person. He would explain how the distance of the path is shortened through their blessings and the goodness of their supervision when a murīd is sincere. He would encourage in particular, the children of the ᶜAlawiyyīn and those who are affiliated with them never to miss their illuminated gatherings. He would encourage them to meet with the Mashā'ikh, even if it was just for receiving the blessing of looking at their pious and righteous faces, quoting the hadith, 'Allah has servants, when gazing upon them Allah is remembered.'

In his reminders, counsels and sermons he would mention many stories of the Mashā'ikh and the benefits of having a sincere connection with them, and the effect of their piercing gazes upon the Seeker who was ready for such blessings. He would seal his gatherings with the blessed *Fātiḥa*, which was amongst the greatest means for those present to receive peace. He would also encourage the Seekers to write the benefits, in particular regarding the sciences of Fiqh and Hadith, and the states of piety of the righteous predecessors.

## *His love for the great Quṭb - Ḥabīb Aḥmad Mashhūr b. Ṭāhā al-Ḥaddād* ﵁

Ḥabīb ᶜAbd al-Qādir had the greatest connection with Ḥabīb Aḥmad Mashhūr, may Allah make us benefit from them both. There was no gathering in which they would meet together but that each would venerate and honour the other. Whenever Ḥabīb ᶜAbd al-Qādir spoke on any occasion, he would end his speech by referring the talk to Ḥabīb Aḥmad Mashhūr to add to what he had said. They would visit each other abundantly. In their gatherings the spirits would unite, which would move the hearts into the rank of *iman* and proximity to Allah and His Messenger. There were many times in Jeddah where they would meet and scatter precious pearls of wisdom and knowledge upon those gathered, such words of wisdom were worthy of being written in gold.

Amongst the signs of their intimate friendship was their trip to the Comoro Islands in 1393AH, to visit Ḥabīb ᶜUmar b. Aḥmad b. Sumait ﵁ where they received from the bounty and effulgence of the Imam. Subsequently they went together to East Africa calling to Allah and His Messenger ﷺ.

## *Towards the end of his life*

Ḥabīb ᶜAbd al-Qādir ﵁ continued his daᶜwa in the Hijaz, travelling between Jeddah and the Sacred Sanctuaries, spreading the knowledge and mercy that he had inherited from his grandfather, the Messenger of Allah ﷺ. Being a great Spiritual Master and heir of the blessed Prophet ﷺ, not only was his service to the ummah through external teaching but also by bearing the burden of their afflictions on his shoulders, and to avert calamities away from the ummah.

Towards the end of his life, he ﷺ even sacrificed the flesh of his body to His Lord. Due to illness and physical weakness he was unable to leave the house, however he continued to receive many visitors.

At the age of 100, his noble spirit left this world, and joined His Lord, on 19th Rabīᶜ al-Thānī 1431AH/4th April 2010CE, prior to the time of Fajr. The funeral prayer took place on the very same night and was attended by thousands in the Masjid al-Haram in Makka. May Allah sanctify his secret, and may we continue to benefit from his life, teachings, and example of his compassionate nature and Lordly presence that remains alive in the hearts of his lovers till this day.[59]

[59] Abū Bakr bin ᶜAlī bin Abū Bakr al-Mashhūr, *Jani ul-qitāf min manāqib wa aḥwāl al-Imam al- ᶜallāma Khalīfat ul-aslāf ᶜAbd ul-Qādir bin Aḥmad bin ᶜAbd ul-Raḥmān al-Saqqāf.*

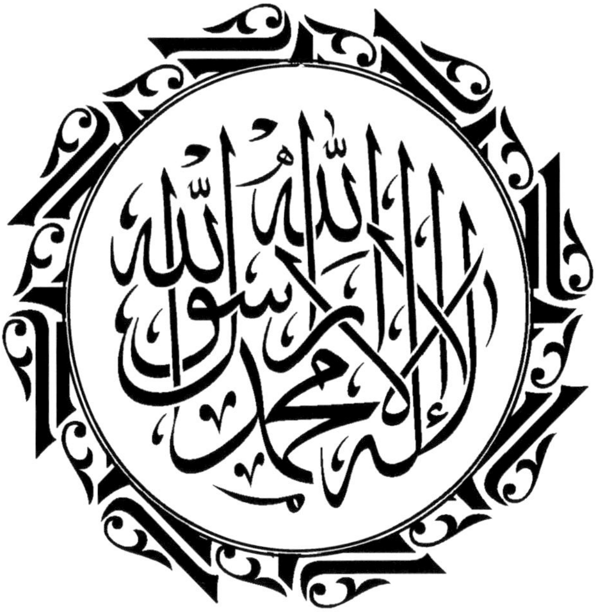


# Volume 2

# The Guide to the Path *of* Righteousness

Path of the Banī ᶜAlawī

Volume 2

# INTRODUCTION

Praise be to Allah, and may peace and blessings be upon His chosen Messenger and his Companions.

The essence of the path is the remembrance of Allah. For the *murīd*, it is his life, akin to the breaths that he takes to sustain his existence. Without it, he is nothing but a corpse. 'The comparison of the one who remembers his Lord and the one who does not is like that of the living and the dead,' – Hadith.

The importance of remembrance has been emphasised in the litanies inspired to the great masters. Each litany is unique in its blessing and outcome, but they all share the reality that it is a needy supplication, a plea from the destitute in the presence of the Al-Mighty King; a recognition of our non-existence and His reality. For this reason the greatest litanies and supplications come from the one with the greatest *fanā'* (annihilation), the one true ᶜ*abd* of Allah, our Master Muhammad, the Messenger of Allah, may Allah send eternal salutations and blessings upon him. Therefore, the first litany that a *murīd* takes is the Sunna of the Messenger of Allah ﷺ, which he never leaves throughout his entire life.

The aspirant establishes himself in this, and then according to the instruction of his teacher adopts the litanies of the masters once permission has been granted. The necessity of adhering to the litanies and reciting them regularly is mentioned by Imam ᶜAbd ul-Wahhāb Shaᶜrānī:

> An aspirant should not become bored of reciting the litanies, which have been instructed by his Sheikh. Allah has placed his *madad* (spiritual help), his secret and the secret of the path within his litanies which the aspirant has been ordered upon. Whoever abandons his litany has broken the agreement with his Sheikh. It is agreed upon that no aspirant has left his litany only that as a result of it the *madad* has been severed from him for that day.

Regarding the connection of the murīd with his Sheikh through the litany and the benefits of reciting them, Sheikh Aḥmad al-Zarrūq has mentioned:

> The litanies of the masters of the people of perfection are mingled with their spiritual states; they have originated from their inspirations and are accompanied with miracles. They contain the outpouring of their knowledge, the etiquette of their direction, and their knowledge of the path. They include the indication to the reality, the remembrance of the majesty, greatness, and exaltedness of Allah, the recollection of the lowliness of the soul and a recollection of their faults, and sins. It is a lesson in facing the approach, and in the approach to facing the magnificence. Therefore, one will not hear anything of their speech except that they will find an effect within themselves, as long as they are not preoccupied with afflictions or fame, may Allah protect us from trials.

Ḥabīb ᶜAlī bin Ḥasan al-ᶜAṭṭās has mentioned in his commentary of the *Wird Rātib al- ᶜAṭṭās:*

> Allah has said: *'And it is He who made the night and the day to follow each other: for such as have the will to remember His praises or to show their gratitude.'* (Al-Furqān: 52)

Some scholars have mentioned that part of this gratitude and remembrance is awareness of time, so that one is able to engage himself in the appropriate type of obedience and good.

The Prophet ﷺ said, "The most beloved of servants to Allah are those that pay attention to the (timing of the) sun and the moon and its phases for the remembrance of Allah." (Tabarānī).

Sheikh al-ᶜUmrī has mentioned:

> The *wird* is the action of drawing water from the places of pure water (*al-mawārid*) at the presence of proximity and witnessing. The means and guide to this connection are the *awrād* (litanies), which polish rusted hearts, remove the filth of desires and the whisperings in the breast. '*Indeed in the remembrance of Allah do hearts find peace.*' (Al-Raᶜad: 28). In a hadith it is mentioned, 'When you pass by the Gardens of Paradise then graze.' The Companions asked, 'O Messenger of Allah what are the Gardens of Paradise?' He ﷺ replied, 'The gatherings of *dhikr*.' Therefore, the *wird* is the means by which one receives purity of heart.

It is mentioned by Ibn ᶜAṭā'illāh:

> Know that Allah has placed the lights of the divine kingdom within the various forms of worship. So

> whoever misses a particular type of worship has missed the light of it by a similar amount. Therefore, do not neglect any form of worship. Do not satisfy yourselves with inspirations over litanies, and do not be content with that which other pretenders are content with; they talk of realities yet their hearts are deprived of its light. The Real in His wisdom has made all continual obedience over worship like the action of knocking at the door of the unseen. So whoever establishes obedience and interaction, along with the condition of etiquette, then the unseen will not be veiled from him.

Purification from faults will open up the door to the unseen. So do not be from those who demand Allah for themselves. For this is the state of the ignorant, who do not understand anything regarding Allah, and neither has the spiritual assistance flowed to them from Allah. The believer is not like this. In fact the believer demands himself for his Lord and does not demand his Lord for himself. Therefore, when the time comes he delays his habit but does not delay his purpose. May Allah grant us all *tawfiq* to follow in the steps of the masters.

# SECTION 1

# THE VIRTUES OF DHIKR

*"Verily in the remembrance of Allah do hearts find tranquility"*

Quran 13:28

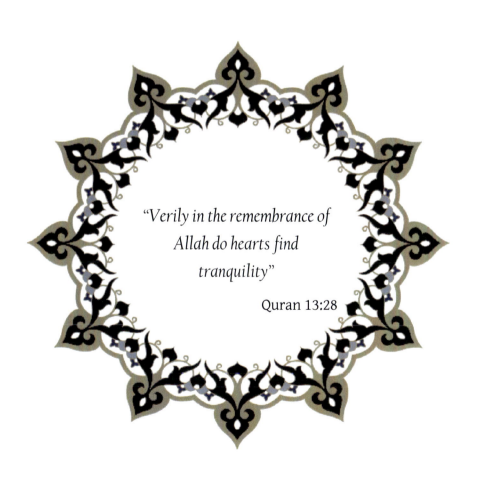

# ~ Chapter 1 ~

## On the Merits of Dhikr

Imam ᶜAlawī the great grandson of Imam al-Ḥaddād has mentioned in his commentary on the Rātib al-Ḥaddād:

‘Imam al-Bayhaqī has related on the authority of Anas ؓ that the Prophet ﷺ said, “To remember Allah ﷻ with a group of people after the Fajr prayer until the rising of the sun is more beloved to me than the world and all that it contains.”

Abū Dāwūd has related that the Messenger of Allah ﷺ said, “To sit with a group of people remembering Allah ﷻ from the ᶜAṣr prayer until the setting of the sun is more beloved to me than liberating four slaves.”

Abū Naᶜīm has related that the Messenger of Allah ﷺ said, “Tranquility descends upon the gatherings of dhikr, angels surround them, mercy encompasses them, and all those that are with them remember Allah.” Imam Aḥmad and Muslim have related that the Messenger of Allah ﷺ said, “A people do not sit to remember Allah only that they are surrounded by angels, covered with mercy, tranquillity descends upon them, and all those that are with them remember Allah.”

Al-Bayhaqī has cited in '*Shu$^{c}$ab al-Īmān*' that the Messenger of Allah ﷺ said, "Increase with the dhikr of Allah until the hypocrites say that you are showing off." In another narration, "Increase with the dhikr of Allah until they call you crazy (*majnūn*)."

Imam al-Bayhaqī has cited on the authority of Sa$^{c}$īd al-Khudrī ؓ, on the authority of the Messenger of Allah ﷺ that he said, "The Lord Mighty and Majestic is He, will say on the Day of Judgement, 'Today the people of congregation will know who the noble ones are (*ahl al-karam*)' He was asked, "Who are the noble ones?" He ﷺ said, "The people who held gatherings of dhikr in the mosques."

Bukhārī and Muslim have related on the authority of Abū Huraira ؓ that the Messenger of Allah ﷺ said,

> Allah has angels that roam the paths in search of the people of remembrance (*ahl al-dhikr*). When they find a people remembering Allah they proclaim: "Come to what you seek!" Then they surround them with their wings going up to the lowest heaven, and when they disperse they ascend to the sky. Then their Lord, Who is more knowing than them, asks them, "Where have you come from?" They reply: "We have come from your worshippers on earth." Then He, Who is more knowing than them, asks them, "What do my worshippers say?" They say, "They glorify You, Exalt You, praise You, laud You and extol You." Then He asks: "Have they seen Me?" They reply: "No by Allah, they have not seen You." Then He asks, "How would it be if they had seen Me?" They say, "If they were to see You they would increase in their worship of You, they would increase in their praise for You and they would increase in their glorification of You." What do they seek from Me?" They say, "They seek Paradise from You." Then Allah asks: "Have they seen it?"

> They reply, "No by Allah they have not seen it." Allah says, "How would it be if they had seen it?" They say, "Had they seen it they would aspire for it even more, they would seek it even more, and their hope for it would be greater." And what do they seek protection from?" They reply: "They seek protection from the Fire." Allah says, "Have they seen it?" They say, "No by Allah they have not seen it." Allah says, "How would it be if they had seen it?" They say, "Had they seen it they would flee from it even more, and fear it even more." And they say, "They seek Your forgiveness". Allah says, "Bear witness that I have forgiven them, and given them what they seek, and rewarded them for the reward they seek." Then one of the angels says, "Lord there is a servant amongst them, who is sinful, he just passed by and joined them." Then Allah says, "And I have forgiven him; they are a people whose companions do not incur misfortune."

Thus, every gathering wherein believers gather to worship Allah ﷻ, Allah shows pride in them to the angels, and He reminds them of what they say, and of what He says to them, and responds to them, like in their gatherings of dhikr, or the Friday prayer, or congregational prayer, working for the sake of Allah, the stopping at ᶜArafa, or gathering for beneficial knowledge and so forth, so understand that these merits are specifically related to congregational worship. The special benefits that are received in the gatherings of dhikr cannot be acquired in isolation and that is the only reason why the *masha'ikh* would recite the Rāṭib in congregation. You should not think that the state of gathering and isolation are the same, were it so, the benefits and rewards for the prescribed prayer in isolation and congregation would be the same. The noble Prophet ﷺ has distinguished between the two: "The excellence of the prayer in congregation over the individual prayer is by twenty seven ranks." In other words the individual prayer is like 1/27th of the congregational prayer, so which one seems better to you?

Al-Bayhaqī has related on the authority of ᶜAbdallāh b. al-Mughaffal, who said that the Messenger of Allah ﷺ said, "There is not a (group) of people that gather to remember Allah عز وجل only that a herald proclaims: 'Stand for you have been forgiven, and your sins have turned into good deeds.'"

The sound Hadith Qudsi relates: "I am with my servant according to his opinion of Me, I am with him when he remembers Me. If he remembers Me within himself then I remember him within Myself, and if he remembers Me in a gathering, then I remember him in a better gathering..." And there are many Hadiths that indicate the merits of gathering for dhikr.'

# ~ Chapter 2 ~

## ON LĀ ILĀHA ILLA ALLĀH

Imam ʿAlawī the great grandson of Imam al-Ḥaddād has mentioned in his commentary on the Rātib al-Ḥaddād:

Regarding the dhikr 'There is no god but Allah, *Lā ilāha illa Allāh*', Imam Qāḍī ʿIyāḍ cited in his book Ash-Shifāʾ on the authority of Ibn ʿAbbās ☙ who said: 'Upon the gate of Paradise is written: 'Verily I am Allah there is no god but I, Muḥammad is the Messenger of Allah, I will not punish he who says it."

It has also been narrated in some traditions on the authority of Ibn ʿAbbās ☙ who said, 'The night and day are twenty four hours, and the phrase *Lā ilāha illa Allāh Muḥammad-ur-Rasūlullāh* (There is no god but Allah, Muḥammad is the Messenger of Allah) contains twenty four letters. Therefore one who says "*Lā Ilāha Illa Allāh, Muḥammad-ur-Rasūllullah,*" for every letter, the sins of one hour will be expiated. No sin will remain with the person if it is recited every day or night.

Our master Imam al-Ḥaddād mentions in his book *An-Nasā'iḥ al-Dīniyya* in the section on belief:

> The faith of a servant is not accepted even if he believes in Allah Most Glorified is He, until he believes in Muḥammad ﷺ and in everything that he came with and all that which he informed us of concerning the world and the afterlife.
>
> There are many excellences to the phrase '*Lā ilāha illa Allāh*'. Of its greatness it suffices to know that it is the greatest pillar of Islam and the principle element of *Tawḥīd*, and he whose last words, at the time of death, are '*Lā ilāha illa Allāh*' enters the Garden.
>
> The Messenger of Allah ﷺ said, "There is no desolation in the grave for the people of *Lā Ilāha Illa Allāh,* or at the Resurrection. It is as though I am looking upon them crying (out of joy) while shaking the dust off their heads saying, 'All praise belongs to Allah who removed grief from us. Our Lord is the Most Forgiving, the Most Appreciative!"
>
> The Prophet ﷺ said on the authority of Abū Huraira ؓ, "O Abū Huraira! Every good that you perform will be weighed on the Scale, on the Day of Judgement, except for the testification: *Lā ilāha illa Allāh*, for this will not be placed on the Scale. If it were to be placed on the Scale of the sincere one, and the seven heavens and earths with all that they contain to be placed (on the other side), then *Lā ilāha illa Allāh* would outweigh them." He ﷺ also said, "Were a man to come with sins that filled the earth but said '*Lā ilāha illa Allāh*' sincerely, Allah would forgive him for it."
>
> The Prophet ﷺ said, "O Abu Hurairah! Prompt your dying ones to say *Lā ilāha illa Allāh*, for it wipes sins away

completely." It was asked, 'O Messenger of Allah! If this is for our dying ones, then how is it for those who are alive?' He ﷺ replied, 'It is more of an effacer, more of an effacer!'"

It is mentioned in *Jāmi*ᶜ *us-Saghīr* on the authority of Ibn ᶜAbbās رضي الله عنه that the Prophet ﷺ said:

Allah opens the doors of Paradise, and it is called out from under the Throne: 'O Paradise! And all the blessings that are within you, to whom do you belong?' Paradise and that which is within it calls out, 'We belong to the people of *Lā ilāha illa Allāh* and we only contain the people of *Lā ilāha illa Allāh*. We are forbidden to the people who did not say *Lā ilāha illa Allāh*, and those who did not believe in *Lā ilāha illa Allāh*.' At this point the Fire and all the chastisement it contains will say, 'Only those who disbelieved in *Lā ilāha illa Allāh* will enter me and I only seek those who deny *Lā ilāha illa Allāh*. I am forbidden to those who say *Lā ilāha illa Allāh*. My anger is only towards those who rejected *Lā ilāha illa Allāh* and I am only filled with those who fought against *Lā ilāha illa Allāh*.'

Then the Forgiveness and Mercy of Allah will come saying: 'We belong to the people of *Lā ilāha illa Allāh*, and we are the supporters of the people of *Lā ilāha illa Allāh*, and we respond to the one who says *Lā ilāha illa Allāh*, and we are the blessings for the people of *Lā ilāha illa Allāh*. Allah ﷻ says: 'I have made Paradise lawful for those who say *Lā ilāha illa Allāh*. I have forbidden the Fire for those who say *Lā ilāha illa Allāh*, I have forgiven the sins of those who say *Lā ilāha illa Allāh*. I do not veil My Forgiveness and Mercy from those who say *Lā ilāha illa Allāh*. I did not create Paradise except for the people of *Lā ilāha illa Allāh*. Do not

> mix the people of *Lā ilāha illa Allāh,* except with that which is in accordance with *Lā ilāha illa Allāh.*
>
> It is mentioned in *Jami ᶜus-Saghīr* that the Messenger of Allah ﷺ said, "Allah has forbidden the Fire from those who say *Lā ilāha illa Allāh,* by it seeking the Face of Allah."

Imam al-Ḥaddād رحمه الله has mentioned in his book *An-Naṣā'iḥ al-Dīniyya:*

> The most noble and excellent litany is the phrase *Lā ilāha illa Allāh.* The Prophet ﷺ said, "The best of what I and the Prophets before me have said is *Lā ilāha illa Allāh.*" And he ﷺ said, relating from Allah ﷻ, '*Lā ilāha illa Allāh* is My fortress. He who enters My fortress is safe from My punishment.' He ﷺ also said, "Renew your faith!" The Companions asked, "How can we renew our faith?" He ﷺ replied, "Exceed in the phrase of *Lā ilāha illa Allāh.*" He ﷺ said, "Transcendent is Allah" (*Subḥān Allāh*) fills half of the Scale, 'All Praise belongs to Allah' (*Al-Ḥamdulillāh)* fills it, and 'There is no god but Allah' (*Lā ilāha illa Allāh*) does not have a veil before Allah."
>
> It has been related that when the servant says *Lā ilāha illa Allāh* it does not pass by a sin in his book only that it erases it until it finds a virtue, then it settles down beside it.

The Sayyid, the pious ascetic, Muḥammad b. Yūsuf as-Sanūsī al-Ḥasanī mentions in the commentary to his text on the creed:

> An-Nasā'ī related that the Messenger of Allah ﷺ said, "Mūsā عليه السلام said, 'My Lord, teach me that with which I can remember You with and call upon You!' Allah ﷻ said, 'O Mūsā, Say '*Lā ilāha illa Allāh*!' Mūsā عليه السلام said, 'All your

servants say *Lā ilāha illa Allāh.* I would like something especially for myself.' Allah replied, 'O Mūsā! Were the seven heavens and earths to be placed on one of side of the Scale and *Lā ilāha illa Allāh* on the other, *Lā ilāha illa Allāh* would outweigh it."

The Messenger of Allah ﷺ said, "A man will be brought to the Scale along with ninety nine scrolls. Each record will have errors and sins as far as the eye can see, and it will be placed in the pan of the Scale. A card, as small as a finger tip will be brought out, upon it will be the testification *Lā ilāha illa Allāh Muḥammad ur-Rasūlallāh* ﷺ, it will be placed in the other pan and will outweigh his shortcomings and sins."

The Messenger of Allah ﷺ said, "No one utters *Lā ilāha illa Allāh,* sincerely from his heart, except that the gates of the heavens open until it reaches the Throne, as long as the major sins are avoided."

The Messenger of Allah ﷺ said, "Someone came to me from my Lord and informed me that he who dies testifying that there is no god but Allah, He is alone and He has no associate, will enter Paradise." Abū Dharr ؓ asked, "Even if he committed adultery and stole?" He ﷺ replied, "Even if he committed adultery and stole."

He ﷺ said, "He who enters the grave with *Lā ilāha illa Allāh,* Allah will save him from the Fire." And he ﷺ said, "The person happiest with my intercession on the Day of Judgement will be the one who said *Lā ilāha illa Allāh* sincerely from his heart." And he ﷺ said, "*Lā ilāha illa Allāh* is the key to Paradise."

It has been related by Anas ؓ that *Lā ilāha illa Allāh* is the price of Paradise. The Messenger of Allah ﷺ said, "You will certainly enter Paradise except those who refuse and run away from Allah like the camel that strays from its family."

The Companions asked, "O Messenger of Allah, who is the one that refuses?" He replied, "He who did not say *Lā ilāha illa Allāh*."

So exceed in reciting the phrase *Lā ilāha illa Allāh* before there is an obstacle between you and it. It is the phrase of *Tawḥīd*, the phrase of sincerity, the phrase of *taqwa*, the most pleasant phrase. It is the call to truth, the firm handhold (*ʿurwat ul-wuthqā*) and the price of Paradise.

On the authority of Abū Dharr ؓ who said, "I said, O Messenger of Allah advise me!" He ﷺ said, "I advise you to be conscious of Allah and if you commit an offence then follow it with a good deed and it will erase it." I said, "O Messenger of Allah is *Lā ilāha illa Allāh* from among those good deeds?" He ﷺ replied, "It is the most excellent of good deeds."

On the authority of Kaʿb ؓ who said, "Allah revealed to Mūsā ﷺ in the Torah, "Were it not for those who say *Lā ilāha illa Allāh* I would have released *Jahannam*[60] upon the people of the world." The Messenger of Allah ﷺ said, "He who says *Lā ilāha illa Allāh* three times in his day, it will be an expiation for all the sins he has committed in that day." And he ﷺ said, "The Throne shakes for three: the believer saying *Lā ilāha illa Allāh,* the words of the disbeliever when he says it, and for the stranger when he dies in a foreign land."

On the authority of one of the Companions ؓ who said that he who says *Lā ilāha illa Allāh* sincerely from his heart and extends it out of glorification, four thousand of his major sins are forgiven. It was asked, 'What if he does not have these sins?' He replied, "The sins of his father, his family and his neighbours are forgiven."

Qāḍī ʿIyāḍ mentioned in the book *Mustadrak* on the authority of Yunus b. ʿAbd ul-ʿAlā that he had been afflicted

---

[60] A level of Hell.

with something, when he saw in a dream someone saying to him, 'The greatest name of Allah is *Lā ilāha illa Allāh,*' so he recited it and wiped it over his face and he was relieved from his affliction.

Ibn Fakihānī said, "Adherence to this phrase when entering the house removes poverty. It has been related from the Prophet ﷺ that he who says *Lā ilāha illa Allāh* seventy thousand times is liberated from the Fire."

Sheikh Abū Muḥammad ᶜAbdallāh b. Asᶜad mentioned in the book *Al-Irshād wa Tatrīz,* in the chapter on the excellence of the remembrance of Allah and the recitation of the Great Book, on the authority of Sheikh Abū Yazīd al-Qurṭubī that:

> I heard related in some narrations that he who says *Lā ilāha illa Allāh* seventy thousand times is liberated from the Fire. So I performed it, hoping for the promised blessing, storing it for myself, and having performed some of it for my family.
>
> Now, we used to have a youth who would sleep in our house and it was said that at times he was able to see Paradise and the Fire by way of unveiling. Many people considered him to have a rank despite his youth. However, I didn't quite believe this. Some brothers decided to invite us to the young man's house. We were eating with the young man when suddenly he screamed outrageously. As he was regaining control of himself he said, 'O uncle, My mother is in the Fire!' He continued to scream outrageously. There was no doubt in the minds of those that heard him that he was greatly disturbed. When I saw what had happened to him I said to myself, 'Today I will test his truthfulness!' Allah reminded me of the seventy thousand recitations of '*Lā ilāha illa Allāh* that I had made; no one other than Allah knew this action of mine. I thought to myself if there is truth in this narration

> and in those that narrated it to us then, O Allah, the seventy thousand are a ransom for this woman, the mother of this youth. I had not finished thinking this within myself, when the young man said, 'O uncle, my mother has come out of the Fire.' *Al-Ḥamdulillāh*! I gained two things from this incident: my faith in the soundness of this tradition and safety in my opinion regarding the young man and his truthfulness.

The Messenger of Allah ﷺ said, "*Lā ilāha illa Allāh* continues to protect the servants from the wrath of Allah ﷻ as long as they are not concerned for that which diminishes from their world." In another narration it says, 'As long as they do not prefer this world over their afterlife. If they do then when they say *Lā Ilāha Illa Allāh*, the Exalted replies, "You lie, you are not sincere."'

It is related in the book *Ghāyat ul-Qaṣd wa'l-Murād* that our master the Axis of poles, Imam al-Ḥaddād - may Allah make us benefit by him - used to exceed in the recitation of the phrase *Lā ilāha illa Allāh* to the extent that he would utter it between his words when speaking to someone, and in his pause before responding.

Imam al-Ḥaddād would recite *Lā ilāha illa Allāh* after the *Ẓuhr* prayer, a thousand times every day. In the month of Ramadan, he would increase it by another thousand and would complete by the end of the six days of Shawwāl seventy thousand recitations of *Lā ilāha illa Allāh*.

It is mentioned in *Bahjat ul-Fawā'id* that Imam al-Ḥaddād once said, 'The Rātib that we have arranged to be read in the evening protects the town in which it is recited.' Therefore, every sincere murīd must recite the Rātib, especially if Imam Al-Ḥaddād is his intermediary to Allah ﷻ. The most perfect way to recite it is after the ᶜIshā prayer and in the morning.

One should recite it with presence of heart and feel as though one sees their Lord, the Exalted. One should begin with the *Fātiḥa* and end with the phrase of *Tawḥīd*. If this phrase is recited a thousand times it is all the more excellent; most certainly something from the lights of the dominion will manifest to him.

The Imam, the Proof of Islam, the *Quṭb*, and *Gawth*, our master Imam ᶜAbdallah b. ᶜAlawi al-Ḥaddād, may Allah make us benefit by him stated in his book *Gifts of the Seeker* (*Ittiḥāf as-Sā'il*):

> You asked, may Allah bestow you with enlightened understanding, regarding the meaning of *Lā ilāha illa Allāh.* Know that all the religious sciences and practical measures are but an unfolding of the meaning of this noble phrase and of the rights it has (over mankind) which take the form of injunctions, prohibitions, promises, warnings and that which follows them. That which is an exposition of its rights is consequently an explanation of it. (The purpose of this statement) is to make you aware that it is impossible to know fully the details (of each) of its sciences, let alone write them all down.
>
> He further expanded upon that until he said, 'Know that there are two halves to this noble phrase. The first is negation: 'There is no god' (*Lā ilāha*). When the negation is uttered, followed by the affirmation by one who associates no other deity to God, this means that he has denied and refuted the illusion of the polytheists that there may be another divinity, and also means that the meaning of this phrase is now present in his heart which will be strengthened through the repetition of these

words. The Messenger of Allah ﷺ said, "Renew your faith by (saying) *Lā ilāha illa Allāh.*"

He ﷺ also mentions in the same book, 'It should suffice you to know in explaining the wisdom and virtue of this phrase that the disbeliever's life and wealth are unprotected through the rejection of this phrase. He is eternally resident in the fire of Hell. Whereas, if a man who lives as a disbeliever for seventy years, and then utters it with faith, renders his life and wealth sacrosanct, and will slough off his sins and become as pure as the day his mother gave him birth. A servant who meets Allah ﷻ with as many sins as all the ancient and modern people combined, but who does not associate anything with Allah, will be forgiven if Allah wills, or else punished for his sins, but this punishment will be temporary, since none of the people of *Tawḥīd* remain in the hell fire forever.'

He further said, may Allah make us benefit by him, 'Know that this phrase is the most comprehensive and most profitable of all litanies, the nearest means to bring spiritual openings and illumining the heart with the light of Allah. It is also the most suitable of litanies for all people, since it includes the meanings of all other litanies, such as 'Praise be to Allah,' 'Transcendent is Allah' and so forth. Each believer should, therefore, make it his inseparable *wird*, his constant *dhikr*, however without abandoning the other litanies, from each of which he should have a portion.'

He says in the book, *Tathbīt al-Fu'ād bi dhikri kalām al-Quṭb al-Ḥabīb al-Ḥaddād:*

We counsel you with *Lā Ilāha Illa Allāh* at all times, especially in times of distress, endless preoccupations, and when enduring hardship; for it increases sustenance and its essence possesses a calming effect, to the extent that one may acquire sleep from it.

# ~ Chapter 3 ~

## On Seeking Forgiveness

Imam ᶜAlawī the great grandson of Imam al-Ḥaddād has mentioned in his commentary on the Rātib al-Ḥaddād:

'Seeking forgiveness is needed, recommended and encouraged. The commandments to seek forgiveness as well as its virtues have been related in the Book of Allah and the Sunna which are so numerous that it is difficult to relate them all. Allah ﷻ says: "*Those who, when they act indecently or wrong themselves, remember Allah and ask forgiveness for their bad actions, and who can forgive bad actions except Allah?*"[61]

"*Anyone who does evil or wrongs himself, then seeks Allah's forgiveness, will find Allah Ever-Forgiving, Most Merciful.*"[62] And "*Allah would not punish them as long as they sought forgiveness.*"[63]

The blessed Prophet ﷺ said, "Blessed is he who finds in his book (of deeds) plenty of *istighfār* (seeking forgiveness)." And he ﷺ said, "Shall I not inform you of your diseases and your cures? Surely your diseases are

---

[61] Sura Āl-ᶜImrān 3:135
[62] Sura an-Nisā' 4:110
[63] Sura al-Anfāl 8:33

sins and your cure is seeking forgiveness." The Messenger of Allah ﷺ said, "Whoever is abundant in seeking forgiveness, Allah dispels every worry of his, he finds a way out of every distress and He grants him sustenance in an unexpected way." And he ﷺ said, "A man who seeks forgiveness is not a persistent sinner, even if he lapses seventy times a day." He ﷺ also said that Allah says, 'O my worshippers all of you are sinful except the one I have granted well being, so seek forgiveness from Me and I shall forgive you. The one who knows that I have the power to forgive, then I will forgive him and I do not care.'

Imam al-Ḥaddād says in his book *An-Nasā'iḥ* that Allah ﷻ says, '*Ask your Lord for forgiveness and then repent to Him. He will let you enjoy a good life until a specified time.*'[64]And Allah says, (which he related to His Prophet Nūḥ عليه السلام) "*Ask forgiveness from your Lord, for He is oft-Forgiving. He will send rain to you in abundance, and will help you with wealth and sons, and will bestow on you Gardens and bestow on you rivers.*"[65]

The Messenger of Allah ﷺ said, "Whoever says, 'I seek forgiveness from Allah and I repent to him' (*Astaghfirullāha wa atūbu ilayhi*) more than seventy times in a day, Allah forgives seven hundred of his sins." He ﷺ also said, "Surely I seek forgiveness from Allah and repent to Him more than seventy times a day." He ﷺ also said, "Iblīs, may Allah curse him said, 'By Your Honour and Your Majesty O Lord, I will continue to mislead Your worshippers, as long as their souls remain in their bodies.' Then Allah said, 'By My Honour and My Glory, I will continue to forgive them as long as they seek forgiveness from Me.'"

[64] Sura Hūd 11:3
[65] Sura Nūḥ 71:10

The Messenger of Allah ﷺ said, "Whoever wishes to be pleased with their book [of deeds] should increase in seeking forgiveness." Tabarānī related on the authority of Mu‘ādh b. Jabal ؓ, "Whoever says, 'I seek forgiveness from Allah the Magnificent' [Astaghfirullāh il-‘Aẓīm], a plant is fixed for him in Paradise." He ﷺ also said, "O people! Seek forgiveness from Allah and repent to Him, surely I seek forgiveness and repent to Him a hundred or more than a hundred times everyday." - Related by Aḥmad and Tabarānī and others. And he ﷺ said, "Surely a covering[66] comes upon my heart until I seek forgiveness from Allah, everyday, one hundred times."

Imam Muḥiyyuddīn an-Nawawī related from the 'Ṣaḥiḥayn', (Al-Bukhārī and Muslim) on the authority of Abū Huraira ؓ, from the Messenger of Allah ﷺ who said, "Allah descends to the lowest heaven when the last third of the night remains. He ﷺ says, 'Who is supplicating to Me so that I can respond to him? Who is asking from Me, so that I can give him? Who is seeking forgiveness from Me, so that I can forgive him?'

Sayyida ‘Ā'isha ؓ said that the Messenger of Allah ﷺ said, "If you commit small sins then seek forgiveness from Allah, surely repentance of sins is through remorse and seeking forgiveness." It has also been related from the Messenger of Allah ﷺ, "Allah raises the rank of the servant in Paradise, who will then ask, 'O Lord! By which virtue have I received this?' Allah says, "It is by your son's seeking forgiveness for you."

---

[66] It should never be understood that this 'covering' is a covering due to sins, or because of a pre-occupation with other than Allah. The Prophet ﷺ was divinely protected from errors and sins. The Lordly scholars have explained it is a 'covering of light' and is due to the constant elevation that Prophet was going through, in that he would consider the previous rank that he was in as being low and deficient before the majesty of His Lord, and so would seek forgiveness for that. And Allah knows best.

It is related on the authority of Abū Huraira ﷺ that the Messenger of Allah ﷺ said, "When a servant commits an offence, a spot appears on his heart and when he becomes fearful and seeks forgiveness and repents from it, his heart becomes polished. If he returns to it, it increases until it covers his whole heart. And that is the seal that Allah ﷻ has mentioned.'[67] - Related by Tirmidhī.

Tirmidhī also related a sound hadith in which Allah says, 'O son of Adam! If your sins reach up to the firmament, and you seek forgiveness from Me, I will forgive you and I do not mind. O son of Adam! If you come to me with the earth filled with your faults and without associating anything to Me, I will return it filled with forgiveness and I do not mind. O son of Adam! As long as you call upon Me and have hope in Me, I will forgive you for that which is from you and I do not mind.'

Al-Ḥākim has related through a sound transmission the following hadith, 'There is not a Muslim who commits a sin except that his angel pauses for three hours. If he seeks forgiveness for it, his sin is not recorded for him, nor will he be punished for it on the Day of Judgement.' Al-Bayhaqī relates the hadith, 'The heart rusts like the rusting of copper and its polish is seeking forgiveness.' The Messenger of Allah ﷺ said, "There is not a bondsman or a bondswoman who seek forgiveness from Allah seventy times a day except that Allah forgives seven hundred of his or her sins. Surely a bondsman or a bondswoman has failed if they perform more than seven hundred sins in a day or night."

Abū Huraira ﷺ relates that when the Messenger of Allah ﷺ would swear an oath he would say, 'No! And I seek forgiveness from Allah.' It was related by Abū Dāwūd.

Ḥākim related a hadith according to the criteria of Bukhārī and Muslim, on the authority of Bara b. ᶜĀzib, that

---

[67] In Sura al-Muṭaffifīn 33:14

the statement of Allah, '*Do not cast yourselves into destruction,*'[68] refers to a man who commits a sin, then says that Allah does not forgive.

On the authority of Khālid b. Maᶜdan - may Allah have mercy upon him – who said that Allah ﷻ says, 'The most beloved servants to Me are those who love each other for My sake, and those whose hearts are attached to the mosques, and those who seek forgiveness in the early hours. They are the ones whom I remember when I wish to punish the people on the earth, and so I leave them and turn the punishment away from them.'

Our master Imam ᶜAlī ؓ (may Allah ennoble his face) said, "I am astonished at the one who perishes when he has salvation with him." It was asked, 'What is it?' He ؓ replied, 'Seeking forgiveness.'" Sufyān b. ᶜUyayna - may Allah have mercy upon him - would say, "My brother passed away and I saw him in my dream after his death, I asked him, 'What did Allah do to you?' He said, 'Allah forgave all the sins that I had asked forgiveness for, and for those sins that I had not sought forgiveness for, He ﷻ did not forgive me.'"

The Messenger of Allah ﷺ said, "If you can increase in seeking forgiveness then do so, for there is nothing more successful with Allah and more beloved to Him than seeking forgiveness."- Related by Ḥākim on the authority Abū Darda. The Messenger of Allah ﷺ said, "(Prayers for) seeking forgiveness in ones' book (of deeds) shine with light."- Related by Ibn Asākir on the authority of Muᶜāwiya b. Ḥaid. He ﷺ also said, "It is worthy of a man to have sittings in which he remembers his sins and seeks forgiveness from Allah for them."

It has been related that Sufyān al-Thawrī - may Allah have mercy upon him - visited Jaᶜfar b. Muḥammad b. ᶜAlī b. Imam

[68] Sura al-Baqara 2:195

Ḥusain b. Imam ᶜAlī b. Abī Ṭālib ☙ conveyed his greetings and sat down. Imam Jaᶜfar said, 'O Sufyān!' He replied, 'At your service.' 'You are a man whom the sultan seeks, and I am a man who escapes the sultan, so leave without having been expelled. Sufyān replied, 'Tell me of a hadith and I will go.' Imam Jaᶜfar said, 'My father told me relating from his grandfather that the Messenger of Allah ☙ said, 'The one whom Allah has bestowed a blessing upon should say 'Praise be to Allah' (Alhamdulillāh). The one who finds his sustenance is slow in coming, should say, 'I seek forgiveness from Allah' (Astaghfirullāh). The one who is grieved over a matter should say 'There is no power or strength besides Allah' (Lā Ḥawla wa lā Quwwata illā billāh).' Sufyān stood up to leave and Imam Jaᶜfar called him, 'O Sufyān!' He replied, 'At your service!' Imam Jaᶜfar said, 'Take these three and what a three they are!' Related by Bayhaqī in the book Shuᶜab al-Īmān.

One of the scholars of language said, 'There are three traits that Allah will not punish you for as long as you uphold them: gratitude (shukr), supplication (duᶜāʾ) and seeking forgiveness (istighfār).' Then he said, 'Why should Allah punish you if you are thankful and have faith?'[69] and My Lord will not be concerned for you, were it not for your supplication[70] and Allah would not punish them as long as they sought forgiveness.[71]

Imam Ḥasan al-Basrī ☙ said, 'Increase in seeking forgiveness in your houses, upon your tables, in your pathways, in your markets, in your gatherings and wherever you may be, for you do not know at what time blessings will descend.'

It is mentioned in the book Adhkār an-Nawawī, in the chapter on seeking forgiveness:

---

[69] Sura an-Nisāʾ 4:147
[70] Sura al-Furqān 25:77
[71] Sura al-Anfāl 8:33

> 'Know that this chapter is one of the most important chapters which should be a priority, and practised continuously. My intention was to place it at the end, hoping that Allah the most Generous will grant us an end upon it. We ask Him for that and for all forms of good.'
>
> He then continued with the subject with citations from the Quran hadith. He said, 'It is mentioned in Ṣaḥīḥ Muslim, on the authority of Abū Huraira ﵁ that the Messenger of Allah ﷺ said, "By the One who holds my soul in His hand, if you did not sin, then Allah would do away with you, and bring forth a people that commit sin, then seek His forgiveness, and thus receive His forgiveness."

Imam Shaʿrānī mentioned in the book *Mashāriq ul-Anwār*:

> An oath was taken from us with the Messenger of Allah ﷺ that we seek forgiveness in abundance, throughout the day and night, whether we can recollect our sins or not. This oath has been violated by many of those who claim to be Sufis and have not been guided by a sheikh. The devil adorned their own desires to themselves, making them believe that they have become true people of Allah and that they have no sins against Allah. None of them are hardly able to recall their sin and seek forgiveness for it. Perhaps he says to himself, 'How unlikely it is that Allah ﷻ would punish someone like me!' However, if Allah granted him insight like that of the gnostics, he would certainly see that he deserves to be swallowed by the earth as a punishment in this world, and entrance into the Fire in the next. For a servant is completely made up of sins and faults. How many times has the servant committed a sin and then forgotten about it? It will be

revealed to him on the Day of Judgement, therefore my brother seek forgiveness in abundance.

Every morning and evening my master ᶜAlī al-Khawwās would inspect his limbs from his head to his feet and would repent for the crime that each limb had committed that day or night, particularly for the ear, eye, tongue and the heart. He would say, 'Surely seeking forgiveness extinguishes the anger of the all-Powerful. Whoever seeks forgiveness, no sin will remain attached to him by the will of Allah. Especially if a man was approaching death, and his chances of performing a righteous action were limited, then there would be nothing more beneficial for him in that state than to seek plenty of forgiveness.

I heard him mention, 'The needs of this world and the hereafter are only held back by the abandonment of seeking forgiveness. Allah ﷻ says: *'Ask forgiveness from your Lord, for He is Oft-Forgiving. He will send rain to you in abundance. And He will help you with wealth and sons and will bestow on you Gardens and bestow on you rivers. What is the matter with you that you do not hope toward Allah for dignity?'*[72]

Know that he who has been dismissed from his job, or been imprisoned for a crime or is in debt, then the most beneficial thing for him is to seek forgiveness in abundance. This is because, dismissal and imprisonment are humiliation and disgrace for a servant who is in a state between intimacy and revenge. If his Lord is pleased that his servant confesses to his mistake, seeks forgiveness, and is pleased with him then He releases him from the situation in due time. If he sought forgiveness but was not released from his situation, it is an indication

[72] Sura Nūḥ: 10-14

> that Allah ﷻ did not accept his repentance, for he still possesses arrogance or an inclination to commit wrongs. He should treat this through seeking plenty of forgiveness and to return anything wrongfully taken, for Allah is the Most Relenting and the Most Merciful.

Imam Shaᶜrānī also said:

> It has been known by experience that the one who closes the door of disobedience in his life completely, his supplication is never rejected as he has become like the angels.'
>
> He said further, 'O brother do not fall into sin and then demand a response to your supplication, as that will not happen, and if it does then it is a means to your downfall. Just as your Lord the Exalted called you to His obedience and you did not respond to it. Likewise, when you call Him, He will not respond to you. But if you speed towards His obedience when He calls you, Allah ﷻ is swifter in responding, by answering you, immediately and rewarding you accordingly.
>
> Sheikh b. Abī an-Najā Sālim, who is buried in the city Quwa, counselled his companions on his death bed saying, 'Know that all of creation will treat you according to that which manifests from you, so look at how you are.'
>
> In summary, we are now halfway through the tenth century, we have reached the time when the signs of the Hour are evident. The signs of the Hour have been fulfilled before us, upon the elders of our community, whether we like it or not. It is not in our hands to turn back that which has been destined for us or to prevent the anxiousness that comes with it, so we say, 'I seek forgiveness from Allah the Great' '*Astaghfirullāh il-ᶜAẓīm,*' for no other reason than in obedience to Him. Whoever

> holds on to this, Allah will remove his grief and show him a way out of every difficult situation. He will receive sustenance from where he did not expect. By Allah, if one sat for the rest of his life saying, 'I seek forgiveness from Allah', (*Astaghfirullāh*) without being inattentive for a moment, he still would not compensate for his previous sins, let alone those that we commit, and Allah is Forgiving and Merciful.

Rabīᶜ b. Subayhin related that a man came to Imam Ḥasan al-Basrī, and complained to him of drought. Imam Ḥasan al-Basrī said, 'Seek forgiveness from Allah.' Another person came and complained of poverty, the Imam replied, 'Seek forgiveness from Allah. Then another came to him and complained of his barren gardens, he said, 'Seek forgiveness from Allah!' Then we asked him, 'Some men came to you complaining of an epidemic and asking you about all kinds of things and you commanded them all to seek forgiveness from Allah?' He said, 'I have not mentioned anything from my own opinion, but I learnt it from the parable whereby Allah mentions His Prophet Nūḥ ﷺ, saying to his people: *'Ask forgiveness from your Lord, for He is Oft-Forgiving. He will send rain to you in abundance. And He will help you with wealth and sons and will bestow on you Gardens and bestow on you rivers.'* [73] - It was reported by Thaᶜlabi.

It has been related that a bedouin came to Caliph Manṣūr asking him for help and said, 'I will not give you money but I will relate to you a hadith that my father narrated to me from my grandfather, who narrates from his father, who heard it from Ibn ᶜAbbās ؓ that the Messenger of Allah ﷺ said, "Whoever seeks forgiveness one thousand times every day for a year, the year will not pass by until he is enriched."

---

[73] Sura Nūḥ 71:12

The bedouin took his advice and at the end of the year while travelling, there was a fall of cool rain, so the man stopped to take shelter in a church. As a result of the rain the ground opposite the church caved in. Hidden beneath the earth was a jar containing thirty six thousand dirhams. His matter was raised to Manṣūr, who, during that time, used to tax a fifth from all hidden treasures but he let the Bedouin off.

It has also been related that a man and his wife only gave birth to daughters. He asked the scholars for a means to supplicate to Allah for sons. They directed him towards seeking forgiveness, after which he had a number of boys one after the other.

Ash-Sharjī ﵀ mentions in his book *Al-Fawā'id:* 'I found in the writing of some scholars that whoever mentions the following *istighfār* twenty five times, everyday and night:

أَسْتَغْفِرُ اللّٰهَ العَظِيمَ الَّذِي لَا إِلٰهَ إِلَّا هُوَ الرَّحْمٰنُ الرَّحِيمُ الحَيُّ القَيُّومُ

الَّذِي لَا يَمُوتُ وَأَتُوبُ إِلَيْهِ رَبِّ اغْفِرْ لِي

*I seek forgiveness from Allah the Great, besides Whom there is no god. The Merciful the Compassionate, the Living the Self-Subsisting, the One Who does not perish. I repent to him. O Lord forgive me.*

He will never see anything undesirable in his wealth, children and himself.' This is tried and tested, in fact it is mentioned in a hadith related by the Prophet ﷺ. It is also one of the litanies of our master Imam al-Ḥaddād ﵀ who would advise and urge people to recite it. Similarly our predecessors used to recommend it to their children and their followers. Just as Sayyid Imam [c]Abd ul-Qādir Jīlānī b. Sheikh al-[c]Aydrūs mentions it in his book, *Az-Zahar al-Basīm Sharhi Risālat-is-Sayyid Hatīm.'*

Imam al-Ḥaddād رضي الله عنه mentions in his book *al-Nasā'ih:*

> The excellence of seeking forgiveness and its benefits are sufficient for you, as Allah says, '*Allah would not punish them as long as they sought forgiveness.*'[74]
>
> And Allah's informing us of His Prophet Nūḥ عليه السلام, '*I say, seek forgiveness from your Lord surely He is forgiving. He will send you from the sky abundant rain. Help you with wealth and sons, and provide you with gardens and flowing rivers.*'[75]
>
> Repentance and forgiveness are from the treasures of good deeds. They are the greatest of good deeds and blessings and the swiftest means to all the good of the world and the Hereafter. So it is up to you to adhere to repentance and seeking forgiveness throughout the night and day. Surely the devil deceives some of the foolish amongst the Muslims, when he says to them, 'How can you repent when you yourself do not know whether you will remain firm and persistent upon the repentance? How many times will you repent and then return to sin?' These are the kind of whispers that the devil whispers. Therefore the Muslim should be cautious of it and not be deceived by him nor duped by his forgery and deception.
>
> The Messenger of Allah ﷺ said, "A man who seeks forgiveness is not a persistent sinner, even if he lapses seventy times a day."
>
> It is up to the servant to repent and ask Allah for assistance. If his soul commands him towards sin again, then he should command it to repent again. And Allah is

[74] Sura al-Anfāl 8:33

[75] Sura Nūḥ 71:12

the One Who grants success. All praise belongs to Allah Lord of the Worlds!

# ~ Chapter 4 ~

## On Invoking Blessings on The Messenger of Allah ﷺ

Fawzī Muḥammad Abū Zaid relates in his book Ḥadīth al-Ḥaqā'iq, 'Our master the Messenger of Allah ﷺ has said in a hadith, "Love for me is not mixed into the heart of a believing servant except that Allah forbids his body from the Fire."[76] Therefore, any believing servant whose heart is mixed with the love of the Messenger of Allah ﷺ his body is forbidden from the Fire. For this reason we want to strengthen and intensify our love for the Messenger of Allah ﷺ. So how is it that we can strengthen our love for him ﷺ?

In order for us to strengthen our love for him ﷺ, a number of things are necessary. Initially, one must get to know his attributes, description, character, and perfections. As a person increases his knowledge in these, he will eventually be lost in love for the Messenger of Allah ﷺ. The unique combination of these attributes of perfection have not come together in anyone other than him ﷺ, neither before him nor after him. It is as our master Imam ᶜAlī رضي الله عنه said, "Whoever saw him at first glance was filled with awe of him and whoever associated with him knowingly, fell in love with

[76] Related by Abū Naᶜīm on the authority of Ibn ᶜUmar. Imam Suyūṭī has indicated towards its authenticity.

him. His portrayer could only say, 'I have not seen anyone like him, neither before him nor after him.'"

It is necessary for every person to love this divine personality, for love of the Messenger of Allah ﷺ is the door to happiness and the door to good pleasure. Our Lord has said, *'Say if you love Allah, follow Me, Allah will love you and forgive you your sins, for Allah is Oft-forgiving, Most Merciful.'*[77] And it is related in a hadith, "By Allah, none of you believe, until I am more beloved to him than his wealth, parents, his self and all the people."[78]

Our master ʿUmar ؓ said, "I love you, O Messenger of Allah, more than everything else besides myself." He ﷺ replied, "Your faith is not complete, ʿUmar." Our master ʿUmar then said, "By Allah, O Messenger of Allah, I truly love you more than everything else, even more than my own soul which is between my two sides." The Prophet ﷺ replied, "Now ʿUmar your faith is complete."

Therefore, in order for a person to gain love for the Messenger of Allah ﷺ there is no doubt that he must know something of his features, his attributes, his manners, and know of his perfections which Allah has bestowed upon him. It is this that will attach him to the Muhammadan essence. Along with conceptualising (or keeping in mind) the Prophetic beauties in his heart and mind, to the extent that he is able to form them in his imagination, so that his thoughts are able to connect with him. His heart will then adore that spiritual Muhammadan image. Adoration necessitates love; this should be coupled with constant salutations upon him ﷺ. As a result he will draw closer to him, and will be in his presence, and with him.

---

[77] Sura Āl-ʿImrān 3: 31
[78] Narrated by Muslim whose wording it is, as well as Nasāʾī, Ibn Khuzaima, on the authority of Anas ؓ

For this reason, Sheikh ᶜAbd ul-Karīm al-Jīlī ﷺ says in his book *Qāba Qawsayn wa Multaqī an-Namusayn*:

> Be in a state of remembering him ﷺ as if you are in front of him during his life, well mannered, in reverence, veneration, in awe, and with shamefulness; for he sees you, and hears you every time you mention him. He is adorned with the attributes of Allah ﷻ, since Allah is the Companion of the one who remembers Him, and the Prophet ﷺ has a massive share of this attribute.

He also says in his book *An-Namūs al-Aᶜẓam*:

> I counsel you my brother, to constantly imagine his image ﷺ and its meaning, even if you have to burden yourself to bring it to mind. For very soon, your spirit will become familiar with him, then he ﷺ will be present before your eyes, and you will find him, converse with him, talk to him and he will respond to you, converse with you and talk to you. Thus you will achieve the rank of the companions, if Allah ﷻ wills.
>
> Know that the gnostics are constantly, even though they may have risen to the highest ranks, in contemplation and bring to mind the master of masters; even at the appearance of Divine Manifestations, they concentrate their energy towards him ﷺ. They receive from the Messenger of Allah ﷺ in accordance to their capacities and they acquire more than that which many people are capable of. All who see him in a robe, they are given that very robe of honour which they have witnessed, and their elevation is magnified, and this is his noble habit ﷺ, with everyone who sees him, a *Muḥammadan* generosity and *Aḥmadiyyan* character.

Regarding this, Sheikh Ibrāhīm Rashīd ﷺ says:

> Amongst the greatest means of arriving (*wuṣūl*) is attachment to the attributes of the beloved and abundant salutations upon him ﷺ until his form is present before the mind's eye wherever that person may be. The compiler of *Dalā'il ul-Khairāt* has described the noble *rawdah* in his composition, so that one who is distant is able to see it on conveying salutations upon the beloved, and would be moved by it, until he visualises the one who is in it ﷺ. When this is repeated constantly with abundant salutations, then his imagination will see it as physical and this is the goal. The goal of the gnostics, in their abundance of salutations upon the Prophet ﷺ is not the reward, or for the sake of their selves, even though they may receive this at the same time.

## *The result of loving him* ﷺ

When a person knows these perfections, then love within him is strengthened, and his approach is increased. When love is increased a little, then one is honoured with receiving the vision in sleep. When one is honoured with a vision in sleep, then the approach is increased, for he wants to see him ﷺ more often.

In order for us to know, how much a person receives from Allah, when a person honours and venerates the Messenger of Allah ﷺ, there is the story of a man from the Banī Isrā'īl who had sinned a lot and lived for a hundred years. After his death, the Banī Isrā'īl threw him onto a rubbish heap and refused to pray over him, and bury him with their dead. Then Allah revealed to Mūsā عليه السلام to go this servant of His, to wash and shroud him, and to pray over him. So he did, which astonished the people, who then asked Mūsā ﷺ to ask Allah what was the reason for this. Allah revealed to him that everytime the Torah was opened and his eyes fell upon the name of My beloved Muḥammad written in it, he kissed the place of his name, and placed it on his eyes and sent salutations upon him. Because of this, I had mercy upon him, forgave his sins, and married him to seventy Hūrs.[79]

ᶜUmar b. Saᶜīd al-Futī mentions in his book *Rimāh Ḥizb ar-Raḥīm*, on the authority of Sufyān al-Thawrī:

> He was once circumbulating the Kaᶜba (and we know that worship around the Kaᶜba consists of dhikr, dua, and seeking forgiveness) when he found a man who did not take a step without sending salutations upon the Messenger of Allah ﷺ. So he asked him about it and said to him, "O man! This is a place of dhikr, supplication and seeking forgiveness, why is it that I see you sending salutations upon the Messenger of Allah ﷺ?" The man replied, "Who are you?" He said, "Sufyān al-Thawrī" (he was a famous scholar of Iraq). The man then said to him, "If you were any other than Sufyān al-Thawrī, I would not have informed you! Sit next to me and I will relate my story." They went to a side and the man said:
>
> > My father and I had intended the Hajj this year, during the journey, death suddenly approached him. When he died I looked at his face and found it to be black, so I covered it. I then sat down grief stricken, distressed and anxious. Then sleep overcame me and I saw a man, with bright white clothes and an extremely white face, he drew nearer until he stood over my father's head.

[79] Abū Naᶜīm related this in his Ḥilya and Suyūṭī in al-Khasā'is on the authority of Wahb.

> He unveiled his face, and wiped his hand over him and his face became white like the moon! He had with him a small piece of paper which he placed next to him. I asked him, 'Who are you? What brings you to my father at such a time?' He replied, 'Do you not know me? I am Muḥammad, the Messenger of Allah! Upon this paper are the salutations that your father would send upon me. When you witnessed what had happened, he sought help from me, and I came to help him.' I then woke up from my sleep, removed the cover from my father's face and found it to be white. This is the reason why I do not take a step except with salutations upon the Messenger of Allah ﷺ.

## *The connection of salutations to him ﷺ*

Another aspect which strengthens love for the Messenger of Allah ﷺ is conveying salutations upon him ﷺ. If we already send salutations upon him, then it is essential to increase the number of salutations, and the statement of the Messenger of Allah ﷺ suffices us, "Whoever sends ten salutations upon me in the morning and ten in the evening, my intercession is binding upon him on the Day of Judgement."[80]

One who sends salutations upon the Prophet ﷺ ten times in the morning, and ten times in the evening, this necessitates his intercession on the Day of Judgement. This can be performed whether one is in a state of ritual purity or not, although it is better to perform it in a state of purity. For this reason one can convey salutations upon the Messenger of Allah ﷺ while walking, sitting, at work or in any place.

[80] Related by Tabarānī on the authority of Abū Darda رضي الله عنه.

It should be known with certainty, that the salutation upon the Messenger of Allah ﷺ is also the dhikr of Allah, because it involves the act of asking Allah to convey blessings upon him ﷺ: 'O Allah send blessings...' We do not know how to send blessings upon him and so we say, 'O Lord' or '*Allāhumma*' meaning 'O Allah send blessings upon him.' Moreover, the Messenger of Allah ﷺ is not needy of our blessings, therefore we should be wary of thinking that he ﷺ is need of it. Our Lord has sent blessings upon him and whoever Allah sends blessings upon is not in need of any other blessing. As Allah ﷻ says, "*Indeed Allah and His angels send blessings upon the Prophet...*"[81]

We have within our litanies, a litany which is the dhikr of Allah and is the best of litanies, and at the same time it is a salutation upon the Messenger of Allah ﷺ and so we say in the morning a hundred times and in the evening a hundred times, '*Lā ilāha illa Allāh Muḥammad ur-Rasūlullāh ṣallallāhu ᶜaleyhi wa sallam*' (There is no god but Allah, Muhammad is the Messenger of Allah, may Allah bless him and grant him peace). As the Messenger ﷺ has said, 'The best thing that I and the Prophets before me have said is *Lā ilāha illa Allāh*.'[82] Hence by reciting *Lā ilāha illa Allāh Muḥammad ur-Rasūlullāh ṣallallāhu ᶜaleyhi wa sallam* we are encompassing all good, as it includes the remembrance of Allah, with the most excellent phrase, the phrase of *Tawḥīd* and salutations upon the beloved of Allah ﷺ.

As a result, one who is abundant in conveying salutations upon the Messenger of Allah ﷺ, while reading his life story, his attributes, perfections and is occupied with him constantly, there is no doubt that he will be honoured, and not deprived, because he ﷺ is the secret of generosity, and

[81] Sura al-Aḥzāb 33: 56

[82] Narrated by Bayhaqī on the authority of Talha b. ᶜUbaydillāh b. Salām ﷺ

honouring. Even though the honouring is from the Generous (*al-Karīm*), glorified and exalted is He, in which case Allah only honours all of the loving believers for his sake ﷺ.

Sheikh Yūsuf Nabahānī has quoted in his book *Sa'ādat ud-Dārayn* on the authority of Imam Muḥammad al-Ghumrī al-Wāsitī, from his book, *Minḥ ul-Minna fī Talabus bis Sunna*:

> Know that salutations upon the Prophet ﷺ are undeniable in relation to the Seeker at the beginning of his affair, constantly by day and night. This will help him in his travel (*sulūk*) upon the path, and it is a means of proximity to the Lord of lords, exclusive from other litanies, for it is an opening to the door of guidance to Allah ﷻ.
>
> For he ﷺ is the means between us and Him ﷻ, and our guide to Him, and the one who knows Him ﷺ. Attachment to the means precedes attachment to the objective. For the means is the cause for entrance to the Greatest King, and the way (*waṣīla*) to the ranks of proximity. Therefore he ﷺ is the means between the creation and their Lord, the Exalted.
>
> Know that assistance to all of creation, including the Prophets and saints is from him ﷺ. And that all of their works are presented to him, and that he ﷺ has a reward from them, since he is the cause of their good.
>
> Salutations upon him are from the greatest of assistances to proximity toward Allah ﷻ and His Messenger, and through it does one acquire light, and darkness is not removed except by light. The meaning of darkness (*ẓulma*) is the filth which is attached to the soul (*nafs*) and that which is the rust upon the heart. Once the soul is purified from filth, and the heart from rust, then impeding obstacles towards good are removed, and all of this is through his blessings, may Allah bless him and

grant him peace. Abundance of salutations upon him ripens a fixation of love for him within the heart.

One does not reach in acquiring to follow his actions and character ﷺ except through an intense concern for him, and one does not reach an intense concern for him except through an exaggeration of love for him, and one does not reach this exaggerated love except through an abundance of salutations upon him ﷺ. Whosoever loves a thing is abundant in its remembrance, for this reason the seeker begins with salutations upon the Prophet ﷺ. He has through it an illumination of the inward, a purification of the soul, wonders which the seeker will find experientially, besides that it contains benefits and secrets, which are impossible to count or limit.

It is enough for the seeker to have a sincere endeavour towards Allah ﷻ through salutations upon His Prophet ﷺ, until he reaps its fruits and its blessings glisten for him. Salutations upon all stages of the path, are nothing but a lantern by which he is guided, a light which illuminates. Therefore, whoever cultivates his heart with salutations upon him ﷺ will see through its lights the secrets of the realities of *Tawḥīd*.

ʿAbd ul-Wahhāb Shaʿrānī ؒ has said in his book *Lawāqiḥ ul-Anwār il-Qudsiyya fī Bayān il-Uhūd al-Muḥammadiyya:*

A general covenant was taken from us, with the Messenger of Allah ﷺ to be abundant in reciting salutations and greetings of peace upon the Messenger of Allah ﷺ by day and night. We will mention for our brothers the reward and good that it contains and to encourage them greatly, so that they manifest love for him ﷺ. If they were to make it a litany everyday and night, morning and evening from a thousand to ten thousand then that would be one of the best actions. Whoever is consistent upon this will have a great reward, and will be the closest in proximity to him ﷺ.

There is no one in the creation that has been granted a connection and a release from Allah, not in the world or the afterlife as has been granted to the Prophet ﷺ. So whoever serves him with sincerity, love and purity, the necks of the tyrants will be subjugated to him, and all the believers will honour him.

He رضي الله عنه also says in the same book:

Therefore, work my brother, on polishing the mirror of your heart from rust and dust, and purify yourself from all filth, until there does not remain within you even one characteristic which wiill prevent you from entering the presence of Allah ﷻ and the presence of the Messenger of Allah ﷺ.

If you increase in salutations and greetings of peace upon the Prophet ﷺ, then perhaps you will reach the rank of seeing him ﷺ, and this is the path of Sheikh Nūr ud-Dīn al-Shūnī, Shaykh Aḥmad az-Zāwī, and Sheikh Aḥmad b. Dāwūd al-Manzalawī and a whole number of masha'ikh from Yemen. They continued to send blessings upon the Messenger of Allah ﷺ and were abundant in it, until they became purified from all sins, and then they were able to meet him ﷺ while awake, at any time they wished, and also conversed with him. Whoever has not reached this rank then he has not yet been abundant in salutations upon the Messenger of Allah ﷺ. Abundance is necessary in order to reach this rank.

Sheikh Aḥmad al-Zāwī told me that he did not reach the rank of meeting with the Prophet ﷺ while awake until he persisted in sending salutations upon him ﷺ, reciting every day and night fifty thousand salutations for a whole year.

I also heard my master ʿAlī al-Khawwās - may Allah have mercy upon him - say, 'The rank of a slave within the rank of gnosis is not complete until he begins to meet with the Messenger of Allah ﷺ at any time he pleases. Amongst the predecessors, that we know of, who used to meet with the Prophet ﷺ while awake and conversed with him are: Sheikh Abū Madyan, Sheikh ʿAbd ur-Raḥīm al-Qinawī, Sheikh Mūsā al-Zūlī, Sheikh Abu'l Ḥasan al-Shādhilī, Sheikh Abu'l ʿAbbās al-Mursī, Sheikh Abū'l-Suʿūd b. Abī'l-Ashʿir, my master Ibrāhiīm al-Matbūlī and Sheikh Jalāl ud-Dīn as-Suyūṭī, (may Allah be pleased with them all).

He also said, "Sheikh Aḥmad al-Zāwī once said to me, 'Our path is to be abundant in salutations upon the Prophet ﷺ, until we begin to sit with him while awake, and we accompany him like the Companions, and we ask him regarding our religious affairs, and the hadith which the *Ḥuffāẓ* have declared weak, so that we are able to implement what he has said ﷺ. If this has not happened to us, then we are not from those who are abundant in salutations upon him, may Allah grant him blessings and peace.'"

Sheikh Aḥmad Dahlān said in his book *Taqrīb al-Usūl*:

For this reason, many of the Imams of the path who have a following have said, "Pursuance with salutations upon the Prophet ﷺ is amongst the greatest means of receiving openings for a servant. It can stand in place of a sheikh in upbringing (*tarbiyya*). Many gnostics have acquired gnosis (*maʿrifa*) of Allah ﷻ by having no sheikh but by conveying salutations upon the Prophet ﷺ."

Abu'l-Mawāhib al-Shādhilī ﵁ would say, "Allah has servants whose *tarbiyya* is undertaken by the Prophet ﷺ himself without any intermediary because of their abundant salutations upon him ﷺ."

~ I ~

# On The Importance Of Maintaining A Connection With The Beloved of Allah ﷺ

Imam Yusuf Nabahānī says in his book *Blessings of Praise*, 'Know that the point of sending blessings upon the Prophet ﷺ is to venerate him and to respect him.'

Imam Fakhr ad-Dīn ar-Rāzī as well as the majority of scholars have commented on the question: "If Allah praises the Prophet, then what need is there for our praise?" The answer they have given is that the Prophet ﷺ is not in need of praise from us, or from the angels but it is Allah's desire to manifest his greatness, which is why He has ordered us to do so. This He did out of affection for us so that he may reward us for it. It is for this reason that the Prophet ﷺ said, 'Whoever sends blessings upon me once, Allah sends ten upon him.'

Imam al-Ḥaddād رضي الله عنه has said in his *Book of Assistance*:

> Adopt a wird of prayer for the Messenger of God ﷺ for this will be a connection between you and the Prophet, and a door through which assistance from his presence flows in abundance to you.

Hence the Ummah, in particular the Gnostics and the Lordly scholars rejoiced in such a command for they had found their salvation, intimacy, hope and refuge in praising and sending blessings upon the Prophet ﷺ. Through this, as enumerated in sound hadith after sound hadith were they promised the best of this world and the best of the hereafter. This promise was expressed on the fortunate tongue of the companion Rabīʿa b. Kaʿab ؓ who when finding that Door of Generosity ﷺ wide open before him, ordering him to 'Ask!' for anything he desired, he simply said, 'Your companionship in Paradise, O Messenger of Allah.'

With the above verse of Allah, the hadith, 'The most beloved to me and the nearest in sitting to me on the Day of Rising are those of you who pray on me the most,' and the saying of Ibn Masʿūd ؓ, 'Make excellent blessings upon your Prophet, for you do not know perhaps it will be presented before him' in front of them, the people of Allah rolled their sleeves up and immersed themselves in seeking the Prophet ﷺ, in their salutations, their prayers, their speech, actions and thoughts, throughout their days and throughout their nights, while awake and even while sleeping, hoping for a glimpse, and a glance from that face which is the most beloved to Allah.

~ II ~

## On The Benefit of Reciting Salutations on The Prophet ﷺ

أَدِمِ الصَّلاَةَ عَلَى الْحَبِيْبِ ۞ فَصَلاَتُــهُ نُورٌ وَطِيبٌ

*Be persistent in your salutations upon the Beloved*
*For salutations upon him are a light and goodness*

أَنْفَاسُ جَنَّاتٍ مَفَاتِيحُ رَحْمَةٍ ۞ نَغَــمٌ حَبِيــبٌ

*They are the breezes of the Gardens, the keys of Mercy,*
*A melody beloved*

تَسْرِي فَتُبْعَثُ بِالنَّدَى وَالرَّيِّ فِي ۞ الرُّوحِ الْجَدِيــبِ

*They travel, and arise like morning dew and a drink*
*For dehydrated spirits*

وَتَطُوفُ بِالرِّضْوَانِ تَنْشُرُهُ ۞ عَلَى كُــلِّ الْقُلُوبِ

*They go round with good pleasure and spread*
*Within every heart*

إِنَّ الصَّلَاةَ عَلَى رَسُولِ اللهِ ۞ شَمْسٌ لَا تَغِيبُ

*Verily the salutation upon the Messenger of Allah*
*Is a sun that never sets*

اللهُ صَلَّى وَالْمَلَائِكَةُ الْكِرَامُ ۞ عَلَى الْحَبِيبِ

*Allah and the noble angels send salutation*
*Upon the Beloved*

وَأَنَالَ مَنْ صَلَّى عَلَيْهِ ۞ الْفَوْزَ وَالْمَدَدَ الرَّحِيبِ

*The one who sends salutations upon him gains*
*Victory and abundant help*

أُدْعُ الْإِلٰهَ كَمَا تَشَاءُ بِهَا ۞ تَجِدْهُ يَسْتَجِيبُ

*Ask Allah by it for whatever you desire*
*You will find Him responding*

وَابْدَأْ دُعَاءَكَ وَاخْتَتِمْهُ ۞ بِالصَّلَاةِ عَلَى الْحَبِيبِ

*Begin your supplication and end it*
*With salutation upon the Beloved*

## ~ III ~

## THE INTENTION BEFORE ṢALAWĀT

Sheikh al-Aḥsāʾī has said, 'This is one of the supplications of our master Imam ᶜAbdallāh bin ᶜAlawī al-Ḥaddād who said, "It is recommended for the one performing salutations upon the Prophet ﷺ to commence with the following supplication for there are great blessings therein."'

اَللّٰهُمَّ إِنِّي نَوَيْتُ بِصَلَاتِي هَذِهِ عَلَى النَّبِيِّ سَيِّدِنَا مُحَمَّدٍ صَلَّى اللهُ عَلَيْهِ وَسَلَّمَ إِمْتِثَالاً لِأَمْرِكَ وَتَصْدِيْقًا بِكِتَابِكَ وَاتِّبَاعًا لِنَبِيِّكَ سَيِّدِنَا مُحَمَّدٍ صَلَّى اللهُ عَلَيْهِ وَسَلَّمَ وَمَحَبَّةً فِيْهِ وَشَوْقًا إِلَيْهِ وَتَعْظِيْمًا لِحَقِّهِ وَتَشْرِيْفًا لَهُ وَلِكَوْنِهِ أَهْلاً لِذَلِكَ فَتَقَبَّلْهَا اَللّٰهُمَّ بِفَضْلِكَ وَجُوْدِكَ وَكَرَمِكَ وَإِحْسَانِكَ وَأَزِلْ حِجَابَ الغَفْلَةِ عَنْ قَلْبِي وَاجْعَلْنِي مِنْ عِبَادِكَ الصَّالِحِيْنَ .

اَللّٰهُمَّ زِدْهُ شَرَفًا عَلَى شَرَفِهِ الَّذِيْ أَوْلَيْتَه وَعِزًّا عَلَى عِزِّهِ الَّذِيْ
أَعْطَيْتَهُ وَنُوْرًا عَلَى نُوْرِهِ الَّذِيْ مِنْهُ خَلَقْتَهُ وَأَعْلِ مَقَامَهُ فِيْ مَقَامَاتِ
الْمُرْسَلِيْنَ وَدَرَجَتَهُ فِيْ دَرَجَاتِ النَّبِيِّيْنَ وَأَسْأَلُكَ رِضَاكَ وَالْجَنَّةَ
وَرِضَاهُ يَارَبَّ الْعَالَمِيْنَ مَعَ الْعَافِيَةِ الدَّائِمَةِ فِي الدِّيْنِ وَالدُّنْيَا
وَالْآخِرَةِ وَالْمَوْتِ عَلَى الْكِتَابِ وَالسُّنَّةِ وَالْجَمَاعَةِ وَكَلِمَةِ الشَّهَادَةِ
عَلَى تَحْقِيْقِهَا مِنْ غَيْرِ تَبْدِيْلٍ وَتَغْيِيْرٍ وَاغْفِرْ لِيْ مَا ارْتَكَبْتُهُ بِفَضْلِكَ
وَإِحْسَانِكَ عَلَيَّ إِنَّكَ أَنْتَ التَّوَّابُ الرَّحِيْمُ وَصَلَّى اللّٰهُ وَسَلَّمَ عَلَى
سَيِّدِنَا مُحَمَّدٍ وَآلِهِ وَصَحْبِهِ وَالتَّابِعِيْنَ أَجْمَعِيْنَ وَالْحَمْدُ لِلّٰهِ رَبِّ
الْعَالَمِيْنَ.

*O Allah, I intend to perform this prayer upon the Prophet Muḥammad ﷺ in compliance to Your command, in affirmation of Your Book, in obedience to Your Prophet Muḥammad ﷺ. Together with love and longing for him, with reverence and honour according to his immense worth.*

*So accept it O Allah, with Your bounty, Your munificence, Your Generosity, and Your Favour, and remove the veil of heedlessness from my heart and make me from amongst Your righteous servants.*

*O Allah, increase him in honour above the honour You have granted him, and exalt his esteem above that which You have bestowed, and illuminate him more than his light from which you created him. Elevate his station amongst the Messengers, and his rank amongst the Prophets.*

*I ask You, O Lord of the worlds for Your Pleasure, the Garden, his pleasure with permanent well being in the religion, the world and the hereafter. I ask You for death upon the Book and the Sunnah and with the congregation, and upon the Words of Testimony and upon accomplishing it without alteration or change.*

*Forgive me with Your Favour and Your Kindness upon me, for that which I have committed, indeed You are the Most Forgiving and the Most Merciful.*

*May blessings and peace be upon our Master Muḥammad, his Family, his Companions and the Successors all of them, and all praise belongs to Allah, Lord of the worlds.*

## ~ IV ~

## ṢALĀT AL-TĀJIYYA
## OF SHEIKH ABŪ BAKR BIN SĀLIM

اَللّٰهُمَّ صَلِّ عَلَى سَيِّدِنَا مُحَمَّدٍ صَاحِبِ التَّاجِ وَالْمِعْرَاجِ وَ الْبُرَاقِ وَ

الْعَلَمِ دَافِعِ الْبَلَاءِ وَ الْوَبَاءِ وَ القَحْطِ وَالْمَرَضِ وَالْأَلَمِ جِسْمُهُ مُعَطَّرٌ

مُنَوَّرٌ مَنْ إِسْمُهُ مَكْتُوْبٌ مَرْفُوْعٌ مَوْضُوعٌ عَلَى اللَّوْحِ وَ الْقَلَمِ شَمْسِ

الضُّحَى بَدْرِ الدُّجَى نُوْرِ الهُدَى مِصْبَاحِ الظُّلَمِ سَيِّدِ الكَوْنَيْنِ وَشَفِيعِ

الثَّقَلَيْنِ اَبِي الْقَاسِمِ سَيِّدِنَا مُحَمَّدٍ بْنِ عَبْدِ اللّٰهِ سَيِّدِ العَرَبِ وَالْعَجَمِ نَبِيِّ

الْحَرَمَيْنِ مَحْبُوْبٍ عِنْدَ رَبِّ الْمَشْرِقَيْنِ وَرَبِّ الْمَغْرِبَيْنِ يَا أَيُّهَا الْمُشْتَاقُوْنَ

بِنُوْرِ جَمَالِهِ صَلُّوْا عَلَيْهِ وَسَلِّمُوْا تَسْلِيْماً.

*O Allah bestow blessings and peace upon our Master Muhammad, the*
*Owner of the Crown, the Ascent, the Burāq and the Banner (of*
*Prophethood). He repels affliction, disease, drought, illness and pain.*
*His body is fragrant and illuminated. His name is inscribed, exalted*

*high, upon the Preserved Tablet and the Divine Pen. He is the Sun of the day, and the Full Moon at night, the Light of guidance, and the Lamp that dispels darkness. He is the Master of both worlds, the Intercessor of men and jinn. He is the Father of Qāsim, our Master Muḥammad, the son of ʿAbdallāh. He is the Leader of the Arabs and the non-Arabs. The Prophet of the two Sacred Mosques, the Beloved of the Lord of the two Easts and the two Wests. O those who yearn for him by the light of his beauty, invoke blessings and peace upon him with a worthy salutation!*

## ~ V ~

# The Salutations of Imam ᶜAbdallāh ibn ᶜAlawī al-Ḥaddād ﵁

It has been related on the authority of Imam Aḥmad al-Mashhūr al-Ḥaddād ﵁ may Allah make us benefit by him, that the one who recites the following seven salutations, by the allocated number, every night, will have the vision of the blessed Prophet ﷺ.

اللَّهُمَّ يَا رَبَّ سَيِّدِنَا مُحَمَّدٍ وَآلِ سَيِّدِنَا مُحَمَّدٍ صَلِّ عَلَى سَيِّدِنَا مُحَمَّدٍ

وَاجْزِ سَيِّدِنَا مُحَمَّدٍ صَلَّى اللهُ عَلَيْهِ وَآلِهِ وَسَلَّمَ عَنَّا مَا هُوَ أَهْلُهُ ﴿11﴾

*O Allah, O Lord of our Master Muḥammad and the family of our Master Muḥammad, send blessings upon our Master Muḥammad and reward our Master Muḥammad - may Allah send blessings and peace upon him and his family - on our behalf, according to his worth.*

اللَّهُمَّ صَلِّ عَلَى سَيِّدِنَا مُحَمَّدٍ وَعَلَى آلِ سَيِّدِنَا مُحَمَّدٍ عَدَدَ مَا عَلِمْتَ وَ
مِلأَ مَا عَلِمْتَ ﴿11﴾

*O Allah, send blessings upon our Master Muḥammad, and upon the family of our Master Muḥammad, by the number of what You know, and by that which Your knowledge encompasses.*

اللَّهُمَّ صَلِّ عَلَى سَيِّدِنَا مُحَمَّدٍ وَ عَلَى آلِ سَيِّدِنَا مُحَمَّدٍ عَدَدَ الشَّفْعِ
وَالوَتْرِ وَكَلِمَاتِ رَبِّنَا الطَّيِّبَاتِ الْمُبَارَكَاتِ ﴿11﴾

*O Allah, send blessings upon our Master Muḥammad, and upon the family of our Master Muḥammad, by the number of the even and the odd and (by the number of) the pure and blessed Words of our Lord.*

اللَّهُمَّ صَلِّ عَلَى سَيِّدِنَا مُحَمَّدٍ وَعَلَى آلِ سَيِّدِنَا مُحَمَّدٍ عَدَدَ كُلِّ ذَرَّةٍ أَلْفِ
مَرَّةٍ ﴿11﴾

*O Allah, send blessings upon our Master Muḥammad, and upon the family of our Master Muḥammad, by the number of each atom, a thousand times.*

اللَّهُمَّ صَلِّ عَلَى سَيِّدِنَا مُحَمَّدٍ وَعَلَى آلِ سَيِّدِنَا مُحَمَّدٍ فِي الأَوَّلِينَ وَصَلِّ عَلَى سَيِّدِنَا مُحَمَّدٍ وَ عَلَى آلِ سَيِّدِنَا مُحَمَّدٍ فِي الآخِرِينَ وَ صَلِّ عَلَى سَيِّدِنَا مُحَمَّدٍ فِي المَلَاءِ الأَعْلَى إِلَى يَوْمِ الدِّينِ ﴿11﴾

*O Allah, send blessings upon our Master Muḥammad and upon the Family of our Master Muḥammad among the first ones. And send blessings upon our Master Muḥammad and upon the Family of our Master Muḥammad among the last ones. And send blessings upon our Master Muḥammad in the presence of the highest company until the Day of Judgement.*

اللَّهُمَّ صَلِّ وَسَلِّمْ وَ بَارِكْ وَ كَرِّمْ عَلَى سَيِّدِنَا وَ مَوْلَانَا مُحَمَّدٍ السَّابِقِ لِلْخَلْقِ نُورُهُ الرَّحْمَةِ لِلْعَالَمِينَ ظُهُورُهُ عَدَدَ مَنْ مَضَى مِنْ خَلْقِكَ وَ مَنْ بَقِيَ وَ مَنْ سَعِدَ مِنْهُمْ وَمَنْ شَقِيَ صَلَاةً تَسْتَغْرِقُ العَدَّ وَ تُحِيطُ بِالحَدِّ صَلَاةً لَا غَايَةَ لَهَا وَلَا انْتِهَاءَ وَلَا أَمَدَ لَهَا وَلَا انْقِضَاءَ صَلَاتَكَ الَّتِي صَلَّيْتَ عَلَيْهِ صَلَاةً دَائِمَةً بِدَوَامِكَ بَاقِيَةً بِبَقَائِكَ لَا مُنْتَهَى دُونَ عِلْمِكَ وَعَلَى آلِهِ وَأَصْحَابِهِ كَذَلِكَ وَالحَمْدُ لِلَّهِ عَلَى ذَلِكَ ﴿11﴾

*O Allah, send salutations, peace and blessings upon our master and guardian Muḥammad and honour him. Foremost amongst the creation by his light, whose appearance is a mercy to mankind. May it be multiplied by the number of all Your past creation and by those that remain. By the number of those who are felicitous and those who are not. A blessing, which is beyond numeration and encompasses all limits, without an extremity, end or termination. May this blessing be in the way that You convey Your blessing upon him, which is everlasting by Your eternal existence, and may the same be upon his Family and Companions and praise be to Allah for that.*

اللَّهُمَّ صَلِّ عَلَى سَيِّدِنَا مُحَمَّدٍ وَعَلَى آلِ سَيِّدِنَا مُحَمَّدٍ صَلَاةً تَكُونُ

لَكَ رِضًا وَلِحَقِّهِ أَدَاءً ﴿33﴾

*O Allah, send blessings upon our Master Muḥammad and upon the descendents of our Master Muḥammad, a blessing that will gain Your pleasure and fulfill his worth.*

It has been related that the one who recites this salutation three times receives the reward of reciting the '*Dalā'il ul-Khairāt*' of Imam al-Jazūlī.

اللَّهُمَّ صَلِّ وَسَلِّمْ عَلَى سَيِّدِنَا مُحَمَّدٍ وَعَلَى آلِ سَيِّدِنَا مُحَمَّدٍ بِعَدَدِ مَا

تَعَلَّقَ بِهِ عِلْمُكَ مِنَ الْوَاجِبَاتِ وَالْجَائِزَاتِ وَالْمُسْتَحِيلَاتِ إِجْمَالًا وَ

تَفْصِيلاً مِنْ يَوْمِ خَلَقْتَ الدُّنْيَا إِلَى يَوْمِ الْقِيَامَةِ فِي كُلِّ يَوْمٍ أَلْفِ مَرَّةٍ

﴿3﴾

*O Allah, send blessings and peace upon our Master Muḥammad and upon the descendents of our Master Muḥammad by the amount that Your knowledge is connected to of that which has to be, that which can be, and that which cannot be in totality and specifically, from the day You created the world until the Day of Judgement, a thousand times every day.*

~ VI ~

# The Salutations of Ḥabib Aḥmad Mashhūr bin Ṭāhā al-Ḥaddād رضي الله عنه

Ḥabīb Aḥmad Mashhūr رضي الله عنه said that these blessings upon the Prophet ﷺ were inspired to him by Allah (*wāridāt ul-Ilāhiyya*)

اللَّهُمَّ صَلِّ وَسَلِّمْ عَلَى سَيِّدِنَا مُحَمَّدٍ حَبِيبِ الرَّحْمٰنِ وَدُرَّةِ الأَكْوَانِ
الحَاضِرِ مَعَ مَنْ صَلَّى عَلَيْهِ فِي كُلِّ زَمَانٍ وَمَكَانٍ وَعَلَى آلِهِ وَصَحْبِهِ وَ
تَابِعِيهِمْ بِإِحْسَانٍ.

*O Allah, send blessings and peace upon our Master Muḥammad, the beloved of the Beneficent, and the most precious in all creation, who is present with the one who sends blessings upon him in every time and place. And may blessings and peace be upon his Family, Companions and Followers.*

اللَّهُمَّ صَلِّ عَلَى سَيِّدِنَا مُحَمَّدٍ سَيِّدِ الكَوْنَيْنِ وَ بَهْجَةِ الثَّقَلَيْنِ وَ جَدِّ الحَسَنَيْنِ وَ اجْعَلْ لِي بِالصَّلاةِ عَلَيْهِ قُرَّةَ عَيْنٍ وَ عَلَى آلِهِ وَصَحْبِهِ وَسَلِّمْ.

*O Allah, send blessings and peace upon our Master Muḥammad, the leader of both worlds, the splendour of the world of jinn and the world of humans, the grandfather of Imam Ḥasan and Imam Ḥusain. With this blessing upon him, make him the light of my eyes, and may the blessings and peace be upon his Family and Companions.*

اللَّهُمَّ صَلِّ عَلَى سَيِّدِنَا مُحَمَّدٍ النَّبِيِّ الأُمِّيِّ وَ آلِهِ وَ سَلِّمْ تَسْلِيماً وَ أَسْتَغْفِرُ اللهَ العَظِيمَ وَأَتُوبُ إِلَيْهِ.

*O Allah, send blessings and peace upon our Master Muḥammad, the Prophet, not taught by man, (but by You), and also upon his Family. I beg forgiveness of Allah, The Incomparably Great and turn to Him repentant.*

اللَّهُمَّ يَا نُورَ السَّمٰوَاتِ وَ الأَرْضِ صَلِّ عَلَى مَنْ خَلَقْتَهُ مِنْ نُورِكَ وَ اغْفِرْ لِي ذَنْبِي وَنَوِّرْ قَلْبِي بِأَنْوَارِ مَعْرِفَتِكَ وَبِمَعْرِفَتِهِ بِكَ وَعَلَى آلِهِ وَ صَحْبِهِ وَسَلِّمْ.

*O Allah, O the Light of the heavens and the earth, bestow blessings and peace upon the one You created from Your Light, and forgive my sins, and fill my heart with the light of Your Knowledge, and with his knowledge of You, and may blessings and peace be upon his Family and Companions.*

اللّٰهُمَّ صَلِّ عَلَى سَيِّدِنَا مُحَمَّدٍ صَاحِبِ الْمَقَامِ الْأَسْنَى الْمَخْصُوصِ بِشَرَفِ الْأَدْنَى مَنْ لَوْلَاهُ مَا كُنَّا وَاغْمِرْنَا بِأَنْفَاسِهِ فِي الْحِسِّ وَالْمَعْنَى وَعَلَى آلِهِ وَصَحْبِهِ وَسَلِّمْ.

*O Allah, send blessings and peace upon our Master Muḥammad, the one who has the highest position, the one singled out to be honoured with closeness to Allah. Were it not for him, we would not exist. Immerse us in his breaths, physically and spiritually, and may blessings and peace be upon his Family and Companions.*

اللّٰهُمَّ صَلِّ عَلَى سَيِّدِنَا مُحَمَّدِ الَّذِي مَا ذُكِرَ اسْمُهُ عَلَى مَرِيضٍ إِلَّا شُوفِيَ وَلَا سَقِيمٍ إِلَّا عُوفِيَ وَعَلَى آلِهِ وَصَحْبِهِ وَسَلِّمْ.

*O Allah, send blessings and peace upon our Master Muḥammad, the mention of whose name before anyone who is sick, cures him and anyone who is ill and in pain is given good health, and may blessings and peace be upon his Family and Companions as well.*

اللَّهُمَّ صَلِّ وَسَلِّمْ عَلَى البَدْرِ المُنِيْرِ البَشِيْرِ النَّذِيْرِ رُوْحِ مَعْنَى الوُجُوْدِ وَ

الرَّحْمَةِ المُهْدَاةِ لِكُلِّ مَوْجُوْدٍ وَعَلَى آلِهِ وَصَحْبِهِ وَ تَابِعِيْهِمْ إِلَى اليَوْمِ

المَوْعُوْدِ.

*O Allah, send blessings and peace upon the bright moon, the bringer of glad tidings, the warner, the soul of all existence, and the merciful gift for all that exists, and on his Family, Companions and Followers till the Promised Day.*

# ~ VII ~

## THREE UNIQUE SALUTATIONS

اَللّٰهُمَّ صَلِّ وَ سَلِّمْ وَبَارِكْ عَلٰى خَيْرِ مَنْ عَرَفَ رَبَّهُ بِالنُّوْرِ وَالْعِلْمِ
وَالْعِرْفَان

*O Allah send salutations, peace, and blessings upon the best who has recognised his Lord; through light, knowledge and gnosis.*

اَللّٰهُمَّ صَلِّ وَسَلِّمْ وَبَارِكْ عَلٰى مَكْنُوْنِ رَحْمَتِكَ فِي الدُّنْيَا وَالْآخِرَة

*O Allah send salutations, peace and blessings upon the hidden treasure of Your mercy in this world and the hereafter*

اَللّٰهُمَّ صَلِّ وَ سَلِّمْ وَبَارِكْ عَلٰى مَنْ لَايُعْرَفُ قَدْرُهُ وَمَقَامُهُ إِلَّا رَبُّهُ
سُبْحَانَهُ وَتَعَالٰى

*O Allah send salutations, peace, and blessings upon the one whose virtue and rank is not known except by His Lord, Glorified and Exalted is He.*

~ VIII ~

# The Salutation of Sheikh Aḥmad bin Idrīs ﵁

اَللّٰهُمَّ إِنِّي أَسْأَلُكَ بِنُورِ وَجْهِ اللهِ الْعَظِيمِ الَّذِي مَلَأَ أَرْكَانَ عَرْشِ اللهِ الْعَظِيمِ وَقَامَتْ بِهِ عَوَالِمُ اللهِ الْعَظِيمِ أَنْ تُصَلِّيَ عَلَى مَوْلَانَا مُحَمَّدٍ ذِي الْقَدْرِ الْعَظِيمِ وَعَلَى آلِ نَبِيِّ اللهِ الْعَظِيمِ بِقَدْرِ عَظَمَةِ ذَاتِ اللهِ الْعَظِيمِ فِي كُلِّ لَمْحَةٍ وَنَفَسٍ عَدَدَ مَا فِي عِلْمِ اللهِ الْعَظِيمِ صَلَاةً دَائِمَةً بِدَوَامِ اللهِ الْعَظِيمِ تَعْظِيماً لِحَقِّكَ يَا مَوْلَانَا يَا مُحَمَّدُ يَا ذَا الْخُلُقِ الْعَظِيمِ وَسَلِّمْ عَلَيْهِ وَعَلَى آلِهِ مِثْلَ ذَلِكَ وَاجْمَعْ بَيْنِي وَبَيْنَهُ كَمَا جَمَعْتَ بَيْنَ الرُّوحِ وَالنَّفْسِ ظَاهِراً وَبَاطِناً يَقَظَةً وَمَنَاماً وَاجْعَلْهُ يَا رَبِّ رُوحاً لِذَاتِي مِنْ جَمِيعِ الْوُجُوهِ فِي الدُّنْيَا قَبْلَ الْآخِرَةِ يَا عَظِيمُ.

*O Allah! I ask You by the light of Your formidable Countenance which has filled the corners of Allah's Throne, and by which the worlds of Allah have been established; to send peace and blessings upon our guardian Muhammad, possessor of a formidable standing and upon the family of the great Prophet of Allah. By the amount of Allah's formidable greatness; send peace and blessings in every moment and every breath by the number of that which is in the knowledge of Allah the Formidable. Send peace upon him and the like upon his family and Companions. Join me with him just as You have joined the soul and the spirit, inwardly and outwardly, when asleep and awake. Make him, O Allah, the spirit of my soul from all dimensions in this world before the Hereafter, O the Formidable!*

This is the salutation of the great Gnostic Sayyid Aḥmad b. Idrīs, may Allah be pleased with him, the sheikh of Ṭarīqa al-Idrīsiyya, which is a branch of the Shādhilī Ṭarīqa. Sayyed Aḥmad b. Idrīs received this salutation from the Prophet ﷺ directly; once without any intermediary and the second time through Sayyidnā al-Khidr عليه السلام.

Sayyed Aḥmad relates that he met the Prophet ﷺ and with him was Khidr عليه السلام. The Prophet ordered Khidr عليه السلام to recite to him the litanies of the Shadhilī Ṭarīqa, so he recited them to him in his presence. Then the Prophet ﷺ said to Khidr عليه السلام: "O Khidr recite to him that which encompasses all litanies, salutations and istighfār, and is the best in reward and the greatest in number." He replied, "What is that O Messenger of Allah ﷺ?" And so he said:

لَا إِلَهَ إِلَّا اللهُ مُحَمَّدٌ رَّسُولُ اللهِ فِي كُلِّ لَمْحَةٍ وَنَفَسٍ عَدَدَ مَا وَسِعَهُ عِلْمُ اللهِ

Then he recited it to me and I said it after him. The Prophet repeated it 3 times, and then said say: "(the above salutation)" then he said:

أَسْتَغْفِرُ اللهَ العَظِيمَ الَّذِي لَا إِلَهَ إِلَّا هُوَ الحَيُّ القَيُّومُ غَفَّارُ الذُّنُوبِ ذُو الجَلَالِ وَالإِكْرَامِ وَأَتُوبُ إِلَيْهِ مِنْ جَمِيعِ المَعَاصِي كُلِّهَا وَالذُّنُوبِ وَالآثَامِ وَمِنْ كُلِّ ذَنْبٍ أَذْنَبْتُهُ عَمْدًا وَخَطَأً ظَاهِراً وَبَاطِناً قَوْلاً وَفِعْلاً فِي جَمِيعِ حَرَكَاتِي وَسَكَنَاتِي وَخَطَرَاتِي وَأَنْفَاسِي كُلِّهَا دَائِماً أَبَداً سَرْمَداً مِنَ الذَّنْبِ الَّذِي أَعْلَمُ وَمِنَ الذَّنْبِ الَّذِي لَا أَعْلَمُ عَدَدَ مَا أَحَاطَ بِهِ العِلْمُ وَأَحْصَاهُ الكِتَابُ وَخَطَّهُ القَلَمُ وَعَدَدَ مَا أَوْجَدَتْهُ القُدْرَةُ وَخَصَّصَتْهُ الإِرَادَةُ وَمِدَادَ كَلِمَاتِ اللهِ كَمَا يَنْبَغِي لِجَلَالِ وَجْهِ رَبِّنَا وَجَمَالِهِ وَكَمَالِهِ كَمَا يُحِبُّ رَبُّنَا وَيَرْضَى.

This is "*Istighfār al-Kabīr*", Khidr عليه السلام repeated it, and I repeated it after him, whereby I gained lights, Muḥammadan strength (*quwwatin Muḥammadiyya*) and Divine assistance. He ﷺ then said, "O Aḥmad, I have given you the keys to the heavens and the earth." i.e. the above dhikr the great salutation and Istighfār al-kabīr.

# SECTION 2

# BENEFICIAL SUPPLICATIONS

*"Dua is the essence of worship"*

The Prophet ﷺ

~ I ~

# Supplications to be Recited after the Prayer

The supplication of the Prophet ﷺ which he received when he was in the rank of "two bows length"[83]

اَللّٰهُمَّ إِنِّيْ أَسأَلُكَ فِعلَ الخَيْرَاتِ وَتَرْكَ المُنْكَرَاتِ وَ حُبَّ المَسَاكِيْنَ

وَأَنْ تَغْفِرَ لِيْ وَتَرْحَمَنِيْ وَتَتُوْبَ عَلَيَّ وَ إِذَا أَرَدْتَ بِعِبَادِكَ فِتْنَةً فَاقْبِضْنِيْ

إِلَيْكَ غَيْرَ مَفْتُوْن.

*O Allah I ask You for the ability to do good, abandon the reprehensible and love for the poor. I ask You to forgive me, be merciful with me, and pardon me. If You will a tribulation for Your servants, then take me to You, unafflicted.*

[83] Sura al-Najm 53:9

Tirmidhī relates from the Prophet ﷺ that he said, "Whoever recites the following supplication after every prayer he will become a scholar without doubt."

رَبِّ زِدْنِي عِلْماً وَوَسِّعْ لِي فِي رِزْقِي وَبَارِكْ لِي فِيمَا رَزَقْتَنِي وَاجْعَلْنِي
مَحْبُوباً فِي قُلُوبِ عِبَادِكَ وَعَزِيزاً فِي عُيُونِهِمْ وَاجْعَلْنِي وَجِيهاً فِي الدُّنْيَا
وَالْآخِرَةِ وَمِنَ الْمُقَرَّبِينَ يَا كَثِيرَ النَّوَالِ يَا حَسَنَ الْفِعَالِ يَا قَائِماً بِلَا
زَوَالٍ يَا مُبْدِئاً بِلَا مِثَالٍ فَلَكَ الْحَمْدُ وَلَكَ الْمِنَّةُ وَلَكَ الشَّرَفُ عَلَى كُلِّ
حَالٍ .

*My Lord increase me in knowledge, increase my sustenance, and bless the sustenance that You have granted me. Make love prevail in the hearts of Your servants for me, and in their eyes make me dear to them. Distinguish me in the world and the hereafter, and make me from the ones that are in close proximity to You. The One abundant in favour! The One so beautiful in acts! The One Who remains without an end! The Incomparable Creator! To You belongs all Praise, Kindness, and Honour, at all times.*

## *Supplication of Āyat ul-Kursī*

Some of the pious predecessors would precede their recitation of *Āyat ul-Kursī* with the following supplication:

اَللَّهُمَّ إِنِّي أُقَدِّمُ إِلَيْكَ بَيْنَ يَدَيْ كُلِّ نَفَسٍ وَلَمْحَةٍ وَخَطْرَةٍ وَطَرْفَةٍ

يَطْرِفُ بِهَا أَهْلُ السَّمَاوَاتِ وَأَهْلُ الأَرْضِ، وَكُلِّ شَيْءٍ هُوَ فِي عِلْمِكَ

كَائِنٌ أَوْ قَدْ كَانَ . أُقَدِّمُ إِلَيْكَ بَيْنَ يَدَيْ ذَلِكَ كُلِّهِ : (اَللهُ لَا إِلَهَ إِلَّا

هُوَ الحَيُّ القَيُّومُ)... إلى (العَلِيِّ العَظِيمِ)

*O Allah, I present to You, in front of every breath, moment, thought, every blink of the eye that the inhabitants of the heavens and the earth take, and everything that Your knowledge beholds, that which is present or in the past, I present to You, in front of that all 'Allah! There is no god but He, the Living, the Self-subsisting...' (until the end).*

It has been related on the authority of the great Quṭb ᶜAlī al-Tamāsīnī al-Tijāni ﷺ that one who recites *Āyat ul-Kursī* ten times after the ᶜAṣr prayer, without moving from their place of prayer, they will receive ten things. They are the following: 1) Repentance before death, 2) blessing in their sustenance, 3) physical well being, 4) love will manifest in the hearts of the believers towards them, 5) absolute certainty, 6) their spirit will depart from the body on the Testification, 7) Allah will expand their grave, 8) they will receive their book of deeds from the right side, 9) they will fly across the Bridge (*Sirāṭ*), 10) they will enter Paradise without reckoning.

It has been related on the authority of a Master of the Tijānī Order that one who recites the following ten times, after the

Fajr and ᶜAṣr prayers, Allah will record them as an inhabitant of *Al-Firdaws* in Paradise:

شَهِدَ اللهُ أَنَّهُ لَا إِلَهَ هُوَ وَ الْمَلَائِكَةُ وَ أُولُوا الْعِلْمِ قَائِماً بِالْقِسْطِ لَا
إِلَهَ إِلَّا هُوَ الْعَزِيزُ الْحَكِيمُ . إِنَّ الدِّينَ عِنْدَ اللهِ الْإِسْلَامُ

## *An encouragement to seek forgiveness*

It is related from the Prophet ﷺ that he said, "Whoever says (the following *istighfār*) 25 times, he will not witness anything which he dislikes in his house, family, or in the houses of his families, or in his town or city." Therefore it is important one should recite this in the mornings and evenings.

أَسْتَغْفِرُ اللهَ الَّذِي لَا إِلَهَ إِلَّا هُوَ الرَّحْمَانُ الرَّحِيمُ الْحَيُّ الْقَيُّومُ الَّذِي لَا
يَمُوتُ وَأَتُوبُ إِلَيْهِ رَبِّ اغْفِرْ لِي .

*I seek Allah's forgiveness. There is no god but He, the Compassionate, the Merciful, the Living the Self-subsisting, the One Who does not perish. I turn to Him repentant, my Lord forgive me!*

## *Ṣalāt ad-Damīr*

It is related from the Prophet ﷺ that whoever recites after the Maghrib and Fajr prayers: "Indeed Allah and His angels send blessings upon the Prophet; O you who believe send blessings upon him and salutations in abundance." And then says: "O Allah send blessings upon him" 100 times, Allah will fulfil 100 of his needs; 30 pertaining to this world and 70 pertaining to the Afterlife.

إِنَّ اللّٰهَ وَمَلَائِكَتَهُ يُصَلُّونَ عَلَى النَّبِيِّ يَا أَيُّهَا الَّذِينَ آمَنُوا صَلُّوا عَلَيْهِ

وَسَلِّمُوا تَسْلِيمًا : اَللّٰهُمَّ صَلِّ عَلَيْهِ

## *Supplication of Sayyidinā Abū Darda*

It is related that a man came to Sayyidinā Abū Darda ؓ and said, 'Your house has burnt down!' He replied, 'No it hasn't.' Then another man came and said, 'O Abū Darda, the fire spread but when it came to your house it went out.' He said, 'I knew that Allah would not do this.' His companions replied, 'O Abū Darda we do not know which of your words are more astonishing, your statement: 'It has not burnt,' or your saying 'Allah would not do that.'

He ؓ said, 'These are words which I heard from the Messenger of Allah ﷺ, whoever says them at the beginning of the day, no calamity will befall him until the evening. And whoever says them at the end of the day, no calamity will befall him till the morning.'

اَللَّهُمَّ أَنْتَ رَبِّيْ لَا إِلٰهَ إِلَّا أَنْتَ عَلَيْكَ تَوَكَّلْتُ وَأَنْتَ رَبُّ الْعَرْشِ الْعَظِيْمِ مَا شَاءَ اللّٰهُ كَانَ وَمَا لَمْ يَشَأْ لَمْ يَكُنْ وَلَا حَوْلَ وَلَا قُوَّةَ إِلَّا بِاللّٰهِ الْعَلِيِّ الْعَظِيْمِ . أَعْلَمُ أَنَّ اللّٰهَ عَلَى كُلِّ شَيْءٍ قَدِيْرٌ وَأَنَّ اللّٰهَ قَدْ أَحَاطَ بِكُلِّ شَيْءٍ عِلْماً اَللَّهُمَّ إِنِّي أَعُوْذُ بِكَ مِنْ شَرِّ كُلِّ دَآبَّةٍ أَنْتَ آخِذٌا بِنَاصِيَتِهَا إِنَّ رَبِّيْ عَلَى صِرَاطٍ مُسْتَقِيْمٍ .

*O Allah, You are my Lord, there is no god but You, upon You I depend, and You are the Lord of the Magnificent Throne. That which Allah wills will be and that which He does not will not come to pass. There is no power or strength but with Allah, the Exalted, the Supreme. I know that Allah is omnipotent over everything and that Allah's knowledge encompasses everything. O Allah, I seek refuge with You from the evil of every creature whom You have taken by the forelock. Indeed Allah is upon a straight path.*

## *The Prayer for the Fulfillment of Needs*

Tabarānī,[84] in his *Al-Muʿjam al-Ṣaghīr*, reports a hadith from ᶜUthmān b. Hunayf ﷺ that during the caliphate of Sayyidinā

[84] The chain of narrators have been established as well authenticated (ṣaḥīḥ) and is also reported in Tirmidhī, Ibn Mājah, Hakim (corroborated by Dhahabī), Nasā'ī, Bukhārī in his '*Tārīkh*', Bayhaqī, Ibn as-Sunnī, and Ibn Khuzaima.

ʿUthmān ﵁, a man repeatedly visited him concerning a need, but Sayyidinā ʿUthmān paid no attention to him or his need.

The man met the companion ʿUthmān b. Hunayf ﵁ and complained to him about the matter – this occurred after the passing away of the Prophet ﷺ and after the caliphates of Sayyidinā Abū Bakr and ʿUmar ﵄ - so ʿUthmān b. Hunayf, who was one of the Companions that collected hadiths and was learned in the religion of Allah, said:

> Go to the place of ablution and perform ablution, then come to the mosque, perform two rakʿas of prayer therein, and say:
>
> *'O Allah, I ask You and turn to You through our Prophet Muḥammad, the Prophet of mercy; O Muḥammad (Yā Muḥammad), by you, I turn to my Lord, that He may fulfill my need.'*
>
> Then mention your need. After that come to me, so that I can go with you [to the caliph ʿUthmān].

So the man left and acted upon the instruction, then went to the door of ʿUthmān b. ʿAffān ﵁. The doorman came, took him by the hand, and led him to Sayyidinā ʿUthmān b. ʿAffān, and seated him on a cushion next to him.

Sayyidinā ʿUthmān ﵁ asked, "What do you need?" The man mentioned his need, and Sayyidinā ʿUthmān accomplished it for him. Then he said, 'I had not remembered your need until just now,' adding, 'Whenever you need something, just mention it.'"

Then, the man departed, and met with ʿUthmān b. Hunayf, and said to him, "May Allah reward you! He didn't see to my need or pay any attention to me until you spoke with him."

[c]Uthmān b. Hunayf replied, "By Allah, I didn't speak to him, but once I saw a blind man who went to the Messenger of Allah ﷺ to complain for the loss of his eyesight. The Prophet ﷺ said, "Can you not bear it?" The man replied, "O Messenger of Allah, I do not have anyone to lead me around, and it is a great hardship for me." The Prophet ﷺ told him, "Go to the place of ablution and perform ablution, then pray two rak[c]as of prayer and make this supplication."

Ibn Hunayf went on, "By Allah, we didn't part company or speak long before the man returned to us as if nothing had ever been wrong with him.""

It is therefore recommended for the fulfillment of needs to ask Allah through the means (*tawassul*) of the Prophet ﷺ, for needs are certainly fulfilled through his name.

After performing ablution, praying two rak[c]as with the intention of the fulfillment of needs, one should recite this supplication:

اَللّٰهُمَّ إِنِّي أَسْأَلُكَ وَأَتَوَجَّهُ إِلَيْكَ بِنَبِيِّكَ سَيِّدِنَا مُحَمَّدٍ صَلَّى اللهُ عَلَيْهِ
وَسَلَّمَ نَبِيِّ الرَّحْمَةِ، يَا سَيِّدَنَا مُحَمَّدُ إِنِّي أَتَوَجَّهُ بِكَ إِلَى رَبِّي فَتُقْضَى لِي
حَاجَتِي. اَللّٰهُمَّ شَفِّعْهُ فِيَّ.

*O Allah, I ask You and turn to You by Your Prophet, our Master Muhammad ﷺ, the Prophet of Mercy. O our Master Muhammad, with you I have turned to my Lord so that my need will be fulfilled. O Allah grant me his intercession...* Then one should mention their need.

## Fātiḥa aṣ-Ṣugrā of Ḥabīb Aḥmad bin Muḥammad al-Miḥdār

Amongst the sayings of Ḥabīb Aḥmad b. Ḥasan al-ʿAṭṭās ﷺ, it has been related that one of the awliyā' of Yemen said that he saw that the Day of Judgement had arrived, and it was said to the people of Yemen: "Enter Paradise!" It was asked: "What is the reason for this?" At that point he heard that they were told to enter Paradise as a reward for departing on the *Fātiḥa*, and for reciting it at the end of their gatherings in the world.

اَلْفَاتِحَةَ لِمَشَايخِ الْقَهْوَةِ الْبَنِيَّةِ وَ السَّادَةِ الْعَلَوِيَّةِ وَالصُّوفِيَّةِ وَكُلِّ وَلِيٍّ

وَ وَلِيَّةٍ وَمَنْ شَرِبَهَا بِنِيَّةٍ أَنَّ اللهَ يُصْلِهُ الطَّوِيَّةَ وَيَقْضِي الْحَوَائِجَ

الدِّينِيَّةَ وَالدُّنْيَوِيَّةَ بِجَاهِ خَيْرِ الْبَرِيَّةِ أَنْ يُسَهِّلَ الْبَتِيْنَ وَالْعُوَيْنَ

وَيَقْضِيَ عَنَّا الدَّيْنَ وَيُصْلِحَ ذَاتَ الْبَيْنِ بِجَاهِ الْحَسَنِ وَالْحُسَيْنِ

وَعِمْرَانَ بْنِ الْحُصَيْنِ وَخَدِيْجَةَ زَوْجَةِ سَيِّدِ الْكَوْنَيْنِ وَإِلَى حَضْرَةِ

النَّبِيِّ سَيِّدِنَا مُحَمَّدٍ صَلَّى اللهُ عَلَيْهِ وَ سَلَّمَ اَلْفَاتِحَةَ.

*Al-Fātiḥa for the Masha'ikh of the coffee tradition,*[85] *the Sāda ʿAlawiyya, the Sufiyya, for every male and female wali. And for those who drink it with the intention that Allah corrects the inward, fulfils the religious needs and those required in the world. By the honour of the best of creation, may children and water be eased for us, may we be relieved of debt and discord, by the honour of Ḥasan and Ḥusayn, ʿImrān ibn il-Ḥuṣayn, Khadīja the wife of the Master of both worlds and to the honourable Prophet our Master Muḥammad ﷺ al-Fātiḥa.*

[85] One of the regular habits for certain Sufi Masters was the use of the coffee drink as an aid to worship. This is further explained in the hadith on page 274.

~ II ~

# Three Special Gifts from Ḥabīb Aḥmad bin Ḥasan bin ᶜAbdallāh al-ᶜAṭṭās ﵁

It is related from the master, Ḥabīb Imam the ᶜĀrif billāh Aḥmad b. Ḥasan b. ᶜAbdallāh al-ᶜAṭṭās ﵁, who said, "I saw our master ᶜAlī b. Abī Ṭālib, may Allah ennoble his face, between the *rukn* and the *maqām* around the Kaᶜba. Firstly, he taught me how to wear a shawl (*ridā'*), saying that one should place one end of the shawl upon one's right shoulder and should pull it across one's chest. One should then bring the end of the shawl under the armpit and then round one's back and then make it hang off one's left shoulder." Our master ᶜAlī, may Allah ennoble his face, then said, "The right is at the front and the left at the back."

Secondly, I then asked him to teach me a supplication, he ﵁ taught me the following:

اَللَّهُمَّ إِنَّا ضَمَّنَّاكَ أَنْفُسَنَا وَأَمْوَالَنَا ، وَأَوْلَادَنَا وَأَهْلِيْنَا وَذَوِي أَرْحَامِنَا

، وَمَنْ أَحَاطَتْ بِهِ شَفَقَةُ قُلُوبِنَا ، وَجُدُرَاتِ بُيُوتِنَا ، وَمَنْ مَعَنَا وَمَا

مَعَنَا ، وَكُلَّ مَا أَنْعَمْتَ بِهِ عَلَيْنَا، فَكُنْ لَنَا وَلَهُمْ حَافِظًا – يَاخَيْرَ

مُسْتَوْدَعٍ – فِي الدُّنْيَا وَ الْآخِرَةِ آمِين .

*O Allah, we entrust ourselves and our wealth, our children, families, relatives, and all those who are encompassed by the affection of our hearts, the walls of our houses, all those who are with us and all that is with us, as well as everything which you have blessed us with. So be a Guardian for us and them, O You who are the best of those entrusted – in this world and the hereafter, amīn.*

Thirdly, the following supplication which is attributed to Ḥabīb Aḥmad b. Ḥasan b. ʿAbdallāh al-ʿAṭṭās ﷺ and it contains immense protection:

حَصَّنْتُ نَفْسِي وَأَهْلِي وَمَالِي وَعِرْضِي  وَدِيْنِي وَدُنْيَايَ وَأُخْرَايَ

وَمَعَاشِي وَمَعَادِيْ وَ أَزْوَاجِيْ وَأَوْلَادِيْ وَظَاهِرِيْ وَبَاطِنِيْ  وَسِرِّيْ

وَعَلَانِيَتِي  وَزَمَانِيْ وَمَكَانِيْ وَوَقْتِيْ وَأَهْلَ وَقْتِيْ وَكُلَّ شَيْءٍ أَعْطَانِيهِ

رَبِّي بِمَا حَصَّنَ بِهِ النَّبِيُّوْنَ وَالْمُرْسَلُوْنَ  وَالْأَوْلِيَاءُ  وَالصَّالِحُوْنَ

أَنْفُسَهُمْ وَأَهْلَهُمْ وَأَمْوَالَهُمْ وَ  أَعْرَاضَهُمْ وَدِيْنَهُمْ وَدُنْيَاهُمْ

وَأُخْرَاهُمْ وَمَعَاشَهُمْ وَمَعَادَهُمْ  وَأَزْوَاجَهُمْ وَأَوْلَادَهُمْ وَظَاهِرَهُمْ

وَبَاطِنَهُمْ وَسِرَّهُمْ وَعَلَانِيَتَهُمْ وَزَمَانَهُمْ وَمَكَانَهُمْ وَوَقْتَهُمْ وَأَهْلَ

وَقِتْهِمْ فِي الدِّينِ وَالدُّنْيَا وَالْآخِرَةِ وَحَسْبُنَا اللّٰهُ وَنِعْمَ الْوَكِيلُ وَصَلَّى

اللّٰهُ عَلَى سَيِّدِنَا مُحَمَّدٍ وَآلِهِ وَصَحْبِهِ وَسَلَّمْ

*I fortify myself, my family, my wealth, my honour, my religion, my world, my afterlife, my life, my death, my wife, my children, my outward, my inward, my essence, my appearance, my time, my place, my era and the people of my era, and everything that My Lord has given to me, with the fortification that the Prophets, the Messengers, the Awliyā', and the Righteous have sought for themselves, their families, their wealth, honour, their religion, their world, their afterlife, their lives, their passing away, their wives, their children, their outward, their inward, their essences, their appearances, their times and places, their eras and the people of their era, in their religion, world and afterlife. Sufficient is Allah for us and an excellent Guardian is He. May Allah bless and send peace upon our master Muhammad, his family, and companions.*

## ~ III ~

# THREE HADITHS GIVEN TO IMAM AḤMAD BIN ᶜALĪ AL-BAHR AL-QADĪMĪ ﵁

The ᶜĀrif billāh, Ḥabīb Aḥmad b. Ḥasan al-ᶜAṭṭās ﵁ reports from his Sheikh the Imam, the ᶜĀrif billāh Abū Bakr b. ᶜAbdallāh al-ᶜAṭṭās ﵁ who says that Ḥabīb, the Imam, the ᶜĀrif billāh Aḥmad b. ᶜAlī al-Bahr al-Qadīmī met with the Prophet ﷺ while in a waking state; he said to him, "O Messenger of Allah, I would like to hear a hadith from you, without any intermediary." The Prophet ﷺ said, "I will inform you of three hadiths:

1) 'As long as the aroma of coffee remains in a person's mouth, the angels will continue to seek forgiveness for them.'
2) 'Whoever picks up a *subha* to remember Allah, Allah will include him among: '*Those who remember Allah abundantly*,' whether he uses it or not!'
3) 'Whoever stands before a walī of Allah ﷻ whether he is alive or has passed away, it is as though he has worshipped Allah in all the corners of the Earth until his limbs have fallen apart.'

# ~ IV ~

## Aqīdat ul-Ḥaq
## (The Creed of Truth)
## by
## Sheikh ʿAlī bin Abū Bakr al-Sakrān رضي الله عنه

أَشْهَدُ أَنْ لَا إِلٰهَ إِلَّا اللهُ وَحْدَهُ لَا شَرِيكَ لَهُ وَأَشْهَدُ أَنَّ سَيِّدَنَا مُحَمَّداً
عَبْدُهُ وَرَسُولُهُ

*I bear witness that there is no god but Allah, He is One, He has no partner and I bear witness that our master Muhammad is His servant and His Messenger.*

آمَنْتُ بِاللهِ وَمَلَائِكَتِهِ وَكُتُبِهِ وَرُسُلِهِ وَبِالْيَوْمِ الْآخِرِ وَبِالْقَدَرِ خَيْرِهِ
وَشَرِّهِ صَدَقَ اللهُ وَصَدَقَ رَسُولُهُ صَدَقَ اللهُ وَصَدَقَ رَسُولُهُ

*I believe in Allah, His angels, His Divine Books, His Messengers, in the Last Day and in the decree both the good of it and the harm of it. Allah has spoken the truth and His Messenger has spoken the truth, Allah has spoken the truth and His Messenger has spoken the truth.*

آمَنْتُ بِالشَّرِيْعَةِ وَصَدَّقْتُ بِالشَّرِيْعَةِ وَإِنْ كُنْتُ قُلْتُ شَيْئاً خِلاَفَ الإِجْمَاعِ رَجَعْتُ عَنْهُ تَبَرَّأْتُ مِنْ كُلِّ دِيْنٍ خَالَفَ دِيْنَ الإِسْلاَمِ

*I believe in the Sharia and I declare the Sharia to be true. If I have said anything which is contrary to the consensus I take it back and I absolve myself from every way which is contradictory to Islam.*

اَللَّهُمَّ إِنِّي أُوْمِنُ بِمَا تَعْلَمُ أَنَّهُ الْحَقُّ عِنْدَكَ وَأَبْرَأُ إِلَيْكَ مِمَّا تَعْلَمُ أَنَّهُ الْبَاطِلُ عِنْدَكَ خُذْ مِنِّي جُمَلاً وَلاَ تُطَالِبْنِي بِالتَّفْصِيلِ

أَسْتَغْفِرُ اللهَ الْعَظِيمَ وَأَتُوبُ إِلَيْهِ ﴿3﴾

*O Allah, I believe in that which You know to be true with You and I absolve myself from that which You know to be false with You. Take me in totality and do not seek the details from me.*
*I seek forgiveness from Allah the Exalted and repent to Him.* (3)

نَدِمْتُ مِنْ كُلِّ شَرٍّ أَشْهَدُ أَنْ لاَ إِلَهَ إِلاَّ اللهُ وَحْدَهُ لاَ شَرِيْكَ لَهُ وَأَشْهَدُ أَنَّ سَيِّدَنَا مُحَمَّداً عَبْدُهُ وَرَسُوْلُهُ وَأَنَّ عِيْسَى عَبْدُ اللهِ وَرَسُوْلُهُ وَابْنُ أَمَتِهِ وَكَلِمَتُهُ أَلْقَاهَا إِلَى مَرْيَمَ وَرُوحٌ مِنْهُ

*I regret every wrong. I bear witness that there is no god but Allah, He is One, He has no partner and I bear witness that our master Muhammad is His Servant and His Messenger. And that ʿĪsā is the servant of Allah, His Messenger, the son of His slave and His word was cast into Maryam. He is a spirit from Allah.*

وَأَنَّ الْجَنَّةَ حَقٌّ وَأَنَّ النَّارَ حَقٌّ وَأَنَّ كُلَّ مَا أَخْبَرَ بِهِ رَسُولُ اللَّهِ صَلَّى اللَّهُ عَلَيْهِ وَسَلَّمَ حَقٌّ وَأَنَّ خَيْرَ الدُّنْيَا وَالْآخِرَةِ فِي تَقْوَى اللَّهِ وَطَاعَتِهِ وَأَنَّ شَرَّ الدُّنْيَا وَ الْآخِرَةِ فِي مَعْصِيَةِ اللَّهِ وَمُخَالَفَتِهِ وَأَنَّ السَّاعَةَ آتِيَةٌ لَا رَيْبَ فِيهَا وَأَنَّ اللَّهَ يَبْعَثُ مَنْ فِي الْقُبُورِ

*I believe that Paradise is true, and that the Fire is true, and everything that the Messenger of Allah, may Allah bless him and grant him peace, has informed us of is true. I believe that the good of the world and the Hereafter lie in having piety of Allah and in His obedience, and that the evil of the world and the Hereafter lie in disobeying Allah and transgressing against Him. I believe that the Hour is true, there is no doubt concerning it, and that Allah will resurrect those in the graves.*

أَشْهَدُ أَنْ لَا إِلَهَ إِلَّا اللهُ وَحْدَهُ لَا شَرِيكَ لَهُ وَ أَشْهَدُ أَنَّ سَيِّدَنَا

مُحَمَّداً عَبْدُهُ وَ رَسُولُهُ

*I bear witness that there is no god but Allah, He is One, He has no partner and I bear witness that our master Muhammad is His Servant and His Messenger.*

لَا إِلَهَ إِلَّا اللهُ أُفْنِي بِهَا عُمْرِي لَا إِلَهَ إِلَّا اللهُ أُدْخُلُ بِهَا قَبْرِي لَا إِلَهَ

إِلَّا اللهُ أُخْلُو بِهَا وَحْدِي لَا إِلَهَ إِلَّا اللهُ أَلْقَى بِهَا رَبِّي

*With Lā ilāha illa Allah I expend my life. With Lā ilāha illa Allah I will enter my grave. With Lā ilāha illa Allah I will be left alone. With Lā ilāha illa Allah I will meet my Lord.*

لَا إِلَهَ إِلَّا اللهُ قَبْلَ كُلِّ شَيْءٍ . لَا إِلَهَ إِلَّا اللهُ بَعْدَ كُلِّ شَيْءٍ . لَا إِلَهَ إِلَّا

اللهُ يَبْقَى رَبُّنَا وَيَفْنَى كُلُّ شَيْءٍ

لَا إِلَهَ إِلَّا اللهُ نَسْتَغْفِرُ اللهَ ﴿3﴾

*There is no god but Allah before everything. There is no god but Allah after everything. There is no god but Allah, our Lord will remain and everything will finish.*
*There is no god but Allah, we seek forgiveness from Allah.* (3)

لَا إِلٰهَ إِلَّا اللّٰهُ وَنَتُوبُ إِلَى اللّٰهِ . لَا إِلٰهَ إِلَّا اللّٰهُ مُحَمَّدٌ الرَّسُولُ اللّٰهِ صَلَّى اللّٰهُ عَلَيْهِ وَسَلَّمَ

*There is no god but Allah and we repent to Allah. There is no god but Allah Muhammad is the Messenger of Allah, may Allah bless him and grant him peace.*

اَلْفَاتِحَةُ إِلَى رُوحِ سَيِّدِنَا وَقُدْوَتِنَا إِلَى اللّٰهِ الْإِمَامِ اَلْحَبِيْب عَلِي إِبْنِ أَبِي بَكْرِ السَّكْرَان بِأَنَّ اللّٰهَ يُقَدِّسُ رُوحَهُ فِي الْجَنَّةِ وَيَنْفَعُنَا بِأَسْرَارِهِمْ وَبِعُلُومِهِمْ وَبِجَاهِهِمْ فِي الدِّيْنِ وَالدُّنْيَا وَالْآخِرَةِ... اَلْفَاتِحَة

*Recite al-Fatiha for the spirit of our master and role model to Allah, the Imam, Habib ʿAli bin Abī Bakr al-Sakrān that Allah may sanctify his spirit in Paradise, and benefit us from his secrets, knowledge and rank in our religion, world and hereafter....al-Fatiha!*

# SECTION 3

# DAILY SUPPLICATIONS

*"The best of actions are those which are small and consistent"*

The Prophet ﷺ

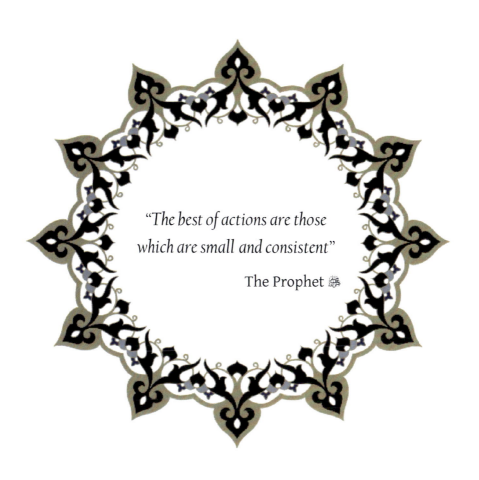

## LITANIES TO BE RECITED THROUGHOUT THE DAY AND EVENING

One should make an effort to maintain a state of purity and remain in a state of ablution at all times. After performing ablution recite the following supplication:

أَشْهَدُ أَنْ لَا إِلٰهَ إِلَّا اللّٰهُ وَحْدَهُ لَا شَرِيْكَ لَهُ وَ أَشْهَدُ أَنَّ مُحَمَّداً عَبْدُهُ وَ

رَسُولُهُ سُبْحَانَكَ اللّٰهُمَّ وَ بِحَمْدِكَ أَشْهَدُ أَنْ لَا إِلٰهَ إِلَّا أَنْتَ

أَسْتَغْفِرُكَ وَ أَتُوبُ إِلَيْكَ اللّٰهُمَّ اجْعَلْنِي مِنَ التَّوَّابِيْنَ وَ اجْعَلْنِي مِنَ

الْمُتَطَهِّرِيْنَ وَاجْعَلْنِي مِنْ عِبَادِكَ الصَّالِحِيْنَ.

*I bear witness that there is no god but Allah, alone without any associate, and I bear witness that Muḥammad is His (most perfect) worshipper and Messenger. Glory be to You, O Allah with Your praise! I bear witness that there is no god but You, I seek Your forgiveness and turn to You in repentance. O Allah make me amongst the repentant, the purified and amongst Your Righteous Servants.*

After the ablution, two *rak ᶜah* of prayer should be performed; this superogatory prayer is called *Taḥiyyat ul-wuḍū'*. One should not speak in between the ablution and the performance of this prayer.

## *After Fajr*

- Recite Sura Yāsīn, followed by the supplication of Sura Yāsīn by Imam al-Ḥaddād.
- Recite Wird ul-Laṭīf.
- Recite Aqīdat ul-Ḥaq of Sheikh ᶜAlī b. Abū Bakr al-Sakrān.
- Recite Wird of Imam Abū Bakr b. ᶜAbd al-Raḥmān al-Saqqāf.
- Recite Wird of Imam al-Nawawī.
- Recite Ayat ul-Kifāya and Ayat ul-Ḥifẓ

For those who have the opportunity should perform the mid-morning prayer (*Ṣalāt al-Ḍuḥā'*), either: 2, 4, 6, 8 or 12 rak ᶜah. Thereafter recite this supplication:

اَلحَمْدُ لِلّٰهِ رَبِّ العَالَمِيْنَ اللّٰهُمَّ صَلِّ عَلَى سَيِّدِنَا مُحَمَّدٍ وَآلِهِ وَ سَلِّم

يا اللهُ يَا وَاحِدُ يَا أَحَدُ يا وَاجِدُ يا جَوَّادُ انْفَحْنَا مِنْكَ بِنَفْحَةِ خَيْرٍ

﴿3﴾

فِي كُلِّ لَحْظَةٍ أَبَداً عَدَدَ خَلْقِهِ وَ رِضَى نَفْسِهِ وَزِنَةَ عَرْشِهِ وَمِدَادَ

كَلِمَاتِهِ.

With arms raised up high in supplication, say 10 times:

يَا بَاسِطُ ﴿10﴾

Then lower your hands to the level of normal supplication and say:

أُبْسُطْ عَلَيْنَا الخَيْرَ وَ الرِّزقَ وَ وَفِّقْنَا لِإصَابَةِ الصَّوَابِ وَ الحَقِّ وَ زَيِّنَّا

بِالإِخْلَاصِ وَالصِّدْقِ وَ أَعِذْنَا مِنْ شَرِّ الخَلْقِ وَاخْتِمْ لَنَا بِالحُسْنَى فِي

لُطْفٍ وَعَافِيَةٍ.

اَللّٰهُمَّ إِنَّ الضُّحَاءَ ضُحَاءُكَ وَ البَهَاءَ بَهَاءُكَ وَالجَمَالَ جَمَالُكَ

وَالقُوَّةَ قُوَّتُكَ وَالقُدْرَةَ قُدْرَتُكَ وَالسُّلْطَانَ سُلْطَانُكَ وَالعَظْمَةَ

عَظْمَتُكَ وَالعِصْمَةَ عِصْمَتُكَ.

اَللَّهُمَّ إِنْ كَانَ رِزْقِي وَ أَحْبَابِي وَالمُسْلِمِينَ أبَداً فِي السَّمَاءِ فَأَنْزِلْهُ وَ إِنْ كَانَ فِي الأَرْضِ فَأَخْرِجْهُ وَ إِنْ كَانَ بَعِيداً فَقَرِّبْهُ وَ إِنْ كَانَ قَلِيلاً فَكَثِّرْهُ وَ إِنْ كَانَ مَعْدُوماً فَأَوْجِدْهُ وَ إِنْ كَانَ حَرَاماً فَطَهِّرْهُ بِحَقِّ ضُحَائِكَ وَبَهَائِكَ وَ جَمَالِكَ وَقُوَّتِكَ وَ قُدْرَتِكَ وَسُلْطَانِكَ وَعَظْمَتِكَ وَعِصْمَتِكَ.

اللهُمَّ آتِنَا فِي كُلِّ حِينٍ أَفْضَلَ مَا آتَيْتَ أَوْ تُؤْتِي عِبادَكَ الصَّالِحِينَ مَعَ العَافِيَةِ التَآمَّةِ فِي الدّارَيْن آمِين.[86]

## *After Ẓuhr*

- Read: *Lā ilāha illa Allāh ul-Malik ul-Haqq ul-Mubīn,* 100 times.
- Recite Ḥizb ul-Naṣr of Imam al-Ḥaddād (this can be recited either after Ẓuhr or ᶜAṣr).

[86] This supplication can be found in *al-Khulāsa fī awrād wa ad'iya wārida wa ma'thūra*, compiled by Umar b. Muḥammad b. Ḥafīẓ

## *After ᶜAṣr*

- Recite Sūra al-Wāqi ᶜa, followed by the supplication of Sūra al-Wāqi ᶜa.
- Recite Rāṭib ul- ᶜAṭṭās.
- Recite Ḥizb ul-Baḥr, (this is only for those who have received the permission to recite it).

## *After Maghrib*

- Recite Wird ul-Laṭīf

## *After ᶜIshā'*

- Recite Rāṭib ul-Ḥaddād
- Recite Sura Mulk

## *Friday*

Recite the following sūras:

- Sura al-Kahf, Sura al-Sajda, Sura Yāsīn, Sura Dukhān,

Sura Mulk, Sura Takwīr, Sura Burūj, Sura Ṭāriq, Sura al-A[c]lā, Sura al-Ḍuḥā', Sura al-Inshrāḥ

With the exception of Sura al-Kahf, it is of great benefit if the above suras are recited daily.

The following prayer upon the Prophet ﷺ should be read after the [c]Aṣr prayer, whilst remaining seated. It should be recited 80 times on the fingers. One should try their utmost not to miss this:

اللهُمَّ صَلِّ عَلَى سَيِّدِنَا مُحَمَّدٍ النَّبِيِّ الأُمِّيِّ وَ عَلَى آلِهِ وَ سَلِّمْ تَسْلِيماً.

The following prayer upon the Prophet ﷺ can be recited anytime after [c]Aṣr but before Maghrib:

اللهُمَّ صَلِّ عَلَى سَيِّدِنَا مُحَمَّدٍ عَبْدِكَ وَ نَبِيِّكَ وَ رَسُولِكَ النَّبِيِّ الأُمِّيِّ.

In general, prayers upon the Prophet ﷺ should be recited throughout the day as much as possible.

- Recite Muḍariyya when able.

## *Daily awrād that can be recited at anytime*

- The verses of protection (*Ḥizb ul-Wiqāya wa'l-Ḥifẓ*)

- The following *istighfār* at least 100 times:

أَسْتَغْفِرُ اللهَ العَظِيمَ الَّذِي لَا إِلَهَ إِلَّا هُوَ الحَيُّ القَيُّومُ وَأَتُوبُ إِلَيْه.

- The following *istighfār* of Imam al-Ḥaddād should be recited 27 times, in the morning and evening:

أَسْتَغْفِرُ اللهَ الَّذِي لَا إِلَهَ إِلَّا هُوَ الرَّحْمَانُ الرَّحِيمُ الحَيُّ القَيُّومُ الَّذِي لَا يَمُوتُ وَأَتُوبُ إِلَيْهِ رَبِّ اغْفِرْ لِي.

## *Qasā'id of Imam al-Ḥaddād:*

- *Yā Rabbi Yā ᶜĀlim ul-Ḥāl*

- *Qad kafānī ᶜilmu Rabbī*

- *Yā Nafaḥāt-illāhi, Yā ᶜatafātihī*

## *Supplications of Imam ᶜAlī al-Ḥabshī:*

- *Rabbi innī yā dha'l-ṣiffāt il-ᶜaliyya.*

- *Qad tammam Allāh maqāṣidanā*

- Fātiḥa al-Ṣugrā of Ḥabīb Aḥmad b. Muḥammad al-Miḥdār [87]

- Fātiḥa al-Kubrā of Ḥabīb ᶜAbdallāh b. ᶜAydrūs b. ᶜAlawī al-ᶜAydrūs to be recited on Monday, Wednesday and Friday.[88]

[87] This can be found in *Mukh ul-ibāda li ahl il-sulūk wa'l-irāda,* p.735
[88] Ibid, p.736

# THE SPECIAL WAY OF RECITING THE RĀTIB AL-ḤADDĀD

It was the habit of Imam al-Ḥaddād ﵁ on Sunday, Wednesday and Thursday nights, after the ᶜIshā prayer to recite the following:

- The Rātib of Imam al-Ḥaddād.
- After completion one should say (اِعلَمْ أنَّهُ) and then recite five hundred times:

لَا إِلٰهَ إِلَّا اللهُ

- Recite a further three times slowly with concentration:

لَا إِلٰهَ إِلَّا اللهُ

- Recite once:

لَا إِلٰهَ إِلَّا اللهُ مُحَمَّدٌ رَسُولُ اللهِ

- Recite three times:

اَللّٰهُمَّ صَلِّ عَلَى سَيِّدِنَا مُحَمَّدٍ اَللّٰهُمَّ صَلِّ عَلَيْهِ وَسَلِّمْ

- The Fātiḥa and Āyat ul-Kursī once.

- Sura al-Ikhlās eleven times.

- Sura al-Falaq and Sura al-Nās once.

- Then to offer the reward of what has been recited to the Prophet ﷺ, his family and companions, and the righteous; may Allah be pleased with them all; and all the Muslims by saying:

اَلْحَمْدُ لِلَّهِ رَبِّ الْعَالَمِيْن اَللَّهُمَّ صَلِّ عَلَى سَيِّدِنَا مُحَمَّدٍ وَعَلَى آلِ سَيِّدِنَا

مُحَمَّدٍ وَسَلِّمْ اَللَّهُمَّ اجْعَلْ ثَوَابَ مَا هَلَّلْنَاهُ مِنْ لَاإِلَهَ إِلَّا اللّٰهُ وَمَا

قَرَأْنَاهُ مِنَ الْقُرْآنِ الْعَظِيْمِ فِي هَذَا الْمَجْلِسِ هَدِيَّةً وَاصِلَةً وَرَحْمَةً

نَازِلَةً إِلَى حَضْرَةِ سَيِّدِنَا وَنَبِيِّنَا وَشَفِيعِنَا مُحَمَّدٍ صَلَّى اللّٰهُ عَلَيْهِ وَسَلَّمَ

وَإِلَى رُوْحِ الْفَقِيْهِ الْمُقَدَّمِ مُحَمَّدٍ بْنِ عَلِي وَإِلَى رُوْحِ سَيِّدِنَا الشَّيْخِ

صَاحِبِ الرَّاتِبِ الْحَبِيْب عَبْدَاللّٰهِ الْحَدَّادِ وَأُصُوْلِهِمْ وَفُرُوْعِهِمْ

وَجَمِيْعِ سَادَاتِنَا آلِ بَاعَلَوِيْ اَللَّهُمَّ اجْعَلْهُ فِدَاءً لَهُمْ مِنَ النَّارِ وَاجْعَلْهُ

فَكَاكًا لَهُمْ مِنَ النَّارِ  اَللّٰهُمَّ اغْفِرْ لَهُمْ وَارْحَمْهُمْ وَ وَالِدِيْنَا وَ وَالِدِيْهِمْ

وَجَمِيْعِ الْمُسْلِمِيْنَ.

تَقَبَّلَ اللّٰهُ مِنَّا وَمِنْكُمْ وَيَجْعَلُهُ خَالِصًا لِوَجْهِهِ الْكَرِيْمِ - اَلْفَاتِحَةَ أَنَّ اللّٰهَ

يَغْفِرُ لَهُمْ  وَيَرْحَمُهُمْ وَيُسْكِنُهُمُ اَلْجَنَّةَ  وَيَجْمَعُنَا وَإِيَّاكُمْ فِيْ مُسْتَقَرِّ

رَحْمَتِهِ مَعَ اللُّطْفِ وَالْعَافِيَةِ  وَإِلَى حَضْرَةِ النَّبِيِّ صَلَّى اللّٰهُ عَلَيْهِ وَسَلَّمْ

اَلْفَاتِحَة.

- Finally one should make *du<sup>c</sup>ā*, which will be *inshā Allāh*, answered.

# COMMEMORATING THE ANNIVERSARIES OF THE SAINTS OF ALLAH

It is the practice of Sāda Bā ᶜAlawī, when gathering in remembrance of the mashā'ikh that have passed away to recite in the following manner.

❧ Recite Sura Yāsīn

❧ Recite 50 times:

لاإلهَ إلّاَ اللّه

❧ Recite 50 times:

سُبْحَانَ اللّهِ وَ بِحَمْدِهِ سُبْحَانَ اللّهِ العَظِيْمِ

❧ Recite 50 times:

أَسْتَغْفِرُ اللّهَ لِلْمُؤْمِنِيْنَ وَ الْمُؤْمِنَات

❧ Recite the qasīda 'Fa yā Nafaḥātullāhi' by Imam al-Ḥaddād on page 299.

- Recite the qasīda of Imam ᶜAlī b Muḥammad al-Ḥabshī on page 304.

- Recite the qasīda of Imam Aḥmad b Abū Bakr b. Sumait on page 307.

- Finally recite the Fātiḥa.

# Section 4

# Qasā'id

*"In eloquence there is magic and in poetry there is wisdom."*

The Prophet ﷺ

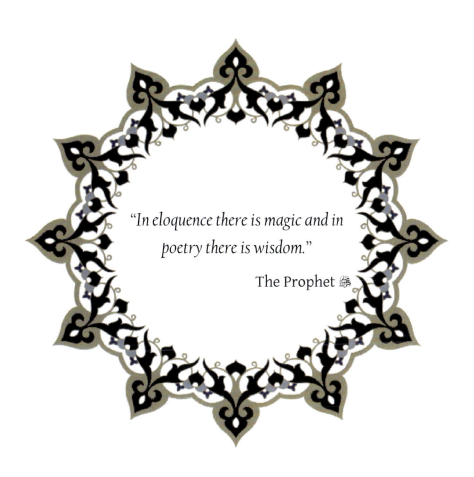

~ I ~

# QASĪDA: *Fa Yā Nafaḥātullāhi* BY IMAM ᶜABDALLĀH AL-ḤADDĀD

بِسْمِ اللهِ الرَّحْمٰنِ الرَّحِيمِ

فَيَا نَفَحَاتِ اللهِ يَا عَطَفَاتِهِ

*O Divine breaths of Allah, O His affections*

وَيَا جَذَبَاتِ الْحَقِّ جُودِي بِزَوْرَةِ

*O Attractions of the Real, honour us with (Your) visit,*

وَيَا نَظَرَاتِ اللهِ يَا لَحَظَاتِهِ

*O Divine gazes of Allah, O His glances*

وَيَا نَسَمَاتِ اللُّطْفِ أُمِّي بِهَبَّةِ

*O breezes of kindness, lead me with a gust.*

وَيَا غَارَةَ الرَّحْمَانِ جِدِّي بِسُرْعَةٍ

*O host of the Merciful, grant me swiftly*

إِلَيْنَا وَحُلِّي عَقْدَ كُلِّ مُلِمَّةِ

*Relieve us from the knots of every misfortune.*

وَيَا رَحْمَةَ الرَّبِّ الرَّحِيمِ تَوَجَّهِي

*O compassion of the Merciful Lord, look towards me*

وَأَحْيِي بِرُوحِ الْفَضْلِ كُلَّ رَمِيمَةِ

*And grant life with the spirit of Your Favour to everything that has perished*

وَيَا كُلَّ أَبْوَابِ الْقَبُولِ تَفَتَّحِي

*O every door of acceptance, open!*

فَإِنَّ مَطَايَا الْقَصْدِ نَحْوَكَ أَمَّتِ

*Verily the means of intent are directed towards You*

وَيَا سُحْبَ الْجُودِ الْإِلَهِيِّ أَمْطِرِي

*O Divine clouds of generosity, pour forth*

فَإِنَّ أَكُفَّ الْمَحْلِ تِلْقَاكَ مُدَّتِ

*The empty palms of my hands are extending to You.*

بِحُرْمَةِ هَادِينَا وَمُحْيِي قُلُوبِنَا

*By the honour of our Guide, the Reviver of our hearts,*

وَمُرْشِدِنَا نَهْجَ الطَّرِيقِ الْقَوِيمَةِ

*Our Leader, who demonstrated the Straight Path*

دَعَانَا إِلَى حَقٍّ بِحَقٍّ مُنَزَّلِ

*He called us to Truth with Truth Revealed*

عَلَيْهِ مِنَ الرَّحْمَانِ أَفْضَلُ دَعْوَةِ

*From The Merciful he has the best call (to the religion)*

أَجَبْنَا قَبِلْنَا مُذْعِنِينَ لِأَمْرِهِ

*We have answered and accepted in submission to his command*

سَمِعْنَا أَطَعْنَا عَنْ هُدًى وَبَصِيرَةِ

*We hear and obey the guidance and see*

فَيَا رَبِّ ثَبِّتْنَا عَلَى الْحَقِّ وَالْهُـدَى

*My Lord, make us firm upon the truth and guidance*

وَيَا رَبِّ اِقْبِضْنَا عَلَى خَـيْرِ مِلَّةٍ

*My Lord hold us in the best of assemblies*

وَعُـمَّ أُصُوْلاً وَالْفُرُوْعَ بِرَحْمَةٍ

*Encompass the forefathers and descendants with mercy*

وَأَهْـلاً وَأَصْحَـابـاً وَكُلَّ قَرَابَةٍ

*Families, companions and every relative*

وَسَـائِرِ أَهْلِ الدِّيْنِ مِنْ كُلِّ مُسْلِمٍ

*And all the people of religion, every Muslim*

أَقَـامَ لَكَ التَّوْحِـيْدَ مِنْ غَيْرِ رِيْبَةٍ

*Are established, for Your sake, in monotheism without doubt*

وَصَـلِّ وَسَـلِّمْ دَائِمَ الدَّهْرِ سَرْمَداً

*May continual, everlasting and eternal blessings and peace*

عَلَى خَــيْرِ مَبْعُوثٍ إِلَى خَــيْرِ أُمَّةٍ

*Be upon the best emissary of the best nation*

مُحَــمَّدٍ الْمَخْصُوصِ مِنْكَ بِفَضْلِكَ الْـ

*Muhammad, the one chosen by You, with Your immense favour*

ــعَظِيمِ وَإِنْزَالِ الْكِتَابِ وَحِكْمَةٍ

*With the Revelation of the Book and Wisdom*

## ~ II ~

## QASĪDA
## BY IMAM ᶜALĪ AL-ḤABSHĪ

بِسْمِ اللهِ الرَّحْمَنِ الرَّحِيمِ

يَا رَبِّ صَلِّ عَلَى النَّبِي مَنْ جَاءَنَا بِالرِّسَالَة

طٰهَ مُحَمَّد وَ آلِهِ مَنْ كَلَّمَتْهُ الْغَزَالَة[89]

*O Lord send blessings upon the Prophet, upon him who*
*brought us the Message*
*Ṭāhā, Muḥammad and his Family, the one whom the Gazelle*
*conversed with*

تَحْتَ بَابِ الْعَطَا قَاصِدُهُ فِي كُلِّ حَالَه

وَالرَّجَا فِيهِ يَجْعَلُ خَاتِمَتْنَا الْجَمَالَه

*Under the door of bestowal does the aspirant*
*desire to be at all times*
*And hope in it will make our end beautiful*

---

[89] This is the chorus and is repeated after two couplets.

أَيْشِ لَكْ بِلْكَدَرْ بَاتَعْبُرْ إِلاَّ سَهَالَه

بَخْتَ مَنْ كَانَ فِي حُسْنِ الرَّجَا رَأْس مَالَه

*Why is it that you tire yourself with this grief when you can*
*traverse through it with ease!*
*Fortunate is the one whose capital is good hope*

يَا سَمِيْعَ الدُّعَا حَيْرَانْ يِبْغِي دِلَالَه

رَبِّ دِلْهُ وَجَنِبْهُ الرَّدِيْ وَالضَّلَالَة

*O the One Who hears the supplication,*
*the perplexed one seeks guidance*
*My Lord guide him and avert him from ruin and misguidance*

وَإِنْ سَأَلْ يَا كَرِيْمَ الْوَجْهِ فَاقْبَلْ سُؤَالَه

يَا الله إِرْحَمْهُ وَاجْعَلْ فِي جِنَانِكْ حِلَالَه

*When he seeks from (You), O Generous One, accept his request*
*O Allah, have mercy upon him and make*
*Your gardens his abode*

اَلْحَبِيْبِ الَّذِي سَيْفُه عَلَيْهِ الْجَلَالَه

النَّبِيُّ الَّذِي مَا قَطُّ تَلْحَقْ مِثَالَه

*The Beloved, his sword reflects his majesty*
*The Prophet, the likes of whom there has not been before*

هُوَ وَأَهْلُهُ وَأَصْحَابُهُ وَجُمْلَةُ عِيَالِهْ

وَالصَّلَاةُ عَلَى الْمُخْتَارِ خَتْمِ الرِّسَالَهْ

*He, his family, his companions and all of his dependants*
*May blessings be upon the Chosen One,*
*the one with the final Message*

خَيْرِ دَاعٍ إِلَى التَّقْوَى بِصِدْقِ الْمَقَالَهْ

وَالصَّحَابَهْ وَنِعْمَ الْآلِ فِي النَّاسِ آلَهْ

*The best caller to piety with truthful speech*
*And upon his companions,*
*And the best of families amongst mankind!*

رَيْتَنَا عِنْدَهُمْ نَحْضُرْ نَهَارَ الْكِيَالَهْ

وَالصَّلَاةُ عَلَى مَنْ كَلَّمَتْهُ الْغَزَالَهْ

*If only we were amongst them we would have received our*
*portion in full measure*
*May blessing be upon the one*
*whom the Gazelle conversed with.*

## ~ III ~

## QASĪDA: *Nad ʿūka lā nad ʿūka siwāka*
## BY ḤABĪB AḤMAD BIN ABŪ BAKR BIN SUMAIT

بِسْمِ اللَّهِ الرَّحْمَٰنِ الرَّحِيمِ

نَدْعُوكَ لَا نَدْعُوكَ سِوَاكَ إِلَهَنَا

فَالْطُفْ بِنَا وَاجْعَلْ رِضَاكَ شِعَارَنَا

*We call upon You, we do not call upon*
*anyone other than You, our Lord*
*So be gentle with us and make Your pleasure our feature*

يَا رَبِّ قَدْ ضَاقَ الْخِنَاقُ وَهَالَنَا

خَطْبُ الْكُرُوبِ وَحَادِثَاتُ زَمَانِنَا

*My Lord we are overwhelmed by oppression and fear*
*Fearful situations and adversities*

يَا رَبِّ قَدْ عَزَّ النَّصِيرُ وَمَالَنَا

إِلَّاكَ نَرْجُوهُ لِكَشْفِ كُرُوبِنَا

*My Lord strengthen the support and sympathise with us*
*It is only You that we have hope in to remove our troubles*

هَلْ ثَمَّ غَيْرُكَ يَا إِلٰهِي يُرْتَجِي

أَوْ هَلْ لِغَيْرِكَ نَشْتَكِي أَحْوَالَنَا

*Is there anyone else, my Lord whom hope can be placed in!*
*Or is there any other we can complain to of our condition?*

أَوْ هَلْ يَخِيبُ رَجَاؤُنَا بِكَ سَيِّدِي

كَلَّا فَلَيْسَ يَخِيبُ فِيكَ رَجَاؤُنَا

*Would our hopes in You fail, our Master?*
*Most certainly not, our hopes in You would not fail*

فَبِحَقِّ رِفْعَةِ سِرِّكَ الْمَوْدُوعِ فِي

أَسْمَائِكَ الْحُسْنَى بِلُطْفِكَ حُفَّنَا

*By the honour of the rank of Your secret in Your*
*Beautiful Names with Your kindness that surrounds us*

يَـــا رَبَّـــنَا إِنَّا تَوَسَّلْنَا بِمَنْ

بِـهُدَاكَ لِلدِّيْنِ الْقَوِيْمِ هَـدَيْتَنَا

*Our Lord, our request is by the one who guided*
*Us with Your guidance to the correct religion*

الْمُصْطَفَى الْمُخْتَارِ مَنْ فَاقَ الْوَرَىٰ

وَرَقَ إِلَى الرُّتَـــبِ الْعُلَى لَـمَّا دَنَا

*Al-Mustafa, the Chosen One who surpassed mankind*
*And ascended to the sublime ranks when he drew near*

لَوْلَاهُ لَمْ نَشْهَدْ سَنَا بَرْقِ الْهُدَىٰ

كَلَّا وَلاَ سَطَعَتْ شُمُوْسِ يَقِيْنِنَا

*Had it not been for him, we would not have witnessed*
*the radiant flash of guidance*
*Certainly not, and neither would the suns of our certainty ever risen*

هُوَ أَصْـــلُ كُلِّ فَضِــيْلَةٍ وَجَـمِيْلَةٍ

هُوَ أَشْرَفُ الرُّسُلِ الْكِرَامِ حَبِيْبُنَا

*He is the origin of every virtue and beauty*
*He is the most honorable amongst the noble Messengers, our Beloved*

يَـــارَبِّ وَفِّـــقْـــنَا لِمَا تَـرْضَى وَلَا

تَجْعَلْ إِلَى سُوْءِ الْحِسَابِ مَصِيْرَنَا

*My Lord, grant us success in that which pleases You and do not Grant us a bad end*

وَاجْعَلْ تَوَكُّلَنَا عَلَيْكَ وَلَا تَكِلْ

لِسِوَى جَــنَابِكَ يَــا إِلَهِي أَمْرَنَا

*Make our reliance upon You and do not entrust our affairs to any other than in Your honour my Lord*

وَاصْلِحْ فَسَادَ قُلُوْبِنَا وَاجْعَلْ لَنَا

مِنْ كُلِّ هَمٍّ مَخْرَجًا وَارْأَفْ بِنَا

*Correct the corruption of our hearts and grant us Relief from every worry and have mercy upon us*

وَتَعَــطَّفِ اللَّــهُمَّ فِيْ غُفْـرَانِ مَا

قَدْ كَانَ مِنَّا مِنْ قَبِيْحِ ذُنُوْبِنَا

*And sympathise, O Allah in forgiving our shameful sins*

وَاصْلِحْ عَوَاقِبَنَا وَسَهِّلْ أَمْرَنَا

وَانْصُرْ وَأَيِّدْ مَنْ يُؤَيِّدُ دِيْنَنَا

*And rectify our end and ease our affair*
*Assist and support those who support our religion*

وَاشْمَلْ جَمِيْعَ الْحَاضِرِيْنَا مُرَادَهُمْ

مِنْ كُلِّ مَا تَرْضَىٰ بِهِ يَا رَبَّـنَا

*Include the intentions of all those present*
*And grant them everything that pleases You O our Lord*

وَأَفِضْ عَلَيْنَا سُحْبَ عَفْوِكَ وَاسْقِنَا

كَأْسًا رَوِيًّا مِنْ حِيَاضِ نَبِـــيِّنَا

*Pour upon us the clouds of Your pardon and give us to drink*
*A thirst quenching cup from the reservoirs of our Prophet*

وَاخْـــتِمْ بِخَاتِمَةِ الرِّضَا أَعْـــمَالَنَا

وَاجْعَلْ عَلَى التَّوحِيْدِ آخِرَ عُمْرِنَا

*Make our end with (Your) approval of our deeds*
*Let the end of our life be upon the Testification*

وَأَفِضْ عَلَى الْعَبْدِ الذَّلِيْلِ مَوَاهِباً

وَانْشُلْهُ مِنْ أَوْحَــالِهِ بِمَّا جَنَا

*Pour gifts upon the humiliated servant*
*Rescue him from the filth of what he has committed*

وَعَلَى الرَّسُوْلِ أَبِي الْبَتُوْلِ مُحَمَّدٍ

خَــيْرِ الْأَنَامِ صَــلَاتُنَا وَسَلَامُنَا

*May our blessings and peace be upon the Messenger*
*The father of chaste (Fatima), Muhammad the best of creation*

وَعَلَى جَمِيْعِ الْآلِ وَالْأَصْحَابِ مَنْ

هُمْ أَنْجُمُ ظَهَرَتْ بِآفَاقِ السَّنَا

*And upon all the Family and Companions who*
*Are the stars that manifest the radiance of the horizons*

~ IV ~

# QASĪDA: *Ya Rabbi Ya ᶜĀlim ul-Ḥāl*

## IMAM ᶜABDALLĀH AL-ḤADDĀD

بِسْمِ اللهِ الرَّحْمٰنِ الرَّحِيمِ

يَا رَبِّ يَا عَالِمَ الحَالْ    إِلَيْكَ وَجَّهْتُ الآمَالْ

فَامْنُنْ عَلَيْنَا بِالإِقْبَالْ    وَكُنْ لَنَا وَاصْلِحِ البَالْ

*O Lord, Knower of my state! I direct my hopes towards You,*
*Favour us with a response, be for us and rectify our state*

يَا رَبِّ يَا رَبَّ الأَرْبَابْ    عَبْدُكْ فَقِيرُكْ عَلَى البَابْ

أَتَى وَقَدْ بَتَّ الأَسْبَابْ    مُسْتَدْرِكاً بَعْدَمَا مَالْ

*My Lord, The Lord of lords! Your needy servant is at the door,*
*Who has (come to You), as all other means have failed, having realized this after what has passed*

يَا وَاسِعَ الْجُودِ جُودَكْ    الْخَيْرُ خَيْرُكْ وَعِنْدَكْ

فَوْقَ الَّذِي رَامَ عَبْدُكْ    فَادْرِكْ بِرَحْمَتِكْ فِي الْحَالْ

*O Most Generous! Grant us Your generosity, (grant us) the good, Your good and that which is with You*
*It is more than what Your servant aspires, so save us now with Your mercy.*

يَا مُوجِدَ الْخَلْقِ طُرًّا    وَمُوسِعَ الْكُلِّ بِرًّا

أَسْأَلُكَ إِسْبَالَ سِتْرًا    عَلَى الْقَبَائِحِ وَالْأَخْطَالْ

*O Originator of the whole creation! And the One most Beneficient!*
*I ask You to cast a veil over my enormities and folly.*

يَا مَنْ يَرَى سِرَّ قَلْبِي    حَسْبِي اطِّلَاعُكَ حَسْبِي

فَامْحُ بِعَفْوِكَ ذَنْبِي    وَاصْلِحْ قُصُودِي وَالْأَعْمَالْ

*O The One who sees the secrets of my heart, Your awareness suffices me, suffices me,*
*Erase my sins with Your pardon, and correct my aims and actions.*

رَبِّ عَلَيْكَ اعْتِمَادِي    كَمَا إِلَيْكَ اسْتِنَادِي

صِدْقًا وَأَقْصَى مُرَادِي    رِضَاؤُكَ الدَّائِمُ الْحَالْ

*My Lord, upon You is my reliance, just as my confidence is upon You*
*My truthful and utmost desire is Your lasting pleasure.*

يَارَبِّ يَارَبِّ إِنِّي    أَسْأَلُكَ الْعَفْوَ عَنِّي

وَلَمْ يَخِبْ فِيكَ ظَنِّي    يَا مَالِكَ الْمُلْكِ يَاوَالْ

*My Lord, My Lord, I ask for Your pardon*
*I have not become disappointed in You, O King and Ruler of all kings*

أَشْكُو إِلَيْكَ وَأَبْكِي    مِنْ شُؤْمِ ظُلْمِي وَإِفْكِي

وَسُوءِ فِعْلِي وَتَرْكِي    وَشَهْوَةِ الْقِيلِ وَالْقَالْ

*I grieve to You and cry for the evil of my wrongs and lies,*
*My bad actions, and my forsaking and my desire towards idle talk*

وَحُبِّ دُنْيَا ذَمِيمَهْ    مِنْ كُلِّ خَيْرٍ عَقِيمَهْ

فِيهَا الْبَلَايَا مُقِيمَهْ    وَحَشْوُهَا آفَاتْ وَاشْغَالْ

*And (my) love of the world is blameworthy, it renders all good useless*
*In it are lasting tribulations, filled with harms and occupations*

يَاوَيْحَ نَفْسِي الْغَوِيَّهْ    عَنِ السَّبِيلِ السَّوِيَّهْ

أَضْحَتْ تُرَوِّجْ عَلَيَّهْ    وَقَصْدُهَا الْجَاهْ وَالْمَالْ

*Woe to my straying soul, which has deviated from the straight path!*
*Which begins to circulate upon me, its aim is status and wealth.*

يَا رَبِّ قَدْ غَلَبَتْنِي وَبِالأَمَانِي سَبَتْنِي

وَفِي الحُظُوظِ كَبَتْنِي وَقَيَّدَتْنِي بِالأَكْبَالِ

*My Lord, it has overwhelmed me, and made idle my security*
*And in my fortunes it has suppressed me and fettered me in shackles*

قَدِ اسْتَعَنْتُكَ رَبِّي عَلَى مُدَاوَاةِ قَلْبِي

وَحَلِّ عُقْدَةِ كَرْبِي فَانْظُرْ إِلَى الغَمِّ يَنْجَالُ

*I seek assistance from You my Lord for the treatment of my heart*
*And to untie the knot of my depression, so gaze towards my grief for it to be removed*

يَا رَبِّ يَا خَيْرَ كَافِي أَحْلِلْ عَلَيْنَا العَوَافِي

فَلَيْسَ شَيْءٌ ثَمَّ خَافِي عَلَيْكَ تَفْصِيلٌ وَاجْمَالُ

*O Lord, the best of Sufficers! Grant us well being and pardon*
*For there is nothing hidden from You, to You belongs (everything in) detail and totality*

يَا رَبِّ عَبْدُكَ بِبَابِكَ يَخْشَى أَلِيمَ عَذَابِكَ

وَيَرْتَجِي لِثَوَابِكَ وَغَيْثُ رَحْمَتِكَ هَطَّالُ

*O Lord, Your servant is at Your door, fearing the torment of Your punishment*
*And hoping for Your reward and the rain of Your mercy to pour forth.*

وَقَدْ أَتَاكَ بِعُذْرِهْ وَبِانْكِسَارِهْ وَفَقْرِهْ

فَاهْزِمْ بِيُسْرِكَ عُسْرَهْ بِمَحْضِ جُودِكَ وَالإِفْضَالْ

*He has come to You with his excuses, his brokenness and destitution*
*Overcome his hardship with Your ease, with Your affectionate kindness and bounty.*

وَامْنُنْ عَلَيْهِ بِتَوْبَهْ تَغْسِلُهُ مِنْ كُلِّ حَوْبَهْ

وَاعْصِمْهُ مِنْ شَرِّ أَوْبَهْ لِكُلِّ مَا عَنْهُ قَدْ حَالْ

*Favour him with Your forgiveness, as You cleanse him from all misdeeds*
*Protect him from the evils of all diseases, and all that he has at this moment*

فَأَنْتَ مَوْلَى الْمَوَالِي الْمُنْفَرِدْ بِالْكَمَالِ

وَبِالْعُلَا وَالتَّعَالِي عَلَوْتَ عَنْ ضَرْبِ الْأَمْثَالْ

*As You are the Master of masters, unique in Perfection*
*And by Grandeur and Exaltedness You transcend similitudes*

جُودُكْ وَفَضْلُكْ وَبِرُّكْ يُرْجَى وَبَطْشُكْ وَقَهْرُكْ

يُخْشَى وَذِكْرُكْ وَشُكْرُكْ لَازِمْ وَحَمْدُكْ وَالْإِجْلَالْ

*Your Benevolence, Favour and Good are hoped for, while Your grasp and overpowering are*
*Feared, Your remembrance and gratitude is incumbent with Your praise and Your Veneration*

يَـــارَبِّ أَنْتَ نَـــصِيْرِيْ فَلَقِّنِيْ كُــلَّ خَيْرِ

وَاجْعَلْ جِنَانَكَ مَـصِيْرِيْ وَاخْــتِمْ بِـالإِيْمَانِ الآجَالْ

*My Lord, You are my Helper so instruct me to all good*
*Make Your Gardens my destiny, and my end upon faith*

وَصَـــلِّ فِيْ كُـــلِّ حَالَهْ عَلَى مُزِيْـلِ الضَّـلَالَهْ

مَنْ كَـلَّمَتْهُ الْغَزَالَهْ مُحَمَّــــدِ الْهَــادِيْ الدَّالْ

*And send blessings in all states upon the one who removes misguidance*
*The one to whom the gazelle spoke, Muhammad the Guide, the one who shows the way*

وَالْحَـمْدُ لِلّٰهِ شُكْرًا عَلَى نِـعَمْ مِـــنْهُ تَتْرَى

نَحْمَدُهُ سِرًّا أَوْجَهْرًا وَبِـــالْغَدَايَـــا وَالْآصَالْ

*Praise be to Allah out of gratitude for His continual blessings*
*We praise Him secretly and openly, by morning and by evening.*

~ V ~

# QASĪDA: *Qad kafānī ʿilmu Rabbī* BY IMAM ʿABDALLĀH AL-ḤADDĀD

بسم الله الرحمن الرحيم

قَدْ كَفَانِي عِلْمُ رَبِّي مِنْ سُؤَالِي وَاخْتِيَارِي

*My Lord's knowledge is enough for me*
*from asking or choosing*

فَدُعَائِي وَابْتِهَالِي شَاهِدٌ لِي بِافْتِقَارِي

*For my supplication and my begging*
*attest to my neediness*

فَلِهَذَا السِّرِّ أَدْعُو فِي يَسَارِي وَعَسَارِي

*By this secret I supplicate*
*in times of ease and in times of difficulty*

أَنَا عَبْدٌ صَارَ فَخْرِي ضِمْنَ فَقْرِي وَاضْطِرَارِي

*I am a slave whose pride is in his poverty and need*

قَدْ كَفَانِي عِلْمُ رَبِّي    مِنْ سُؤَالِي وَاخْتِيَارِي

*My Lord's knowledge is enough for me*
*from asking or choosing*

يَا إِلَهِي وَمَلِيكِي    أَنْتَ تَعْلَمُ كَيْفَ حَالِي

*O my Lord, my King*
*You know the state I am in*

وَبِمَا قَدْ حَلَّ قَلْبِي    مِنْ هُمُومٍ وَاشْتِغَالِ

*And what has overwhelmed my heart*
*of distress and preoccupations*

فَتَدَارَكْنِي بِلُطْفٍ    مِنْكَ يَا مَوْلَى الْمَوَالِي

*Behold me with a kindness*
*from You, O Lord of Lords!*

يَا كَرِيمَ الْوَجْهِ غِثْنِي    قَبْلَ أَنْ يَفْنَى اصْطِبَارِي

*O Countenance of Generosity! Save me!*
*Before my patience is exhausted*

قَدْ كَفَانِي عِلْمُ رَبِّي    مِنْ سُؤَالِي وَاخْتِيَارِي

*My Lord's knowledge is enough for me*
*from asking or choosing*

يَا سَرِيعَ الْغَوْثِ غَوْثًا    مِنْكَ يُدْرِكُنَا سَرِيعًا

*O Swift in aid! Grant us aid*
*from You which will reach us quickly!*

يَهْزِمُ الْعُسْرَ وَيَأْتِي بِالَّذِي نَرْجُو جَمِيعًا

*Defeating all difficulty*
*and bringing all that we hope for*

يَا قَرِيبًا يَا مُجِيبًا يَا عَلِيمًا يَا سَمِيعًا

*O the One who is Near! O the One who answers!*
*O the All-Knowing! O the All-Hearing!*

قَدْ تَحَقَّقْتُ بِعَجْزِي وَخُضُوعِي وَانْكِسَارِي

*I acknowledge my incapacity,*
*my lack of power and my brokenness*

قَدْ كَفَانِي عِلْمُ رَبِّي مِنْ سُؤَالِي وَاخْتِيَارِي

*My Lord's knowledge is enough for me*
*from asking or choosing*

لَمْ أَزَلْ بِالْبَابِ وَاقِفْ فَارْحَمَنْ رَبِّي وُقُوفِي

*I remain standing at the door,*
*so have mercy, my Lord on my standing*

وَبِوَادِي الْفَضْلِ عَاكِفْ فَأَدِمْ رَبِّ عُكُوفِي

*And I reside to the valley of generosity,*
*So make my retreat here abiding*

وَلِحُسْنِ الظَّنِّ لَازِمْ فَهْوَ خِلِّي وَحَلِيفِي

*With a good opinion (of my Lord) which is binding*
*For He is my Friend and my Ally*

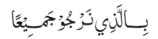

وَأَنِيْسِي وَجَلِيْسِي طُـوْلَ لَيْلِي وَنَهَـارِي

*And He is my Intimate and the One Who is with me,*
*throughout the day and throughout the night*

قَـدْ كَفَانِيْ عِلْمُ رَبِّي مِنْ سُؤَالِي وَاخْتِيَارِي

*My Lord's knowledge is enough for me*
*from asking or choosing*

حَاجَةً فِيْ النَّفْسِ يَارَبّ فَاقْضِهَا يَـا خَيْرَ قَـاضِيْ

*The need in my soul, O Lord!*
*Grant it, for You are the best of those who grant*

وَأَرِحْ سِرِّيْ وَقَلْبِي مِنْ لَظَاهَـا وَالشُّوَاظِ

*And bring ease to my heart*
*from the burning fire inside me*

فِي سُرُوْرٍ وَحُبُوْرٍ وَإِذَا مَـا كُنْتَ رَاضِيْ

*With contentment and happiness*
*and with what You are pleased with*

فَالْهَنَا وَالبَسْطُ حَالِي وَشِـعَارِي وَدِثَـارِي

*And make joy and expansion my state*
*and my disposition and that which I am enveloped with*

قَـدْ كَفَانِيْ عِلْمُ رَبِّي مِنْ سُؤَالِي وَاخْتِيَارِي

*My Lord's knowledge is enough for me*
*from asking or choosing*

## ~ VI ~

## QASĪDA: *Bashshir Fu'ādaka*
## BY IMAM ᶜABDALLĀH AL-ḤADDĀD

❁❁❁

بِسْمِ ٱللَّهِ ٱلرَّحْمَٰنِ ٱلرَّحِيمِ

بَشِّرْ فُؤَادَكَ بِالنَّصِيبِ الْوَافِي

مِنْ قُرْبِ رَبِّكَ وَاسِعِ الْأَلْطَافِ

*Give glad tidings to your heart for the abundant fortune (it has received) by nearness to your Lord Who is copious with favours*

الْوَاحِدِ الْمَلِكِ الْعَظِيمِ فَلُذْ بِهِ

وَاشْرَبْ مِنَ التَّوْحِيدِ كَأْساً صَافِي

*The One, the Great King, seek sweetness with Him*
*And drink a pure glass from the Oneness (Tawḥīd)*

وَاشْـــهَدْ جَـمَالاً أَشْرَقَتْ أَنْوَارُهُ

فِي كُـــلِّ شَيْءٍ ظَاهِراً لاَ خَـــافِي

*Witness the beauty that shines with His lights*
*Which manifests in everything and is not concealed*

وَعَلَى مَنَصِّ الْجَمْعِ قِفْ مُـتَخَلِّياً

عَنْ كُـــلِّ فَـــانٍ لِلتَّفَرُّقِ نَـــافِ

*And upon annihilation, stand withdrawn*
*From all things that perish so that your separation may be sublime*

وَالْبَسْ لِرَبِّ الْعَرْشِ فِي أَقْـــدَارِهِ

ثَـــوْبـــاً مِنَ التَّسْـــلِيمِ وَافٍ ضَافِي

*Dress yourself completely and abundantly*
*In a garment of submission for the Lord of the Throne*

وَاسْـتَكْفِ رَبَّـــكَ كُـــلَّ هَمٍّ إِنَّـــهُ

سُبْحَـــانَهُ الْبَرُّ اللَّطِيفُ الْكَـــافِي

*And find sufficiency in your Lord for every worry*
*Surely He is transcendent, Whose benevolence and kindness suffices*

وَاسْأَلْهُ أَنْ يُلْبِسَكَ ثَوْبَ إِنَابَةٍ

وَهِدَايَةٍ وَسَلَامَةٍ وَعَوَافِي

*And ask Him to dress you in a garment of awareness,*
*Guidance, safety and well being*

وَاشْكُرْ عَلَى النَّعْمَاءِ وَاصْبِرْ لِلْبَلَا

وَتَحَلَّ بِالْإِفْضَالِ وَالْإِنْصَافِ

*Thank Him for the favours and be patient on affliction,*
*In which you should dwell upon the favours and (act) with justice*

وَعَلَيْكَ بِالْإِخْلَاصِ وَالصِّدْقِ وَبِالْ

زُّهْدِ وَجَانِبْ مُنْكَرَ الْأَوْصَافِ

*You must have sincerity and truthfulness (ṣidq),*
*Abstinence (zuhd) and refrain from reprehensible characteristics*

وَاسْتَصْحِبِ التَّقْوَى وَكُنْ ذَا هِمَّةٍ

وَفُتُوَّةٍ وَأَمَانَةٍ وَعَفَافِ

*Take taqwā as a companion, and be a person of determination*
*Chivalry, trust, and chastity*

وَأَنِبْ إِلَى دَارِ الْكَرَامَةِ وَالْبَقَا

وَعَنِ الدَّنِيَّةِ كُنْ أَخِي مُتَجَافِي

*And return to the abode, the everlasting abode of honour,*
*My brother, and refrain from vile (acts)*

وَالْزَمْ كِتَابَ اللهِ وَاتْبَعْ سُنَّةً

وَاقْتَدْ هَدَاكَ اللهُ بِالأَسْلَافِ

*Adhere to the Book of Allah and follow the Sunna*
*Adopt the way, may Allah guide you, of the (pious) predecessors*

أَهْلِ الْيَقِيْنِ لِعَيْنِهِ وَلِحَقِّهِ

وَصَلُوْا وَثَمَّ جَوَاهِرُ الْأَصْدَافِ

*The people of certainty, who had both, the eye and the Truth of certainty.*
*They arrived and there were treasures of pearls*

رَاحُ الْيَقِيْنِ أَعَزُّ مَشْرُوْبٍ لَنَا

فَاشْرَبْ وَطِبْ وَاسْكَرْ بِخَيْرِ سُلَافِ

*The wine of certainty is the most precious drink to us*
*So drink, enjoy and be intoxicated with the best of wines*

هَذَا شَرَابُ الْقَوْمِ سَادَتِنَا وَقَدْ

أَخْطَا الطَّرِيقَةَ مَنْ يَقُلْ بِخِلَافِ

*This is the drink of the people, our masters,*
*And one who says anything other than this has mistaken the path.*

## ~ VII ~

## Du$^{c}$Ā: *Rabbī innī yā dha'ṣ-ṣifāt il-$^{c}$aliyya*[90]
## by Imam $^{c}$Alī al-Ḥabshī

بِسْمِ اللَّهِ الرَّحْمَٰنِ الرَّحِيمِ

رَبِّ إِنِّي يَـــا ذَا الصِّـــفَاتِ العَـــلِيَّةْ

قَـــائِـــمٌ بِـــالفِنَا أُرِيدُ عَـــطِيَّةْ

*My Lord, One with Sublime Attributes I am in extinction, desiring a bequest*

تَحْـــتَ بَـــابِ الرَّجَـــا وَقَفْتُ بِذُلِّي

فَـأَغِثْنِي بِـــالقَصْدِ قَـــبْلَ المَـــنِيَّةْ

*By the door of hope, I stand in humility, So help me with my goal before my demise.*

---

[90] Recited during the last part of the night

وَالرَّسُوْلُ الْكَرِيْمُ بَابُ رَجَائِي

فَهُوَ غَوْثِي وَغَوْثُ كُلِّ الْبَرِيَّةْ

*And the Noble Messenger is the door of my hope*
*He is my aid and the aid of every being*

فَأَغِثْنِي بِهِ وَبَلِّغْ فُؤَادِي

كُلَّ مَا يَرْتَجِيْهِ مِنْ أُمْنِيَّةْ

*So aid me by him and grant my heart,*
*Everything that it desires and aspires*

وَاجْمَعِ الشَّمْلَ فِي سُرُوْرٍ وَنُوْرٍ

وَابْتِهَاجٍ بِالطَّلْعَةِ الْهَاشِمِيَّةْ

*And gather us in happiness and light*
*Rejoicing with the appearance of al-Hāshimi*

مَعَ صِدْقِ الْإِقْبَالِ فِي كُلِّ أَمْرٍ

قَدْ قَصَدْنَا وَالصِّدْقِ فِي كُلِّ نِيَّةْ

*With sincere acceptance for every affair*
*We intend with sincerity in every intention*

رَبِّ فَــاسْلُكْ بِــنَا سَبِيْلَ رِجَــالٍ

سَلَكُوْا فِي التُّقَى طَرِيْقًا سَوِيَّةً

*O Lord, take us upon the path of Men who*
*Travelled the Straight Path with piety*

وَاهْدِنَا رَبَّنَا لِمَا قَـدْ هَدَيْتَ السَّـ

ـــادَةَ الْعَارِفِـيْنَ أَهْـــلَ الْمَزِيَّةْ

*And guide us, our Lord, the way You guided our*
*masters, The Gnostics, the people of virtue.*

وَاجْـعَلِ الْعِلْمَ مُقْـتَدَانَا بِحُكْمِ الدَّ

وَقِ فِي فَـهْمِ سِرٍّ مَعْنَى الْمَـعِيَّةْ

*And make knowledge our guide by tasting the*
*secret meaning of nearness*

وَاحْـفَظِ الْقَلْبَ أَنْ يُلِمَّ بِهِ الشَّيْـ

ـطَانُ وَالنَّفْسُ وَالْهَوَى وَالدَّنِيَّةْ

*And protect the heart from satanic whisperings*
*of reproach, the ego, and loathsome desires.*

## ~ VI ~

## Du$^{c}$ā: *Qad tammam Allah maqāsidnā*
## by Imam $^{c}$Alī al-Ḥabshī

بِسْمِ اللهِ الرَّحْمٰنِ الرَّحِيْمِ

قَدْ تَمَّمَ اللهُ مَقَاصِدَنَا

وَزَالَ عَنَّا جَمِيعُ الهَمّْ

*Allah has fulfilled our intentions*
*And has removed every anxiety from us*

بِبَرَكَةِ النُّورِ شَافِعِنَا

جُودُهُ وَفَضْلُهُ عَلَيْنَا عَمّْ

*By the blessing of the light of our Intercessor.*
*Whose generosity and bounty have encompassed us*

طَابَتْ بِذِكْرِهِ مَشَارِبُنَا

وَكَمْ مِنَنْ لَهُ عَلَيْنَا كَمْ

*Our way has become sweet through mentioning him*
*And how many favours of his are upon us!*

وَكَمْ تَفَضَّلْ وَكَمْ أَغْنَى

وَكَمْ تَكَرَّمْ وَكَمْ أَنْعَمْ

*How much has he honoured and enriched us!*
*How much has he ennobled and blessed!*

ذَا وَعْدْ جَانَا بِلَا سَهْنَا

سُبْحَانْ مَوْلَايْ مَنْ أَلْهَمْ

*This is a promise which has been given to us without any effort*
*Glorified is the Protector Who has inspired*

مَبْنَى الْهَوَى عِنْدَنَا مَبْنَى

بِشَّانْ دَاخِلْهُ أَنْ يَسْلَمْ

*The building of love, which we have, is the building*
*The marvel of the interior is through submission*

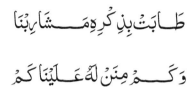

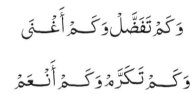

وَلَهُ حَقِيقَةٌ وَلَهُ مَعْنَى

قَلِيلٌ تِلْحَقُهُ مَنْ تَرْجَمْ

*He has a reality and an inner meaning*
*How few are they, who have ever described him?*

لَيْلَةٌ صَفَا قَدْ صَفَتْ مَعْنَا

وَنُورُهَا بَيْنَنَا يُقْسَمْ

*The night of clarity has purified with us*
*And its light is being apportioned amongst us*

وَضَرْبَةِ الطَّبْلْ تُطْرِبْنَا

وَرَاجِي اللهَ مَا يُحْرَمْ

*The beating of the Tabl is moving us*
*And the one with hope in Allah is not denied.*

حَاشَا إِلَهِي يُخَيِّبْنَا

وَلَهُ مَوَاهِبْ عَلَيْنَا جَمّْ

*Allah forbid that He should ever disappoint us*
*His divine gifts are plentiful upon us*

حُسْنُ الرَّجَا فِيهِ قَائِدُنَا

لِلْخَيْرِ فِي ذِهْ كَذَا فِي ثَمَّ

*Excellent hope in Him is our way*
*Towards good; now and in the future*

عَسَى بِفَضْلِهِ يُعَامِلُنَا

مِنَ الْعَطَبْ وَالْغَضَبْ نَسْلَمْ

*Perhaps He will treat us with His bounty*
*And from destruction and wrath we will be saved*

فِي جَنَّةِ الْخُلْدِ يُدْخِلُنَا

مَعَ النَّبِيِّ الْمُصْطَفَى الْأَكْرَمْ

*Forever in the Garden, He will enter us*
*with the noblest of Prophets, al-Mustafa*

وَعَاقِبَتُنَا تَقَعْ حُسْنَى

فِي حِينِ مَا عُمْرُنَا يُخْتَمْ

*Our outcome will end as good*
*At the time when our lives come to an end*

صَلُّوا عَلَى مَنْ بِهِ سُدْنَا

عَلَى فَصِيحٍ كَذَا أَعْجَمْ

*Send blessings upon the one by whom we ascended*
*Over all races, Arab and foreign*

مَا حَرَّكَ الطَّبْلَ مَنْ غَنَّى

وَنَاحَ بِالصَّوْتِ وَتَرَنَّمْ

*May the blessings continue as long as the Tabl moves*
*for the one who sings*
*And calls with the melodious voice*